The Man in the Arena

It is not the critic who counts; not the man who points out how the strong man stumbles, or where the doer of deeds could have done them better. The credit belongs to the man who is actually in the arena, whose face is marred by dust and sweat and blood; who strives valiantly; who errs, who comes short again and again, because there is no effort without error and shortcoming; but who does actually strive to do the deeds; who knows great enthusiasms, the great devotions; who spends himself in a worthy cause; who at the best knows in the end the triumph of high achievement, and who at the worst, if he fails, at least fails while daring greatly, so that his place shall never be with those cold and timid souls who neither know victory nor defeat.

—Theodore Roosevelt

FOREWORD BY ANGUS WINCHESTER

HOSPITALITY DNA

★★★★★

CAREER JOURNEYS WITH
UNPRECEDENTED INSIGHTS FROM
INDUSTRY AWARD WINNERS

---

from the authors of **The Bar Shift**

DAVE NITZEL AND DAVE DOMZALSKI

Copyright © 2023 by Dave Nitzel and Dave Domzalski

All rights reserved. No part of this book may be used or reproduced in any manner whatsoever without prior written consent of the author, except as provided by the United States of America copyright law.

Published by Best Seller Publishing®, St. Augustine, FL
Best Seller Publishing® is a registered trademark.
Printed in the United States of America.

ISBN: 978-1-959840-93-0

This publication is designed to provide accurate and authoritative information with regard to the subject matter covered. It is sold with the understanding that the publisher is not engaged in rendering legal, accounting, or other professional advice. If legal advice or other expert assistance is required, the services of a competent professional should be sought. The opinions expressed by the author in this book are not endorsed by Best Seller Publishing® and are the sole responsibility of the author rendering the opinion.

For more information, please write:
Best Seller Publishing®
53 Marine Street
St. Augustine, FL 32084
or call 1 (626) 765-9750
Visit us online at: www.BestSellerPublishing.org

Contents

FOREWORD 1
INTRODUCTION 5
1 KNOWLEDGE 15
2 PROFESSIONAL DEVELOPMENT 29
3 CLARITY 41
4 BRANDING 55
5 IMMERSION 69
6 DETAILS 85
7 TRAINING 97
8 EXECUTION 109
9 COMMUNITY 119
10 THE POWER OF GIVING 133
11 INFORMATION SYSTEMS 147
12 DISCIPLINE 167
13 SCALING 187
14 MENTORSHIP 201
15 PARTNERSHIPS 221
16 HELIX DISCOVERY 249
THE HELIX SEQUENCE 253

CONCLUSION 307
ACKNOWLEDGMENTS 309
ONLINE RESOURCES 311

Foreword

by
Angus Winchester

I never wanted to be a career bartender, and I believe that you would struggle to find many people of my age who did. While Hospitality is becoming more recognized as a profession — first led by chefs, then sommeliers then later followed by the mixologist — in the past, working in a bar or restaurant was a sign of some sort of dysfunction. A poor academic record. A poor attitude. A lack of other options. A rest home for the socially broken and societal misfits or a resting place for the uncertain who still needed to pay rent. It was not a career most parents wished for their children.

No, I wanted to be a sportsman. And the best route for me to get noticed was, oddly, to go to one of the best academic universities in the world — Oxford. But before entering that cauldron of academic and sporting expertise, I wanted to travel, and to do that, I had to earn some money, so I worked in a department store in my gap year between school and university.

Someone helpfully suggested that I also get an evening job to speed things along, and so one fateful night, I became a bartender at a slightly dodgy nightclub. Pulling pints, using optics to pour Southern Comfort and lemonade and shots of Pernod and blackcurrant: I treated it not like a possible career but as just

Hospitality DNA

another sport. You had a team who all had different roles to play, an opposition consisting of drunk and dismissive customers, and you had a scoreboard (the cash register). I loved it, but I did not see it as a long-term career. My parents agreed — hoping that I would become a lawyer or a diplomat or a doctor.

Part of my initial reluctance to commit to Hospitality was because I had fallen into the trap that many civilians fall into of totally misunderstanding the Service part of the Service Industry. I, like so many guests, thought that working in the Service Industry meant I was a servant: a lackey, whose role was to run around giving the guest whatever they asked for — beaten relentlessly with "The customer is always right" mantra observed by unenlightened customers and alas management too. I was nobody's lackey, and this job was not for me.

Yet as my skill grew, my experience — not just of my own job but of how other people did theirs — made me change my mind toward the concept of Service. I moved from a nightclub to a "cool" Mexican restaurant and felt I was now a skilled artisan, serving delicious food and drink to my fellow man.

> Soon, I realized the true nature of this branch of the Service Industry: I was being Of Service to my fellow human. My job may have been serving food and drink, but my real purpose — and the real purpose of bars and restaurants — was to make people feel better.

I was sharing my skills and my knowledge and being paid for the chance. People would come in and sit at my bar and be amazed by the attentive and knowledgeable service I provided. They liked my drinks so much they became that most precious of commodities to our industry — the Regular. They brought in friends and asked for — not demanded — the best drinks and chat that I could provide ... now, this was a possible career.

Soon, I realized the true nature of this branch of the Service Industry: I was being Of Service to my fellow human. My job may have been serving food and drink, but my real purpose — and the real purpose of bars and restaurants — was to make people feel better.

Service is not what you do to people or even for people; it's about how you make people feel when they are with you. Four human feelings became the driver for much of what I did: I, and most other Hospitality "pros," wanted you to feel Comfortable, Welcome, Important, and finally, Understood.

We understood that by living up to the dictionary definition of Hospitality — the friendly and generous reception and entertainment of guests, visitors, or strangers — not only would we make others feel better, but our bank accounts would swell too.

In over 30 years in this industry, I have had a life that many of my peers at university would envy. Hospitality is truly a global profession, and thanks to that, I have traveled the world, met royalty and rock stars, and endeavored to learn as much as I can about Drinks, Drinkers, and those who serve them.

But so much of my learning has been what not to do. There is no real formal education or certification process for our industry beyond staid and expensive hotel management schools. I have watched and endured mistake after mistake within our industry and have both bemoaned them and, at the same time, profited by running training courses. Which is why this book is so fresh and necessary.

The longer I have spent in this industry, and the more I have studied it, the more I have noticed amazing Hospitality and the people who exemplify it. From backstreet dives to Michelin-lauded palaces of opulence, these people stand out both for their rarity and brilliance. Yet to manage to gather their thoughts into one book is both a magnificent gift and a precious resource, and one quickly sees that though these often unrecognized people may hail from different backgrounds and work in different settings, there are similarities and patterns that emerge. They are not just skilled at their jobs but are amazing humans who embody Hospitality and make us feel better when we leave their establishments than when we arrived.

I write this during the COVID-19 pandemic, when the role of Hospitality venues as not just places to eat and drink but as places where human relationships are built, and communities, as well as individuals, are nourished and supported, is being talked about daily. As human interaction has slowed, our desire for those simple and meaningful gestures and interactions that great Hospitality provides has grown. Bar and Restaurant people are being hailed as essential, and long may that last.

Angus Winchester
Photo by JP Quant

Now go and buy this book, or stop reading the foreword and instead enjoy the sumptuous banquet that lies in the pages ahead. You will be informed and charmed. Enlightened and educated. Like great Hospitality itself, it will seem effortless but has taken much effort, and Dave and Dave should be commended for their continuing efforts to showcase brilliance and educate an industry.

Introduction

The Bar and Restaurant industry is one of the largest, most socially crucial, and individually unique in the world. The scope of its workforce is such that it trails only those working in government and the entire health care sector across the globe, which accounts for an extraordinary number of people. Dominated by independent Bar and Restaurant owners, the Hospitality industry is filled with people who tend to run isolated business models in an effort to find their own way to personal measures of success. Where most other business sectors have significant schooling programs along with well-developed peer and coaching networks, those who strive to create and own one of the 15 million restaurants[1] on the planet largely do so in silos and, when they succeed, tend to do so through sweat, hard-fought lessons, and sheer force of will. There are pockets of people who work to support each other and, of course, those who have an innate drive to seek out mentorship, partnership, and support; however, the vast majority of these operators will either shut down their operation within three years or spend a lifetime fighting to break even.

With over 50 years of combined business and hospitality experience, meeting both those who beat the trend and those who struggled within this framework, we have been fortunate

---

[1] https://thewebminer.com/blog/how-many-restaurants-are-in-the-world/

to forge meaningful careers around looking for ways to help. One truth we have come to realize is that, unlike publicly traded companies that have access to an absolute glut of said public data and information, these independent operators just don't have easy access to the same success-multiplying resources and information. With that in mind, we started writing books. Our first, *The Bar Shift*, was a frontline best-practice effort to help bar managers run their venues more effectively. For our second endeavor, the beginning was somewhat unclear as to how we could deliver value to the industry in our next effort. The question we had to answer was, What was our purpose? A very similar question we find ourselves often asking our clients!

Our honest answer was that it started out as a meandering exploration of fascinating people and, candidly, at the outset, we didn't intend to write *this* particular book. We initially had something totally different in mind. We were out to write a book on the guest experience and how owners and operators planned and executed their specific service strategies.

With that set as our target, we found many people we spoke with had concepts in mind and a feel they were intent on delivering to their guests, but it was much less systematized than what we expected; it seemed to be more an idea than a process. While pushing for an answer to the question we *thought* needed to be answered, a funny thing happened: our interviewees simply began to opine on what they felt actually drove their success — things outside of customer service — and so we kept going, asking people to tell us their stories. Tell us more!

The most extraordinary answers can come from the most ordinary questions.

"Talk to us about your journey; how did you get started?" led to content and information our Bar and Restaurant friends were willing to share with us that, quite frankly, blew us away.

Once we realized we no longer had a very specific book about customer service, Dave and I started treating this as a pure research project; in fact, neither of us would have come to the conclusions we did at the outset. Many of our assumptions going in would have been wrong, in some cases very wrong. We were fully committed to letting the research, the interviews, be our guide.

What we came to understand was that there are so many extraordinary stories to be told in our industry and that it is rife with amazing talent. That our interviewees were so very willing to share in the name of lifting others up both touched and impressed us. You would be hard pressed to find a group of owners in any other industry, "competitors" if you will, who would be willing to share their journeys, talents, and "secrets" with others in hopes of helping their peers and the industry overall. We quickly started to feel the weight of our discovery. This information and insight was so much more valuable than anything we could have expected. It turns out, quite obviously to many, that one of beautiful things about the Hospitality industry is its willingness to share; it's in our DNA!

Dave and I are deeply honored to not only be able to share both our and their insights but to bring you their stories, which are compelling and brilliant in ways that we never imagined. The depth to which these amazing people are willing to go and the consideration they give in order to deliver truly special experiences for others is extraordinary, and the fact that they did so with zero hesitation seems to contradict the apparent isolated nature of the independent restaurant scene.

It was these realizations, that there are so many out there who need this knowledge and yet another group who were more than willing to give just that ... that is what led us to realize why we were doing this.

Simply to help.

While it is not uncommon for our industry to be categorized as "the service industry," as we were writing this book, we learned that calling the restaurant industry "the service industry" is a misnomer. This felt like a revelation to us, but you already saw this idea was obvious to Angus in his eloquent foreword. It was yet another point of converging ideas found throughout this book-writing.

To serve suggests a sense of obligation. When you hear these stories and how committed these industry leaders are to their profession, you realize that Hospitality is not an obligation — which is suggested by the idea of service — but rather is a gift, and gifts are given freely from the heart out of a desire to bring joy to others. The passion and desire to bring joy to others comes from a place of "want to," not a place of "have to," which makes this a truly beautiful industry to be a part of. We hope this book is in keeping with those aspirations.

It was this innate and intense desire to share and help that we continually ran into that started forming our understanding that we were no longer looking for a set of rules and processes, but instead we were looking at the beginnings of our understanding of Hospitality DNA. It quickly became clear that we were speaking with a group of superstars who cracked the code and who were more than willing to share everything about themselves that enabled them to achieve their success.

As we began to reconstruct our ideas into the concept of a book, we realized we were really writing about Hospitality DNA of the most successful operators in our industry; what people were sharing was as much about who they were as it was about what they've created. These two things were clearly inseparable. It was in those conversations that Dave and I began to discuss the ideas of what it really meant to have Hospitality DNA and how we might be able to provide insight for ourselves and others as to what that really means.

The work of interviewing, discussing, writing, re-discussing, and re-writing led us to the *Hospitality HELIX*. We believe that the HELIX ultimately shows what the core makeup of Hospitality DNA really looks like. We've discovered the five key attributes each award-winning person in Hospitality has in common and understands intuitively, yet which lack definition. We will not only share these findings with you but take you on our journey of discovery as well. We believe that you will at the very least be intrigued and hopefully somewhat surprised and, if we're lucky, enlightened at some of our conclusions.

To start with the HELIX is to start in reverse, as before we got to the HELIX, we started discovering Building Blocks. The idea of a Building Block is a talent or skill that, when mastered or owned, propels one toward award-winning success. The combination of these blocks is not the same for everyone. If we use a superhero analogy, some can fly, some have telekinesis, some have special equipment, and perhaps others can do things like time travel. In the end, they have a certain power(s) that makes them special.

We'll reveal these attributes through a series of stories and examples that we believe you will find both captivating and motivational. These Building Blocks in and of themselves are not Hospitality DNA; they are a part of the makeup. They relate to and interact with the HELIX.

As we worked through these Building Blocks, we found that the idea of the classic DNA double helix allowed us to work out how the different blocks interacted.

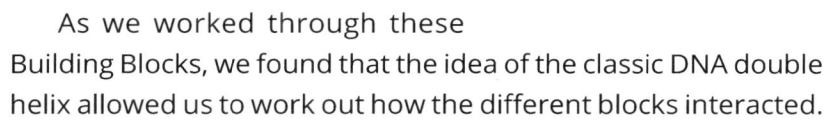

We came to think of the Building Blocks as the individual gifts and the HELIX as the common threads.

It worked out like this ...

Stories and journeys led to figuring out the Building Blocks.

Recurring Building Blocks led us to the discoveries of the HELIX.

The HELIX became the five defining traits of Hospitality DNA!

Once we had the Building Blocks figured out, we organized our book into a series of chapters that profile the journeys of award winners. Within each chapter, we worked to create unique coaching relative to the stories we heard from our interviewees, summing up these coaching ideas at the end of each chapter framed within the five recurring traits of the HELIX. As with DNA, these traits represent the very essence of what these award winners have in common. We have hundreds of hours of recorded interviews and research material that we relied upon to check and recheck our findings.

After all the time we spent, we'll be just a little disappointed if you can guess all five traits that make up the HELIX prior to the reveal. If you like, go ahead now and write down your core five traits that you think make up the most important components of award-winning success in our industry and see if you match our findings. *No cheating!* We've asked two questions of several people in the industry whose opinions we value.

1. What would you consider the core traits for hospitality industry success?

    We would then reveal what we discovered and follow up with a really simple second question.

Introduction

2. Do you agree?

In every case, they were at least somewhat surprised by our findings and, upon further reflection, completely agreed. We can't tell you how reassuring that felt, all things considered!

It is important to note that you can be very successful in our industry without demonstrating all five HELIX traits we're about to unveil. The HELIX outcome seems specific to what we found all of the award winners we interviewed to have in common. What we do know is this: the more of this you get right, the more certain your success.

In each chapter, we will share a Building Block by molding the stories of our interviewees. At the conclusion of each chapter, we will sequence the HELIX of the Building Block in a way we hope will allow you to make it your own.

We conclude the book with five chapters dedicated to each specific HELIX trait; however, we've opted to reveal the five key HELIX traits here and now, and not force you, our reader, to wait until the end of the book.

We want and welcome you to challenge our findings as you read the profiles and coaching points. The main idea of our content is to help. It doesn't matter how the information reaches you, so long as it does. We have found the five traits that define Hospitality DNA — our Hospitality HELIX, if you will:

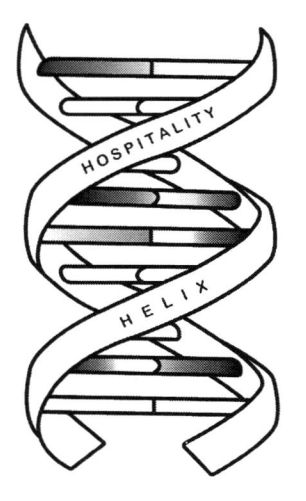

- **H**umble Nature
- **E**xplorer's Pursuit
- **L**ifetime of Experience

- **I**ndomitable Spirit
- **X**traordinary Culture

By the time you get to the end of our book, we hope you will agree (and, if you don't, we would love to discuss your thoughts with you).

Our Criteria

Dave and I are incredibly fortunate to have within our sphere of friends and clients hundreds of world-class, award-winning, super-talented Bar and Restaurant operators. There are way too many we were not able to stuff into this book, so please accept our apologies if you feel we missed you. Dave and I agreed that we had to set specific criteria for every person we interviewed. They needed to have or exemplify two or more of the following.

- Award-winning venues
- Award-winning teams
- Individual award winners
- Individuals of accomplishment
- A speaker, coach, or mentor of professional acclaim

Some of the specific awards that many of our interviewees shared were

- World's Best Bartender
- World's Best Bar
- Most Influential Bar/Owner
- Local and regional recognitions and awards
- Diageo World Class competition winners
- James Beard Award winners
- Bacardi Legacy winners
- Drinks International — Bar World 100

- Tales of the Cocktail award winners

Though many are unassuming, these are all industry greats by any measure.

There are a few final thoughts we wanted to share before you get into the soul of our passion project.

First, award-winning Bar and Restaurant operators tend to do many things very well. One does not simply rise to the very top of this industry by scraping by, in terms of talent. As we worked through our hundreds of hours of interviews, notes, and follow-up conversations, we had to pick and choose which example served as the very best for a particular subject. There are people we talk about in one chapter who easily could have served as a shining example in six others. You will likely find examples of stories told in one chapter that perfectly exemplify the framework of another. While this was not necessarily by design, it is certainly not surprising when you take into account the caliber of the people we have spoken with.

Secondly, Dave and I certainly didn't always agree. It should be noted that we do not process information the same way, so some guidance would resonate with one of us more powerfully than it did the other. What might not be obvious is that we included multiple pieces of advice and guidance within each chapter in an attempt to reach as many diverse ways of learning and thinking as possible. What will stand out more is that Dave and I write in terms of "we" and "us," though in a couple of instances, we do tell some individual stories in the book. This is intentional, as this was very much a team effort.

Finally, you can easily hire consultants — extremely talented people — who can help in any given situation. You can also attend industry or professional seminars where you might find great guidance as to best practices and where you can access amazing talent. This is all readily available, and we strongly encourage those engagements.

What is not so readily available are direct insights into the success drivers of industry champions. That is where this book comes into play.

Please enjoy!

Chapter 1

Knowledge

> The more you know, the dumber
> you think you are.
> —Costin Gache

During our interview process of successful Bar and Restaurant owners, we looked for commonalities and trends with the goal of discovering the essence of Hospitality DNA. One that jumped out at us rather immediately was knowledge and experience. A great number of our success stories involve owners and operators who have either a lifetime of experience or weighty knowledge working with or in bars of significance with the highest standards.

It seems that in a world that lacks structured training programs, there's a heavy reliance upon trial and error and tribal knowledge. It's not uncommon for very successful operators to have started in our industry as early as their teenage years — generally those that are truly formative — and after amassing years of experience have become grounded in a series of fundamental processes they simply do not deviate from. These fundamentals are vital to the success these operators enjoy.

If you attempt to challenge these learned fundamentals, our very successful interviewees will stand resolute in their belief systems as they are often learned through trial by fire and are not to be abandoned. That is not to say they did not have their failures; however, both the successes and failures strengthen what they have learned firsthand, the results of why their way of doing things is so personal to them.

One of the best examples of this is the story of Julio Cabrera. Julio is both the creator and owner of the acclaimed Cafe La Trova in Miami. If you're from South Florida, you know the place. Condé Nast did a piece on the restaurant, and it was featured on an episode of *Live with Kelly and Ryan*. *The Miami Times* voted it the "Best Mojito," and Julio won Bartender of the Year at the Spirited Awards in 2019 and regularly adorns global top 50 lists. But this cafe and these accolades did not come overnight.

Julio was born in Cuba during the early years of the Castro regime. He was raised running around the bar his father built and owned, *El Sacrificio*. Because of the nature of Castro's government, it was just a matter of time before they confiscated the place, forcing Julio's father to walk away from his dream. Well, you can confiscate the bar from the family, but you can't take the family out of the bar. Even in dark circumstances and at a young age, Julio was still infected by his father's generous spirit and love for hospitality.

When the time came for Julio's continued education, his family wanted him to get a practical degree like engineering. He complied with their wishes but shied away from electrical or structural engineering and set his sights on agricultural engineering. True to his roots, he learned how to roast coffee beans and how to turn sugar into rum. These skills would turn out to serve him well.

Later, he trained to be a *cantinero*. *Cantinero* translates directly as "barman," but it's so much more. The concept originated in Spain but became a part of the fabric of the Bar and Restaurant culture in Cuba. *Cantineros* are expected to have 200 cocktail recipes memorized and to know how to toss the drink they are mixing from one tin to another without spilling a drop. They wear a red vest and a tilted fedora and are known for their playful wink of the eye. Beyond drinks, they are trained to pull each customer into an experience to remember.

From the first time Julio wore the legendary outfit, it was a perfect fit. For him, it was a lifestyle, not a job or a career. Not just a certified *cantinero*, he also became a cultural ambassador. He spent his days and evenings speaking to tourists about coffee and rum and the cultural wonders of his homeland.

Next, he traveled around the world to learn about the intricacies of his industry. His stops included places like Cyprus and Italy. Julio's perspective widened. His knowledge expanded.

Returning to Cuba, he was restricted by the government in expressing the passion and knowledge that he had gained through his education and travel. He wanted to create, own, and operate much the same way his father had and he knew that would never be in the cards if he stayed in his homeland. He came to the conclusion that his only option was to escape with his family. In 1989, that chance came.

In that year, Julio received a short-term job offer in Cancun, Mexico. This was his chance! He winded his way north to the U.S. border town of Brownsville, Texas. At that time, U.S. foreign policy granted political asylum to anyone who escaped the Castro regime. Julio crossed the border and put himself at the mercy of the U.S. government. They detained him, questioned him, and then welcomed him and his family into the country. He had made it! His dream was within reach. It was also in Cancun where he met his longtime and current friends and partners Michelle Bernstein and David Martinez.

After entering the country, Julio made his way to Miami. His extended family was there. His people were there. His culture was there. For 17 years, the dream of starting his own place slowly developed. Like his father, Hospitality was in his blood. For 17 years he thought about what he had learned. His mind hearkened back to the countless years of travel and training he had received. He remembered the atmosphere of his father's bar. He even made detailed notes about the place he would open someday. As he traveled the world, his notebook was always with him and he wrote down every detail, including how the bar lights would look and the style of silverware he would use. He even knew exactly how the footrails should look and perform. Finally, the dream came true in 2017.

Julio Cabrera, La Trova
Photo by Anthony Nader

Cafe La Trova opened that year in Little Havana. Why "La Trova"? It's the name of a unique style of music from Santiago, Cuba. It includes beautiful, quick-fingered guitar music. Once you hear it, you will never forget it. Opening Cafe La Trova has made Julio's dream a reality. La Trova music fills the air anytime the cafe is open. Every detail belongs to Julio. His traditions and culture live on.

Cafe La Trova is more than a restaurant. It's more than a bar. It is an experience that you'll never forget. Vibrant oil paintings adorn the walls. There's cast iron trim around the bar, and the patrons sit on red-topped seats. Toward the front of the restaurant, directly across from the main bar, is the stage. Musicians perform in front of the facade of a Cuban-style house, and a clothesline is strung over the heads of the guests dining, drinking, and dancing. Nothing has been compromised. When you are at Cafe La Trova, you truly feel transported, in every way, to Santiago, Cuba.

Chef and partner Michelle Bernstein, who has designed the quintessential menu for Julio's customers, has also won the prestigious James Beard Foundation Award. The menu features modern twists on classic Cuban dishes. Only certified *cantineros* are allowed behind the bar, each one personally trained by Julio. They have all memorized the 200 drink recipes, and they are all trained to show the utmost in professionalism. In Little Havana, there are countless bars and restaurants. Cafe La Trova stands out because of Julio's passion, vision, and incredible attention to detail. At long last, after years of learning, Julio is the teacher.

I found out for myself that all of this praise was well deserved, during my visit to Cafe La Trova. I had known Julio for a few years but had never got to Miami to visit his masterpiece. In anticipation, I, Dave D, flew my mother in from St. Louis to celebrate her 80th birthday. A few years before, she had spent a month in Cuba and was excited to see what Julio had built; she was not disappointed. I knew immediately, when I walked in, that my family and I were in for an exceptional experience. There, on Julio's "Special Guests" board, was my name. The first things I noticed were the enticing smell of fried plantains and the warm, hospitable smiles all around.

Next, I looked at the bar, and there they were — the *cantineros*. Seeing them behind the stunning, dark wood bar is like being transported to a different time and place. Something important to know about Julio is that you would be more likely to find yourself on a rocket to the moon than to find him unshaven or disheveled. It seemed the same with the staff. They were impeccably dressed and exuded the same generous spirit of the owner. When the hostess informed me that Julio was on a plane returning to Miami, I was afraid I would miss him.

The dinner conversation that evening was lively. My mother started recounting her times in Cuba. Cafe La Trova brought back those memories vividly. A few minutes later, I noticed a man walk into the restaurant wearing a lime green polo shirt and pressed dress slacks. It took me a moment to recognize him as Julio since I had never seen him in such casual dress.

It took me a full ten minutes to decide what to order off Julio's incredible menu. After my family and I ordered, I went to find Julio. I really wanted my mother to meet the man behind this wonderfully alive yet warmly nostalgic cafe. I kept searching the place for the lime green polo shirt, but to my surprise, there was Julio, dressed to the nines in his *cantinero* uniform. His bow tie was tied perfectly, his jacket adorned with the medals he had won at countless competitions. To me, he looked a bit like the world's friendliest general, ready to inspect his troops. What struck me was how natural Julio looked in that formal uniform. I mused to myself that he probably slept in *cantinero* silk pajamas!

I walked up to him and received his warm greeting. He followed me to our table and greeted my mother with respect and appreciation. Even though he spent only a few minutes with my family, we all felt his attention and affection, as if we were the only ones in a restaurant filled to capacity. I saw how charming and charismatic he was in this world that he had created. I realized that I was experiencing the culmination of his years of training and travel. The thousands of hours that he spent behind the bar in his bow tie and fedora, delicate daiquiri glass in hand, had led inevitably to Cafe La Trova.

It was a magical evening. The food was spectacular. The ambiance was irresistible. The music was intoxicating. Even my daughter, who is sensitive to loud music, was so enthralled with the band that she didn't want the night to end. At one point, my daughter's eyes went wide, staring behind me at the bar. Just then, the unmistakable sound of a trombone joined the music being played on the stage. Turning around, I was surprised to see one of the *cantineros* jamming away on a trombone for a few minutes before going back to making drinks for his thirsty guests. Julio created birthday perfection for us.

There are few venues that truly transport you to another place. Cafe La Trova does just that. I think it's because when Julio is in his full *cantinero* regalia, shaking drinks and charming people, he is simply being his truest self. Each night, when he opens his doors, it's like opening night for him. Julio's attitude of supreme execution of a vision exemplifies what it means to be a professional in our industry.

For Julio, being a *cantinero* defines him, drives him, and is a source of great inspiration. He emphatically believes in setting a supreme standard of execution and living up to that standard every night, as if it were opening night. During a lifetime of travels, Julio made detailed notes of all the things he wanted in his eventual dream bar, starting with the people he wanted to surround himself with.

As mentioned in Julio's story, only certified Cuban *cantineros* are allowed to work the front bar at Cafe La Trova. The standards are unwavering. Julio, the former student and eventual university teacher, insists on the ultimate professionalism at his bar, and only fully trained, fully committed, certified *cantineros* are allowed to represent his brand, which has been forged over a lifetime of curation. At Cafe La Trova, there is also a back bar that doubles as a training room for future *cantineros*. For now, you are allowed to work that bar if you are deemed ready to serve but not yet a full *cantinero* ready for prime time up front at the main bar. A lifetime of experience and expectations manifests itself every night at Cafe La Trova in Miami.

Julio's list of accolades is too long to print, but suffice it to say, not many people in our industry end up gracing the cover of *GQ* magazine with the caption "America's most imaginative bartender."

In terms of knowledge and experience, Julio stands above the crowd in many ways, but consider, with all his education and global experience, Julio didn't open his first bar until age 52, and when he did ... oh boy!

As we conducted our interviews, we found overwhelming commonalities related to professionalism. The vast majority of our interviewees already had many years of experience under their belts before opening their first bar and very often had begun in their teenage years or early twenties.

Of course, there are those who buck the trend. There are people like Jack McGarry, who won a "World's Best Bar" award by the age of 30 with the Dead Rabbit. Jack began his career by bussing tables in Belfast and along the way befriended Sean Muldoon, who complemented Jack's youthful exuberance and enthusiasm with knowledge and wisdom. So even though Jack is an outlier unto himself in terms of total personal life experience, when his skills are complemented by a business partner who augments his talents, we are again looking at well over 40 years of combined experience behind driving the Dead Rabbit's award of "World's Best Bar."

In Malcolm Gladwell's book *Outliers*, which we highly recommend, he details the importance of at least 10,000 hours of experience as being a prerequisite for achieving greatness of any kind. I won't relive the examples given in Gladwell's book, but suffice it to say, the research he did there was verified in our work product as well. There are very few operators we work with who experience tremendous success before the age of 30, but it's not only an age thing. Our industry is full of people with years of experience but not necessarily in bars and restaurants. In terms of award-winning success, we found that not all experience counts the same. There are those industries in which experience is almost universal, retail for example. As we interviewed our award winners, only one of them had significant experience in another industry or job and then entered Hospitality as a second career. That by no means suggests you can't do it and enjoy a certain level of success, but our mission was to find commonality among "the best," and chief among them was the knowledge gained through a career of industry experience.

So does that mean you shouldn't open a bar without significant knowledge? Well, candidly, yes! If you don't have that type of knowledge yourself, then you should partner with those who do so that you have a wealth of understanding available to you on your team. We cover this concept in detail in Chapter 15, Partnerships. Based on our research, the relationship between industry experience and success rates looks like this:

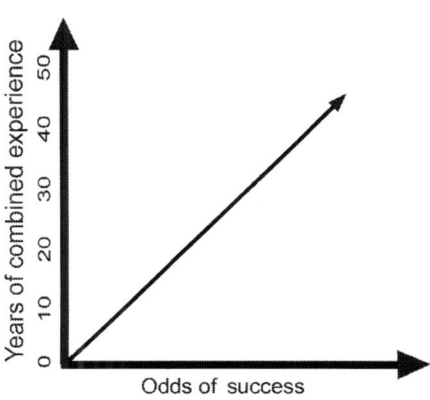

The Experience Continuum

Graph: Y-axis labeled "Years of combined experience" (0 to 50); X-axis labeled "Odds of success"; a diagonal arrow rises from the origin to the upper right.

Does this mean you can guarantee success by having a partner with experience or 10,000 hours of personal experience? No! There are always outliers who defy the norm, but what we do know is, for most, increasing Bar and Restaurant experience leads to exponentially greater chances of success.

We can build on our knowledge with partnerships, but partnerships can be tricky, and the more partners we have, the trickier the alignment and productivity become. There are always trade-offs. Beware of trying to shortcut experience in this industry by simply bolting on partners, because partnerships are complex and require a ton of alignment in order to realize their full potential. In the Partnerships chapter, we are going to highlight how to build successful partnerships and what they look like from the vantage point of the award-winning success. As we followed the stream of thought during our interviews, partnerships were clearly a massive component of success as well and tied in closely with award-winning success, so we've dedicated a chapter to delving into the details of successful partnerships, which becomes a huge force multiplier.

> Increasing Bar and Restaurant experience leads to exponentially greater chances of success.

For a more inverted example, I have a friend who was the CFO of a major U.S. electronics retailer who then went on to become the CEO of the largest auto parts retailer in North America. What did he know about the auto parts industry when he took the job? Nothing, really. He knows business, and he knows it well. He understands publicly traded companies and how to build high-performing organizations.

He could likely go on to be successful in any leadership role of his choosing UNLESS he decided to open up a cocktail bar in, say, lower Manhattan. In this venture, his likelihood of success would be very low. The typical standards simply don't apply to this industry. The expectations are different, the workforce is unique, the guest interactions are different — even the financial parlance is unique to the industry. Specific knowledge is a must, with very rare exceptions.

When I moved into the Hospitality realm, a former colleague of mine called me. He noted that I had moved into the Hospitality realm and wanted to know if we could chat about him buying a bar. He was a big musician as a hobby and had been extremely successful in his primary occupation, enough that he could easily afford to open his very own bar. His "dream" was to buy a space that he'd enjoyed visiting for years. He loved the atmosphere and the vibe and wanted to transition career-wise more into his hobby and start divesting in his current occupation, of which he was very much a leader in his field. I asked him simple questions, which are almost always the best ... "What do you actually know about running a bar, especially one with huge nightlife, music, and large crowds?" His answer: "I think I understand the basics." I simply responded, "I don't think you do, or you wouldn't be calling me."

I didn't get much past the employee turnover issues and staffing dilemmas before I could tell the illusion was starting to curdle. A few more good horror stories, combined with a net profit target, ultimately got him right where he needed to be ... on that day, I was a dream killer, and that was totally okay with me. You have to understand your motives; the *why* always matters. Just because I love racing cars doesn't mean I'll be good at building them. Most of the time, it's exactly the opposite. In the end, he and I agreed he'd be well suited as perhaps a silent partner or perhaps an angel investor to people who had spent a lifetime perfecting their craft.

We add this story because there are tens, if not hundreds of thousands of people out there who own bars and restaurants because they love to cook, have a passion for music, want to be the host of the party, and so on, and all these are singularly bad reasons to get into the Hospitality business. Why? Because the best in our industry have a passion for others over self. It's ultimately not about what we want but in the gift of giving to others. It's not even so much about service as it is giving. That's what's special about Julio: the gift of giving an authentic, memorable experience that transports you to a place like no other.

Not only must you acquire, over significant time, industry-specific knowledge, but the most successful people in our industry realize you do it because you love to give excellent experiences to others. This is not an industry where it's all about us; rather, it's all about the guest, all the time. That's what you have to *love*, and that passion gets pressure tested over time. If you still have a passion for delivering experiences for others after the trials and tribulations that only the years working in bars and restaurants can provide, then, just maybe, you're ready to own your own place.

HELIX Sequencing

> We found varying levels of correlation between the building blocks in each chapter and the DNA points at the end of the book. The strength of the correlation is represented by 1 to 5 circles around our 5-point Hospitality DNA molecule: 1 being a lower correlation and 5 being a higher one.

Humble Nature

Hospitality at its core is about putting others before self. As we came to understand early in our research, it's not so much about the service industry as it is about willful giving. The motivations for this industry in the pursuit of excellence really matter. As it relates to knowledge and Julio's story, the guest experience is at the cornerstone of every consideration, down to the footrails. The core idea behind Cafe La Trova is to deliver on a fully immersive experience for the guest.

Explorer's Pursuit

The entire concept of exploration is discovery. Diverse experiences are where we gain knowledge and perspectives across a wide spectrum. Exploration can lead to a positive experience as often as a negative one, and each needs to be embraced. The positives are obvious, but the negatives "I'll never be like that" or "I'll never do it that way" also pay dividends. Both are priceless learnings in our journey, allowing us to get to a place of excellence that includes a balanced understanding of right and wrong.

Lifetime of Experience

Knowledge takes a lifetime to accumulate. Most of those we interviewed had at least 15 years of personal experience in the industry and over 30 years of combined partnership experience. The caveat: not all experience is created equal. For instance, five years working at Cafe La Trova under the careful tutelage of Julio Cabrera is not going to be the same as five years at your local pub. Learn from the best available whenever possible.

Indomitable Spirit

Gaining knowledge can seem tedious and mind-numbing at times, but it brings with it irreplaceable value. Having the wherewithal and perseverance to acquire knowledge and then the know-how to translate experience to action takes time.

Xtraordinary Culture

Culture is a reflection of our values, and a culture based around the pursuit of knowledge provides near endless value. In the case of Julio, his commitment to professionalism, know-how, and staff development are on display to the staff of Cafe La Trova at all times. You get out what you put in, and there is a specific multiplying effect to living your values.

Chapter 2

Professional Development

> You can't just sit there and wait for people to give you that golden dream. You've got to get out there and make it happen for yourself.
> —Diana Ross

A significant yet unspoken challenge for leaders in our industry is the isolation that comes with being at the top of the food chain in a small business. It can get unmistakably easy to listen only to your own voice and so live in an echo chamber.

This is understandable because, after all, we're in a business with a high failure rate, and those who make it tend to lean heavily on the experience that the industry has taught them. On average, operators earn roughly 7–10% net profit. The top 1% of the industry can make considerably more profits, in the range of 12–17% — a substantial lift! Part of the idea of exploring success is to find out exactly what makes award winners different. Why are they more successful than others?

It's no coincidence that over 90% of the people we interviewed sought out external coaching or mentorship. To us, this couldn't possibly be a matter of chance. Please allow us to introduce Costin Gache! When we first met Costin, he was targeting a net 30% profit for his business — how does that strike you? Many would say it's impossible, and it certainly is a life-changing margin. As we mentioned above, the best many can even dream of achieving is in the neighborhood of 12–17%, but this guy is targeting 30%? Madness! If you find the idea of a 30% net intriguing, you'll want to pay close attention to this chapter and carefully read Costin's story about his commitment to professional growth.

Interbelic — Bucharest

Costin started in the Bar and Restaurant business at the age of 14 in Romania. By the age of 19, he was competing in bartending competitions, mainly on the flair side of things.

Professional Development

Over time, Costin started working on his knowledge in mixology to complement his flair skill set and was gaining a vital set of well-rounded Bar and Restaurant skills. By the time Costin was in his 20s, he was traveling the globe participating in flair competitions and running his own bar, Interbelic. He even started an event management company!

Costin is a deep thinker, and in his competitive travels, he was meeting industry experts, judges, and fellow competitors, thus learning via competition all sorts of ways to improve his business. Many of our interviewees told us unequivocally that travel opens the mind in ways nothing else can and clears the clutter, at least temporarily. In Costin's case, it was certainly the travel experience as well as the multiplying effect of the conversations he was having with experts around the world, where he was absorbing as much knowledge as he possibly could to apply back to his business. He was investing in himself as a way to invest in his business.

The state of mind we're in when we travel revolves around a few factors: we tend to be hyperaware of our surroundings, certain survival instincts kick in, and our heightened senses accelerate intake and learning. When we travel outside our comfort zone, we're exposed to a multitude of new or different ideas and concepts. We can also "turn off" the world as we know it and allow for quiet contemplation that's rarely found in our daily grind. Costin is a true believer and practitioner of travel and how it indispensably impacts learning.

This is what Costin shared with us in terms of how he thinks about learning.

1. Have an idea that becomes a goal
2. Understand that you don't know what you don't know
3. Realize what you don't know

4. Become informed
5. Apply that knowledge to your market
6. Measure for impact

Costin curiously seeks out knowledge and warmly welcomes it in!

In 2009, he began searching for industry experts he could invite to his super-hip cocktail bar located in the heart of Bucharest. His intent was to coach his team. And in walks our very own Angus Winchester — great choice, if we do say so ourselves!

Not only can we seek out opportunities externally to learn, but we can invite opportunities in the form of experts into our venue. This means we can effectively eliminate the middleman and give our teams direct access to knowledge. Experts are available in all forms, from cocktail experts to management specialists to guest experience gurus to marketers, and more. Not only does the team benefit from the direct interface with experts, but it also sets the stage for a culture of learning and development. When owners make these types of commitments to their teams, their teams typically respond in kind. They begin to become actively involved in training ideas and opportunities. They also tend to be more committed to doing things "the right way" versus the way they see fit.

Let's circle back to that crazy 30% profit goal. Costin believed there was more to attain in his business. He enrolled in a coaching program for high performers to go and work on their business with like-minded peers and other experts. *It should be noted, we were also coaches in this program, and several of the people we interviewed for this research project we first met there.* Sometimes the teacher stands to learn from the student!

One issue of great concern was that the class was hosted in Annapolis, Maryland — literally a 15-hour flight from Romania.

Without airport arrival or commuting, Costin was already looking at 30 hours of flight time. That's approximately 34 hours of travel for 48 hours of coaching, which boiled down to just 20 hours of actual classroom exercise. For the vast majority, this trade-off decision would be a nonstarter.

It was not a concern for Costin, however, as he measured it differently. In his mind, he would be thrilled to invest in four days of total time in order to realize the net 30% gain in his business. The net 30% meant thousands of potential dollars per year realized in perpetuity, and he knew he couldn't get there alone. Ultimately, Costin found the coaching so valuable that he made *10 trips* to Annapolis in 2.5 years to work on his business. That's 340 hours of travel for 200 hours of classroom time. It was a colossal commitment for him to see it through and stick to the outcomes.

Today, Costin works a schedule of 50 days on and 10 days off for himself in his business. In those 10 days off, Costin will explore a wide variety of ways to learn — it could be personal, it could be professional. It's basically whatever he feels is best suited to spend his time, but it is all in the name of personal growth. So, did Costin ultimately hit his 30% profit mark? You bet! The only way he finds the money and time to free himself up to do all the things he wants to do on his own terms is by constantly reinvesting in himself, which ultimately has a positive impact on his business. Costin behaves fundamentally differently so that he can live a fundamentally different life!

Another awe-inspiring story is that of Costin's good friend and fellow Diageo World Class award-winning compatriot, Katalin Bene — Kat for short. As with most, her story begins at a very young age, when she was barely old enough to work at a bar. She had an entry-level understanding of the industry and a thirst to learn more.

Hospitality DNA

In the present day, Kat stands as a Diageo World Class champion with a bright future, but things very much did not start out that way. Kat's country of origin is Hungary, and she found her first bar gig in Romania while attending university. She had a typical waitstaff job but was fascinated by the work behind the bar. The bar felt like magic to her, and her inquisitive nature led her to explore that magic while not even being a bartender.

In the early 2000s, according to Kat, there weren't many female bartenders in Romania. She believed she had the savvy and the skills to own the job — she just needed a shot. That opportunity came about just three months into the job. There was an opening to cover a bar shift where she worked, and Kat jumped at the chance. Her first shift wasn't perfect, but her instincts served true. She made cocktails well, she engaged with guests, she had fun, and guests would return. The place was clearly better that night for having her behind the bar, and her talent was noticed. Eventually she became a permanent fixture behind the bar, learning and growing in her craft.

Kat remained committed to her development. She did a lot of reading and engaged in learning beyond her own environment. There were very few books written on the industry of bars and restaurants at that time, let alone those translated into Hungarian or Romanian.

She would need to learn English if she were to evolve her interpersonal skills behind the bar and decided to kill two birds with one stone. She would open a Romanian to English dictionary on one side of the table and a cocktail book on the other — simultaneously learning the English language, all the while enhancing her knowledge of cocktails. This was the first time we had ever

> Kat has come to believe "You work hard and make your own luck" in this life.

heard of someone learning English through cocktail books ... I only wish this is how we had done it in my foreign language classes!

As she continued to research the cocktails of the world, Kat came across a venue called Nightjar, a regular on "The World's 50 Best Bars" list. The more she learned, the more Kat fell in love (virtually) with this London-based bar. At some point, she decided that someday she was going to work there. Not knowing how that would happen, she set the idea firmly in her mind.

As she has continued on her journey, Kat has come to believe "You work hard and make your own luck" in this life. To achieve award-winning success, you have to work hard, take some chances, and relentlessly pursue your dreams. She developed this mindset from real-world experience with one of her industry idols, Marian Beke, the general manager of Nightjar.

A few years after Kat first jumped behind the bar, lo and behold, Marian Beke, of Nightjar fame, was actually hosting an event in Romania! Kat had made it her mission to be sure she would be working at that very same event. At that moment in time, destiny was sealed.

As Kat will tell you, "Where there's a will there's a way." With intent, she hit all her marks that weekend, and when she wasn't working directly with or for Mr. Beke, she ensured her presence was felt.

In the short time he was in Romania, Beke saw the value Kat brought to the bar. Her dedication to the craft and commitment to bettering herself made it clear to him that she would be an asset to any team she joined and, upon leaving, Beke told Kat if she was ever in London, he had a job for her. So, the next journey began — the *curve*, as we call it. It's simply a cute way of describing a learning curve or journey. A few months after returning home, Beke was opening his own bar in London known as The

Gibson, yet another enchanting venue that would regularly adorn The World's Top 50 list.

Upon learning of the opening of The Gibson, Kat became determined to be a part of Beke's new bar! This was something she had been preparing for for years. I was clear to Kat that working in The Gibson would add huge value to not only her career, but her personal growth as well. This was the exact opportunity she had been preparing for all these years! She knew that in order to grow and realize her dreams, she had to make a bold move. Kat reached out to Beke, who remembered her and offered her a job at the new venue in that moment.

Beyond excited and with just a single month's worth of living expenses in her pocket, Kat quickly packed up her belongings into two suitcases and made the daunting trip to a new country. With cocktail books and English dictionary in tow, Kat left Romania with all her worldly possessions without any understanding of what job was being offered to her, no contacts outside of Beke, and no knowledge of where she would be living. She simply knew this was where she needed to be — part of a lifelong dream to play a critical role in the elite London bar scene.

When Kat arrived, she discovered the job she'd been hired for was that of a dishwasher (with a special emphasis on glassware) and as the prep cook, buying and prepping the ingredients needed for the cocktails each night. For most, this would have been soul destroying — an unrecoverable gut punch and a certain deal breaker. For most, this would have been cause to find other opportunities aligned with their skill sets. But not for the resilient Kat — she embraced the curve!

> Kat described her learning curve as a bar manager for a world-renowned, award-winning venue as "working from morning to almost morning."

Kat conquered the role just as she had with every other challenge bestowed upon her up to that point in her career. She approached the purchasing and prepping of the ingredients with sincere professionalism, taking pride in finding the freshest herbs and produce, and preparing them in such a way that the entire bar staff would be proud to use them in their creations. With conviction, her efforts paid off rather quickly as Katalin went from prep cook to bar manager in three short months. Kat described her learning curve as a bar manager for a world-renowned, award-winning venue as "working from morning to almost morning." She was treading water to keep up with all the demands of working in this business and yet still excelling at every step.

In 2018, it was suggested to Kat by friends and colleagues alike that she enter the Diageo World Class competition. World Class is a massive annual bartending competition hosted by Diageo, which has local, regional, and ultimately global winners. The competition is graded similarly to Olympic diving. Participants are scored based on difficulty levels, execution, and creativity. It's considered to be the most elite competition of its kind, and we're proud to boast of many champions, judges, and coaches in this book! To be a Diageo World Class winner is to plant a professional flag atop the Mount Everest of mixology.

Of course, Kat became a World Class winner. We're sure you saw that coming, and it's not hard to see how or why. It is no accident that her career has

Katalin Bene

continued to evolve as she relentlessly invests in her professional development. We share her story as another perfect example of commitment to personal growth: the understanding that it's usually NOT easy, convenient, or comfortable, but it is deeply rewarding. You will grow and improve if you're truly committed to the idea.

Like many whom we interviewed, Kat's and Costin's stories led to lessons that revolve around having a vision, dealing with adversity, overcoming obstacles, and relentlessly pursuing dreams. There are countless ways to invest in yourself, whether you are learning English from a cocktail book or traveling across the world to learn with masters of the industry. The trick of the trade is to stay the course and not become jaded by the journey.

HELIX Sequencing

> We found varying levels of correlation between the building blocks in each chapter and the DNA points at the end of the book. The strength of the correlation is represented by 1 to 5 circles around our 5-point Hospitality DNA molecule: 1 being a lower correlation and 5 being a higher one.

Humble Nature

Pursuing your goals can be a long and arduous journey. It is easy to focus on and even get lost in the external aspects of what it is you are striving to achieve. The incomplete tasks, along with the overall facets of your vision that are not working, tend to be more obvious as you get them all in front of you to examine. There is also a certain sense of self that drives us to focus more on what is wrong with the rest of the world rather than looking inside. Embracing the humility required to look inside and develop oneself, however, is incredibly rewarding and pays off factors above working on the external.

Explorer's Pursuit

The best professional development tends to come from taking chances. However, we must stress that you take intelligent, calculated chances. This is especially true early in your career when you have little to lose in the pursuit of improvement! Discover new places, new ideas, new people, and new opportunities to learn wherever you are and wherever you go. Our award winners have a natural curiosity and desire to learn born of a certain self-awareness that is strongly encouraged.

Lifetime of Experience

Avoid being a know-it-all. Success can create hubris, which only serves to limit your ongoing potential, and there is always room to grow. Our award winners demonstrate great appreciation for the growth they achieve during their lifelong journeys, and they never give up in pursuit of bettering themselves.

Indomitable Spirit

Don't be the biggest obstacle to your success. Compete with yourself first, and challenge your personal status quo. Growing personally, spiritually, and professionally is wrought with rewards you have yet to imagine.

Xtraordinary Culture

Personal growth is ... personal. However, you can also encourage personal growth throughout your organization. All the same rules that apply to you apply to your team. Don't forget where you came from and invest accordingly. We'll cover this in more specific detail in the HELIX Sequencing section at the end of the book, so please read on.

Chapter 3

Clarity

> Everything we do is in support of
> creating a "holy shit" moment.
> —Dave Kaplan

One thing we've come to learn from running our own businesses that has become increasingly more obvious in writing this book is the vital role that clarity plays in award-winning success. It's an amazing concoction of inspiration, discipline, know-how, and grit that seems to create this wonderful amalgamation that allows unprecedented success. Time and time again in our interview process, we were shocked by just how certain our award winners were in their mission. Sometimes you might even say it was "success be damned; I knew what I wanted to do and how I wanted to do it." Perhaps we can better explain through a couple of awesome examples.

Liliana Lovell — or just Lil, if you please — had just graduated high school and moved to New York City to attend NYU. As many college students do, Lil happily worked in waitressing and bartending.

As Lil became more comfortable behind the bar, she discovered her natural talent for entertaining. Whether it was witty banter with a guest or standing on the bar singing songs from the jukebox, it didn't matter much. It was all part of who she is.

After mounting pressures from Mom and Dad, Lil stepped away from the Bar and Restaurant business and took a dry job as an apprentice stock trader on Wall Street. These are unpaid gigs and, to Lil, they had a decidedly un-American feel to them. The days were long, slow, and in terms of a bank account, expensive. So it wasn't long before Lil was back behind a bar doing what she loved.

Lil eventually took a job at the Village Idiot, a well-known, lively cowboy bar in New York City's East Village.

"During the night I would dance on the bar, sing to the crowd, and insult anyone who wasn't man enough to take me on in a drinking contest. As a consummate salesperson, I was very good at this. To this day, the people who were around from the very beginning say that I was the best bartender we ever had."

Lil Lovell
Photo by Leejon Killingsworth

An idea sparked within Lil during her time at the Village Idiot. Like many before and after her, Lil decided that she wanted to open her own bar! She had built a significant following, so she felt she could do it. The only questions were where and how.

One day, lo and behold, a vacant location became available across the street — how serendipitous! If you put it in a movie, no one would believe it.

Lil's work experience, along with a keen eye for detail, allowed her to develop great clarity around what she wanted to create. She had a very specific vision based around an understanding of why people flooded the bar to see her. It wasn't the drinks or the food. It wasn't even the venue or the concept. They were coming for a unique experience they couldn't quite get anywhere else. Shifts with Lil were entertaining as hell, and people couldn't get enough.

Great clarity is a gift! What we learned from our time with Lil aligns well with our first chapter on knowledge. Lil leveraged her experience and learning to attain tremendous clarity on exactly why customers came to the venue during her shifts.

Imagine for a moment that someone comes to you with the following idea, asking you to invest. They want to open a bar but with no draft beer. Well, okay, tell me more. Then they say AND no cocktails … hmm, you may start to think this is starting to sound decidedly unbar-like. No draft, no cocktails, and we certainly won't be serving any food either. Now you're thinking, well, if you're going to do all that, then absolutely you must be treating customers like pure gold if there is any hope of making it, right? NOPE! In fact, if they dare ask for water, what we plan to do is spray them in the face and insult them just for asking. How much would you like to invest?

Even if you were to build out the perfect business plan on paper around this concept, the savviest investor would run away at full speed. Yet, this model ended up becoming known as the most famous bar in the world. It generated articles in *GQ*, which led to a hit movie, then turned into a TV show, and finally culminated in 29 franchises around the world.

In writing this book, it was very important to us to speak and learn directly from Lil as we have long been fascinated by what she created.

How can you possibly know a thing will work? If we could only be absolutely certain, decision-making becomes elementary. We find many of the world's best and most successful operators have this gift of great clarity, but it's crucial to know that this does not come from simply wanting a thing to be true or even just having a good idea. It comes from an element of hard proof born of real-world experience.

Lil did not flinch! It was rather amazing that she had no doubt this would work. That isn't to say it wasn't without challenges. For example, how do you replicate exactly what Lil, the singular bartender, does? How do you create a true culture and not a cult of personality based on and requiring Lil's direct and constant interaction?

You must find beautiful women who can sing, dance, and spar with the boys. Where can you find people with all these unique skill sets? In time, Lil came to this same realization. She was in fact searching for unicorns. What she had to do was build teams of performers with complementary skill sets who could work as a cohesive unit.

This system began to work so well it eventually led to a TV show called *The Ultimate Coyote Ugly Search*, which ran from 2006 to 2007. The show highlighted the need to work as a team and put the candidates through the paces to determine what made "The Ultimate Coyote."

Once Lil figured out the formula for replicating her talent, Coyote Ugly became a scalable entity and a worldwide phenomenon.

What we came to realize was that throwing a hell of a party, night in and night out, was serious business.

> What appear to be random rules and specials written on the bar mirrors and a "let it rip" feel to the place that suggests there is no need to play it safe is actually carefully orchestrated.

You could easily get the wrong idea, however. As you walk into a Coyote Ugly, you'll find discarded bras tossed about and remnants of past good times all over the venue. What appear to be random rules and specials written on the bar mirrors and a "let it rip" feel to the place that suggests there is no need to play it safe is actually carefully orchestrated.

Contrary to the carefree veneer, the look and feel of a Coyote Ugly is meticulously thought out and has a decidedly unique feel that plays right to their brand.

Lil realized that a good ole time with serious escapades and piles of money was all to be had! All this good-natured fun, offered in an atmosphere where everyone was safe, could take having a blast right to the edge but not go over it.

The Coyote Ugly brand is one of a kind! To our knowledge, there's nowhere else you can go to elicit the same experience you get at Lil's places. You won't find a stronger presence than Lil in the industry. She's as tough as nails — a demanding diva with super-high expectations as well as a woman who knows exactly what she wants. Before building her brand, she started with her own proof of concept with her style and talents, a personal brand she developed as a bartender that led to her designing a culture, and finally a reworking of that idea until she had the extreme clarity needed to allow that culture to be sustained without her. It was the clarity that the ladies needed to be a complete, highly competent unit that owns the room, and besides being a bar, Coyote Ugly would very much be an epic show.

To protect those stars, the expectations are set tremendously high that you'd better not mess with a Coyote, no matter how good of an idea it may seem to be at the time. These concepts and more were crafted over time, to a point where Lil could get anyone up to speed quickly and easily on how it all works.

> Productivity is time and time is money.

We've also come to understand that a wonderful side benefit of clarity comes in the form of increased productivity. When we know what we want, how we want to do it, and whose job it is, we eliminate all the wasted time that comes with uncertainty. In the end, this becomes a huge force multiplier, which you'll hear us discuss a few different times throughout the book. Remember: *productivity is time and time is money*. Management productivity is something rarely discussed in our industry, but those who have it are able to multiply success at a higher rate!

Clarity can start from many places and plays a part in strengthening many of our other Building Blocks. In Chapter 5, our Immersion chapter, you will hear in exquisite detail about our visit to Copenhagen and our night out at a bar named Curfew. When you read it, you may think that it was just a damn good night. Perhaps we got lucky and had precisely the right bartender on exactly the right evening, surrounded by the right guests, the right drinks, and the right music, and so on. It may also be true that it was the predictable outcome of 15 years of meticulously developing clarity of a concept.

For Humberto Marques, the founder and owner of Curfew, the journey began at 16 years of age, working as seasonal help where he began to learn the basics of working in a bar and cafe environment. He caught the bug. His journey of falling in love with the enticing flavors of a cocktail began to unfold. He was intrigued by the bar tools and the shakers, and he recalled the first time he saw his brother mixing a magnificently crafted libation. Humberto thought to himself, "Now that's cool," and so the die was cast.

The mystery of one's purpose was over early for Humberto. He knew what he wanted to do with his life, and he was gravely aware of the importance of enhancing his understanding of the industry. At that time, in the early 2000s, Humberto felt he had two choices to help him grow and develop more skills in the industry for which he was destined: work either in the United States or the United Kingdom. So, Humberto gathered up the courage to leave his native Portugal and head to Scotland, a land known for its picturesque green landscapes and old-world castles.

He found work at a four-star hotel that eventually led to a job at a five-star hotel, called Gleneagles. Gleneagles is a legendary venue, well known for its golfing lineage. It had also been owned by Diageo for a period of 31 years, including while Humberto worked there. As you can imagine, in the heart of scotch country, there were expectations. Fine scotch is not to be shot, chugged, or mixed. Anyone serving this storied beverage would need to know the history of each bottle, the proper way to enjoy it, and how each specific step and ingredient of the production process contribute

> As he recalled, his first glass of good scotch "tasted like a dose of medicine to me." As many of us know, scotch is an acquired taste, but Humberto began to grow in appreciation for exactly what can be done with flavors.

to its flavor. This was the pivotal place where Humberto began to really appreciate taste sensations that made his palate come alive! As he recalled, his first glass of good scotch "tasted like a dose of medicine to me." As many of us know, scotch is an acquired taste, but Humberto began to grow in appreciation for exactly what can be done with flavors.

Humberto, who had been used to blue, fruity cocktail drinks from the beaches of his home, realized there was a whole world of flavors out there that touched the palate very differently. He was exposed to fascinating flavor profiles. He began socializing with the cooks to understand flavors and ingredients better so that he could apply the same general, mouthwatering principles to the bar business. It was a very smart and interesting way to develop knowledge around how he could enhance the flavors of a cocktail.

In humble preparation for his next big step, Humberto worked on both his craft and his English while at Gleneagles. Unlike many of the people featured in our book, he had to learn English as part of his professional journey. Humberto was working hard to not only learn the world of spirits but also become fluent in a language that would enable him to communicate and connect with guests effectively.

One of these connections came by way of a gentleman named Tony Singh, whom Humberto met one day at Gleneagles. Tony had owned a critically acclaimed bar named Oloroso in Edinburgh, Scotland. As the two hit it off, he decided to eventually offer Humberto a position at the venue.

It was at Oloroso that Humberto truly found his professional footing. For several years, he worked to develop a strong sense of how flavors interact with one another to create unique taste sensations within the confines of a cocktail.

In 2015, the time had come to venture out on his own. While over the past 15 years Humberto had been accumulating a wealth of knowledge on the art of mixology, he was indulging another hidden passion as well: antiques.

In 2021, Humberto unexpectedly lost his mother — a loss that shook him hard. In working through his grief, Humberto experienced a reconciliation where he felt his antique collections could pay homage to his mother. With this inspiration, he delved into an adventurous antique collection for his bar. He collected cabinets, stools, tools, photographs, and anything else he could find that really spoke to the vision he was creating of a museum in a bar, specifically a U.S. pre-Prohibition museum, in part as tribute to his late mother.

His U.S. pre-Prohibition cocktail bar would also incorporate elements from not only the Chicago gangster era but also places like Berlin and Paris during that same period. A rare combination of unique and authentic permeates the rooms at what would become known as Curfew, in Copenhagen.

Humberto Saraiva Marques and his Coles shaker
Photo by Alexander Banck-Petersen

Curfew would go on to become a highly regarded bar for all the right reasons, and Humberto would land several cocktails on top 100 lists around the world, most notably his succulent Eucalyptus Martini, which was featured in Gary Regan's *The Joy of Mixology*.

Some may say that Humberto has a gift for creating taste in a glass. This is true; I can attest firsthand. Humberto's creations are undoubtedly a glorious gift, but the whole package is a carefully engineered passion that swells the senses.

As a self-described "detail guy," Humberto focuses the same care and attention into the detail of the bar, as the bartenders stow their bar tools in pre-Prohibition gun holsters. For Humberto's museum-in-a-bar concept, every detail is carefully curated — from stools, couches, tables, pictures, and cabinets all the way to glassware and napkins — meticulously contemplated to establish exactly the right tone.

These types of clarity are unambiguous and allow for powerful outcomes.

> For Humberto's museum-in-a-bar concept, every detail is carefully curated — from stools, couches, tables, pictures, and cabinets all the way to glassware and napkins — meticulously contemplated to establish exactly the right tone.

The magic at Curfew comes seemingly easy, putting the guest at ease and the staff at full attention, which we believe is in part due to the certainty and productivity that clarity creates. When one knows exactly what they want to do and how they want to do it, the only obstacle in the way becomes creation. It's an important reminder that many of these award-winning global brands aren't a product of corporations and deep pockets. These success stories are born in most cases of one person with a dream, a vision, a wish, and more than a few higher-power prayers.

We feel compelled to add some nuance to this piece as well. It would be natural to assume clarity is completely a product of experience. While to some extent that is true, it isn't always the case, precisely. Confused? Yeah, us too. It's hard to pin down. For some, there was great clarity in terms of a concept — "What type of bar do I want to open?" — but not great clarity in terms of how to finance it or how to operate it. For others, there was great clarity on wanting to own a bar and how to run it but perhaps a lack of clarity on what the concept would be or where to open it. Perhaps one's clarity isn't about owning a bar but about the journey to become an award-winning bartender, no matter the sacrifice. Very rarely did even our award winners have total clarity in every aspect of their ventures. Many will tell you, if you wait to have all the answers, you'll never start anything, but they did possess enough that they could begin their pursuit with great confidence. This is also where you link up with a great partner or — as you read on — you connect with a mentor. The idea isn't necessarily that everyone created their own clarity on every issue, but they were able to find their way to it, often with help.

HELIX Sequencing

> We found varying levels of correlation between the building blocks in each chapter and the DNA points at the end of the book. The strength of the correlation is represented by 1 to 5 circles around our 5-point Hospitality DNA molecule: 1 being a lower correlation and 5 being a higher one.

Humble Nature

Have the humility to recognize when you're not ready versus when you are. Uncertainty leads to self-doubt but should not be confused with humility. Clarity breeds confidence, which allows for input and intelligent adjustments. Additionally, while it may seem counterintuitive, the confidence created by clarity allows us to give credit to others and receive feedback in a productive way that leads to additional success.

Explorer's Pursuit

Until you are sure, keep looking and keep refining. In addition to your own designs, make sure you also take into account what your market is asking for. Many people launch a concept born solely from what it is *they* want to do, completely ignoring the interests of their community. It is important to ask the question, "What is the unmet need where I want to open my venue?" In your pursuit, you should endeavor to discover what it is that people are thirsting for, combining that with what you want to create to meet that need with confidence and enthusiasm. The explorer's pursuit teaches us to pay attention to the wants and needs of the community and when the timing is right, meet the demand.

Lifetime of Experience

If you don't have great clarity, you may not be ready. Having clarity doesn't guarantee success nor does it suggest you won't need to adapt, but going in without clarity almost guarantees a struggle and increases the potential for failure. Our past informs our future. We learn from the success and failures of others and build our plans accordingly. A lifetime's experience allows us to know the answer to certain questions without having to experience the pains of trial and error. That lifetime can be a bolt-on as well, in the form of mentors and partnerships.

Indomitable Spirit

People won't always agree with your vision or your dreams, but you should still dare to have them. Pursue your vision. Believe in yourself, provided you have done the work. You have the experience, and you know you are meeting a need in the market. You also have the clarity of purpose to achieve your highest aspirations. An indomitable spirit in itself is not enough; but when supported by clarity, it becomes a powerful force for success.

Xtraordinary Culture

Your vision must translate to your team; it must not simply dwell within you. The people around you will need the same clarity of purpose you have, and to give that, you must be able to share. Clarity comes not only in the form of an idea but also in your ability to communicate your vision and ideas to others so that they may execute with the same confidence you enjoy. Our teams must be an extension of the culture we wish to create, and that creation comes from our ability to provide clarity to our teams.

Chapter 4

Branding

> A brand is not a product or a promise
> or a feeling. It's the sum of all the
> experiences you have with a company.
> —Amir Kassaei

    Hiring in our industry can cause a lot of anxiety as the amount of trust, training, and detail involved can be immensely time-consuming. We put our reputation in the hands of a person we hope will handle it with great care. This is immensely true of our business and certainly true of the industry at large. We always seem to be one bad review away from people making an alternative choice as to where to spend their dining dollars. We have a fun intersection of hiring, culture, and branding to share with you.

    One day, I met with someone who appeared to be a great candidate for one of our account manager roles in our inventory business. We met at a halfway point that was convenient for both parties — a busy local sports pub with lots of regulars, located on a corner of two major thoroughfares. I opted for a table tucked away in a corner for privacy with my fingers crossed that this guy — let's call him Brian Moyers — was as good as he seemed on paper. He showed up 10 minutes early — a huge early win for Brian. We introduced ourselves and began the interview process.

Hospitality DNA

> "I don't know who Dave and Alex are, but I'm a huge fan of Death & Co."

About halfway in, he hiked up his long-sleeved shirt to the elbow, revealing a few tattoos, the largest of which was a large Death & Co tattoo, center mass, on his forearm. I smiled and asked, "So you're a pretty big fan of Dave and Alex?" He paused to process the question. I was asking about Dave Kaplan and Alex Day of Death & Co fame. Dave and Alex are owners of the globally acclaimed bar Death & Co, located in New York City, as well as authors of three of the most critically acclaimed cocktail books of all time, *Death & Co: Modern Classic Cocktails, with More Than 500 Recipes*; *Death & Co Welcome Home: [A Cocktails Recipe Book]*; and *Cocktail Codex: Fundamentals, Formulas, Evolutions [A Cocktail Recipe Book]*: which are all prominently featured at my bar at home!

"I don't know who Dave and Alex are, but I'm a huge fan of Death & Co," he said. And I asked, "Why?" He quickly began to talk about their commitment to the industry and the respect he had for the brand as he understood it. He may not have known their names until I told him, but he knew the brand, which is exactly how Dave would want it! Brian believed the Death & Co brand stood for something special which, in his mind, was intensely purposeful and authentic. He felt like the brand represented the best the industry had to offer, despite never having visited the venue.

For the record, I jokingly asked him if he would be willing to put our logo on a body part — I had requested a more intimate location, of course. He laughed and promptly told me no, at which point I told him he was fired. To which he was quick to remind me I hadn't hired him yet. We were off to a great start!

Brian joined the team and quickly became a star in the business. The bigger story is about building a brand that is so compelling that people want to permanently mark their body with your logo and mantra. I'm just old enough to remember when tattoos were mostly reserved for people in the military. And the tattoos they adorned themselves with were associated with their military exploits, representing a sense of belonging.

In this chapter we will discuss the power of a brand and at the end supply you with a tool we call the *Inception Archetype*, to help you begin your branding strategy. There are entire books written on this topic, and we realize we simply don't have the space to do a full analysis on brand building. Rather, we'll frame the importance of a brand relative to how an award-winning business thinks about branding as a strategy and provide you with a tool to get started for yourself.

Dave and I often talk in our consulting business about creating your tribe in terms of marketing. Take, for instance, Harley-Davidson. It's not at all uncommon for a Harley owner to have a Harley jacket and, most likely, the name of their club accompanying a massive company logo on the back. There's a reasonable expectation they may be branded with a company tattoo as well. The tattoo is about the tribe, signifying a certain pride in belonging. These are their people, and the "Hogs" are their ride.

At this point, you would be rightfully wondering, "So how in the hell is some guy halfway across the United States — who has never even been to Death & Co and doesn't know the owners' names or what they look like — proudly displaying the company logo on his forearm, center mass.

You may be surprised to know that Dave Kaplan, the incredibly humble mastermind behind the brand, has never been a bartender, nor has he been a director of operations for a bar or anything of the sort. However, like so many of our interviewees,

Dave at a very young age was immersed in Hospitality in his own unique way.

Dave began studying, yes *studying*, the anatomy of spirits while in high school. Dave told us he has strong family DNA in being terrific and gracious hosts. He bore witness to the care and energy his parents displayed whenever hosting or guests were involved, and they truly loved to entertain. While his parents demonstrated a real commitment to hospitality, it wasn't really in his line of sight to be a Hospitality professional. Sure, he liked to host a great party at a young age, but to do it professionally? That wasn't necessarily his vocation. We asked him what his parents thought about his intrigue with alcohol, and he simply said, "They never really said anything about it; I'll have to ask them. That's a great question!" We like the parents already!

Dave Kaplan
Photo courtesy of Death & Co

Dave put in a lot of work during his high school years hosting a variety of very notable underage (don't tell anyone) events, as one may expect from a burgeoning world-class operator. Even at an early age, a typical Dave Kaplan event seemed different than most, like the time where he and a friend converted the entire family garage into a badass tiki bar. They did this to capture an atmosphere desperately needed for drinking at the underage level. It featured faux palms, a dry ice waterfall, and assorted tiki accoutrements. Everything a teen demands in a proper garage bar!

Dave found the mystery and intrigue of spirits mentally intoxicating. Combined with a gift of giving great experiences and his parents setting a high standard, this had all the makings of a future industry icon.

It wasn't long before Dave was off to college. Dave's second professional passion is art. After surveying his options, he decided to study the arts at Rochester Institute of Technology's College of Art and Design. So, he made the trek from his family home in Jackson Hole, Wyoming, to upstate New York where he studied and finished his formal education and eventually had to make some major life choices about his future.

Post college graduation, Dave quickly found himself at a career crossroads. He had to choose between pursuing his passion for art or his passion for spirits and hospitality. He was torn. So, Dave sojourned in Las Vegas, which on the surface seems like an odd

> When Death & Co was born, it was the collision of a professional obsession and artistic expression.

choice for someone so grounded in authenticity, but Dave saw it as a real test. To him, if it all made sense after a year in Vegas, then his choice would be clear. If his love for Hospitality endured the year, then the industry is where he belonged.

Not only did his passion endure the year in Las Vegas but it flourished. This is where Dave came to understand how to merge his love of art with his love of spirits. Beautiful things can happen when passion and expertise collide. When Death & Co was born, it was the collision of a professional obsession and artistic expression. The professional obsession he had been nurturing since his teenage years started to round into form. When we asked the question, "Where did the name Death & Co originate from?" it was also the perfect time to ask, "How does my guy end up with your tattoo on his arm?"

At that point, Dave began to describe the painstaking attention to detail he believes drives the brand's success and that, in and of itself, must not only be repeatable in terms of guest experience, but it also must be experiential. He wants to not only deliver on perfect drinks as a matter of routine but also be able to experiment with the guests through spirits and mixology. This too becomes part of the process and part of the brand experience as well. Stay tuned as we will discuss this in deeper detail in our next chapter, on Immersion.

> "A guest experience, when executed properly, should be transformational, an experience unique unto itself and difficult, if not impossible, to replicate elsewhere."

I then asked, "So, we want this wonderful, meaningful, repeatable experience for guests that is warm and authentic, yet the name of the venue is Death & Co, with a black facade and no windows. How does that square?"

Dave explains the name Death & Co is a nod to the pre-Prohibition era when it was common for people to dissuade folks from going to bars as a place of ill repute. In effect, to visit bars was to hang out with the devil, or death itself. Hence the idea of Death and Company. It's a jab at the teetotalers of the time, which again is nothing short of brilliant in our estimation and an easy example of that painstaking detail brought to light. It was at this point I began to understand better why Brian had the tattoo.

One of the most fascinating comments we heard from Dave was this contrast between the outward appearance and the name of the venue relative to the warm, welcoming, hospitable amazement that awaited inside. Dave sought a particular reaction from his guest in which he described the perfect immersion experience as a "holy shit" type of reaction! This was found not only in the quality of the cocktail but also in a mesmerizing experience executed by staff. Indeed, Dave believes that "A guest experience, when executed properly, should be transformational, an experience unique unto itself and difficult, if not impossible, to replicate elsewhere."

Perhaps the most unique idea we heard in our process was how Dave and the Death & Co team want the guest to arrive with "a certain intent." What does this mean? This was new to us, and perhaps the most intriguing concept we heard during the interview process. The intent is that the guest's expectation has been set before the journey to the venue even begins!

The Death & Co guys want their brand experience to begin at inception. That is to say, the experience begins in the mind of the guest at the moment they decide that Death & Co has become the destination of choice on any particular night. It could be that on Monday, you have made plans to visit Death & Co on Friday with friends. That mental marker is where the experience begins in the Death & Co philosophy, because that's when expectations are set! For Dave, they want that imagination of possibility to tantalize the mind's eye, so when guests arrive, they arrive with a certain intent. What have they been imagining all week? When we think about how award-winning operators behave differently, we may find no better example than "a certain intent," which translates to the experience beginning at inception, building through expectations, and being exceeded in execution. Welcome to Death & Co!

When you put that type of thought into your guests, you will quickly build your tribe — that's easily understood. It should then come as no surprise that it's only part of the story.

Dave, along with Alex Day and Nick Fauchald, together wrote a book in 2014 called *Death & Co: Modern Classic Cocktails*, so complete, so extraordinary that it became described as "The definitive guide to the contemporary craft cocktail movement." As if being acknowledged as "World's Best Bar" by The World's 50 Best Bars list by William Reed wasn't enough, the book took the Death & Co brand to newfound acclaim as they became not just a New York City treasure but also a global phenomenon. Just to pour on the success (the puns flow easy here), they had a follow-up book called *Cocktail Codex*, which is stylish, smart, and looks great on the bar. It's another stunning piece of work. It's critical that everything the team produces meets the Death & Co standard of excellence.

Death & Co, Denver

So, what is the branding lesson here? Let's go back to my guy Brian. Why the tattoo? Seems like a silly question now, but let's answer it anyway. When you deliver upon your promise so deliberately that people tattoo your name on their body, buy your books in droves, attend your talks, follow your Instagram in the tens of thousands, and flock to your venue, your brand and marketing transforms from a cost center to a significant profit center. The brand is attracting the exact right people, and it's having the exact desired effect. The quality of the brand has transcended being simply a bar and has become a global phenomenon.

It would be very fair to ask, "So, how do I get started on getting great definition around my brand?" Let us help you get started with a simple and useful project.

We call it the Inception Archetype.

A great way to start understanding your brand better and building a brand strategy is to define your target audience with great clarity.

Who is it that visits your venue or who is it that you want to visit your venue?

Think of an archetype as your typical, or ideal, guest. A couple of classic archetype examples would be "the hero" as portrayed in a movie or "the underdog." Think about how you might envision those characters, and then describe them in detail. That is what we want to do with the guests you aim to attract to your venue. It's best to ask your team or partners to join in the exercise as well. This will help drive deeper clarity into the branding of your business. In order to brand effectively, we need to know with precision who we are building to.

Your branding efforts will also inform how you market and advertise. All three of these things are different, and we think it's important to acknowledge those distinctions. We start with branding, and we'll focus on that here for purposes of this specific conversation.

Have everyone involved make a few archetypes of their own. One of the most interesting things you may find here is whether you all even agree on who your most common or most desired guests are. Are we solving to the right people? Sometimes where we start with our concept and our target demographic isn't who ends up arriving — we've seen that more than a few times. In those instances, it's important we understand why. Did we miss on the demographic during the build phase, did we miss on the demographic during the operating phase, or did we never understand the demographic to begin with? All great questions.

Next, discuss these archetypes in your group setting, and pick a handful that best describe your most typical guest. It's important you all agree because this is how we get great clarity on not only our brand but also on how we will deliver on immersive experiences (next chapter)!

Imagine an entire visit through the lens of your archetype. Give them a name. Describe how they're dressed, their attitude, and their expectations. Really bring them to life. You may also include what kind of day they are having, their kids' names, and so on. The more detail the better!

For example, if you have a bar located in Lower Manhattan (since we've mentioned NYC quite a bit), you may describe a businessman dressed in a dark blue suit coming in somewhat exhausted after a stressful day, looking to blow off steam with colleagues. They work in the trading market, and it took a big hit that day, so negative emotions may be high. That would be an ideal beginning to an archetype description, but don't stop there — build the experience all the way through departure and your visit follow-up mechanisms.

Another may be a family restaurant in the suburbs, and you could describe a family of four coming in for the one meal out they can afford each week on a slim budget. They have tight schedules, hectic children, and just need someone to care for them for a change — another solid archetype.

Perhaps you own a nightclub, and you might describe young people coming in late at night on the weekends looking to have fun, listen to music, dance, and meet other people.

Have fun with the exercise. I would suggest building at least three to five of your most common guest archetypes. This is clearly about who they are. Then, start solving to their expectations. We call this the inception exercise because it helps us get started. It's the beginning phase of planning an award-winning experience for your guest, which leads to building an award-winning brand.

The Inception Archetype

- Give them a name, personality, job, and attitude.
- How do they initially connect with us — a certain intent?
- Why are they coming out that night, or that day?
- What do they enjoy?
- What do they expect from us?
- What do they hope to achieve at our venue?
- How do they feel when they arrive? Be specific.
- What are their concerns, curiosities, and interests?
- Does anything make them nervous or unsure?
- How do we make them feel when they leave?
- What compels a return visit?
- What do they tell their friends?

You can add or subtract from the list of questions. The most important thing here is doing it from the lens of the guest, not as an owner, manager, or staff. Be 100% honest as well. It can be easy to lie to yourself in this exercise, trust me! The clarity derived from this exercise will allow you to build your brand with the right target in mind, which then turns into your marketing and advertising ... that strategy becomes the essence of who you are in the community.

Let's use another real-life example from outside our industry and a masterful example of branding. What do online payment systems, automobiles, and space travel all have in common? Answer: Elon Musk. He is exceptionally good at branding and understanding exactly who his customer is across multiple disparate disciplines. Let's do the exercise above right now from a Tesla lens:

- What's the buyers name?
- Where do they work?
- Why do they want an electric car?
- What concerns might they have?
- How did the buying experience feel?
- How do they feel about ownership?
- What might they tell their friends?

Now let's consider for a second Dave's philosophy of "a certain intent." As a Tesla owner is ordering their Tesla and picking out options, how are they imagining it will look? Will it have that new car smell? What will the first drive be like? How does it feel driving past gas stations? How does it feel not being able to drive long distances? This is just a snippet of how that exercise might look from a non-Hospitality lens, for context.

HELIX Sequencing

> We found varying levels of correlation between the building blocks in each chapter and the DNA points at the end of the book. The strength of the correlation is represented by 1 to 5 circles around our 5-point Hospitality DNA molecule: 1 being a lower correlation and 5 being a higher one.

Humble Nature

Our brand interests always come before self-interest, all the while realizing that it is one and the same when done properly. On scale, it's unhealthy for individuals to be bigger than the brand — dangerous, even!

Explorer's Pursuit

Beautiful things happen when passion and expertise collide. Our brand is very much an extension of who we are and what we believe as seen through the eyes of the guest. Those things are often grounded in our learnings and discoveries. The more learnings and discoveries we have, the more we can translate that to our brand and ultimately our guests.

Lifetime of Experience

Award-winning brands are able to be viewed through an external lens. The creators of these brands perpetually demonstrate that they understand the real-life experiences of their guests and ensure that the brand promise matches those experiences. Keeping your brand and experiences connected is paramount to success.

Indomitable Spirit

Considering the entirety of an experience and putting yourself so far out there as to embrace the idea that a guest experience begins at inception has strength. Brands that are thoughtful endure.

Xtraordinary Culture

People have great pride around brands, employees and guests alike, and will proudly display their loyalty in great brands. Hard Rock Cafe, Harley-Davidson, Apple, and the NFL have all created a fanaticism through dogmatic culture that defines not only the brand but also how the guest experiences the product. The NFL has a concept called "protecting the shield." This means that no matter what side of an issue you may find yourself on, for better or worse, everyone believes in and works to preserve the legacy of the NFL. The NFL players are a unionized group, so the fact that most of them "protect the shield" becomes a profound example of Xtraordinary Culture. Unions create a culture first around protecting the employees; unionized employees who protect the company brand ahead of themselves are uncommon. Employees of the NFL feel that brand represents them as much as it does the ownership group. This is how powerful brand building can be.

Chapter 5

Immersion

> The way the experience feels is even more important than the way the food tastes. It's 49% the way it tastes and 51% how you make them feel; getting just one right is a failing grade. Service is a monologue — how do we do the same thing, the same way, every time for everybody, and make it feel unique just for you?
> —Danny Meyer

Isn't it fascinating just how Hospitality can be viewed so very differently, depending upon one's culture? Consider the tradition known as *melmastia* practiced by the Pashtuns. This is such an integral part of the Pashtun culture that one who does not give freely and willingly of oneself to a complete stranger as a guest risks being disowned by their tribe. It's a tradition that goes back hundreds of years and is an absolute part of their moral code. The Pashtuns may go so far as to give their own life in protection of a guest.

The real-life story told in the book and movie adaptation of *Lone Survivor* recounts the experience of Marcus Luttrell and how Mohammad Gulab puts the lives of his family, his village, and himself at risk in the name of protecting Luttrell, a total stranger and, to some, an enemy combatant. To most, that may seem unconscionable, but such is the culture and the customs of the Pashtuns, and they abide by it without hesitation.

It's the most extreme interpretation of a full commitment to "Hospitality" we could find. We believe it serves as a striking example of just how far one can go in the name of caring for a guest. We give this example to set up the idea that there is no one "right" version of Hospitality — it can vary — and this example is certainly cultural in the broader context. It does, however, exemplify the impact of culture and just how ingrained Hospitality customs and traditions can be.

Traditionally, when people travel abroad, it's very common to research all the local sightseeing experiences and historic sites when visiting a new land, but for my wife and me, as an example, we start with, "Where are the best bars in town and how do we make sure we spend time there?" We can recount countless magical experiences we've had with friends and family abroad — the kind of stuff that makes life worth living, the stories you tell for a lifetime. For us, these exceptional experiences seem to happen regularly on a bar stool or at a table when we visit world-class venues. We happen to find looking at the ocean, statues, and castles somewhat interesting, but living in the here and now is far more intriguing because of the people in this world fully committed to delivering those types of magical experiences professionally. We want to celebrate and learn from a small segment of those special people in this chapter and share their greatness with you, in hopes that it may in some way improve upon your own circumstance. The people who stay up late at night trying to figure out just how to make us a little happier when we visit and how to make their bar or restaurant a little more exceptional so that we might return regularly or discuss how great our visit was are worth learning from.

Immersion

A brief personal story from Dave N. For our 25th anniversary, my wife and I had planned to had planned to do something special. We wanted to go somewhere that would be unique to us, and after much research, we decided to go to Istanbul. The expectation of this trip had us overflowing with excitement! A place with a massively rich cultural and religious history would certainly provide for truly unique experiences, which is ideal medicine to us! We had plans in place — airfare, hotel, sites to see, bars and nightclubs to visit picked out — and were raring to go. Then a funny thing happened the week of our trip … revolution!!! There was a full-on coup attempt to overthrow the Turkish government, as some of you may recall. My wife entered my office and asked, "Have you seen the news?" I said, "No, what is it?" She said, "There's a revolution of some kind in Istanbul; I checked the hotel webcam, and there's a tank parked in front of our hotel!"

The hotel has external cameras where you can view the hotel and its goings-on and sure enough, a big greenish tank sat right there at the front door! Now, there was a lot of turmoil leading up to our trip, and the U.S. government had issued a travel advisory, but we weren't scared off so easily, so in my mind we were still going. In for a dime, in for a dollar, I thought (plus we had prepaid for the hotel to save on the rate and if you're wondering … no, there are no revolution refunds)! What're a few tanks and machine guns anyway? So I said, "Hey, should be easy to get a table now." Jeni didn't quite share my sense of humor and retorted, "Should be easy to change the flight." Since the airport had been shut down as a focal point of the local usurpers, Delta, our airline, was happy to redirect us without financial penalty. Shout out to Delta — very hospitable!

We had to pick somewhere else quick, and we ended up choosing Copenhagen as our destination to celebrate 25 years of pure marital bliss. We had very little time to organize our bar playlist. Now, if there's one person in this world I know I can go to for a great bar recommendation on short notice, it's Angus Winchester! Not only does Angus have one of the all-time greatest names, but he also has an epic bar playlist! It's just one of many reasons we wanted Angus for the foreword, by the way. His experience, knowledge, and perspective, to us, are absolutely priceless.

Anyway, back to the story. We were on night three in Copenhagen, which is an incredible city, yet we just hadn't hit on that magical experience we were looking for and, to be fair, I had ignored Angus's recommendations up to that point. I know ... I know. At any rate, we were strolling through the city — it's not all that big; it's a wonderful, intimate city — and I happened to glance across the street and see a hanging sign that said "Curfew," and I stopped in my tracks. I turned to Jeni and exclaimed, "That's on Angus's list!" Our pace hastened as we strode across the street and right into the bar. There was not much to see on the outside, just a hanging shingle and a simple entryway. However, beyond the threshold, the magic began.

Along with only a few other customers at the time, we were welcomed like visiting dignitaries. Humberto Saraiva Marques, the establishment's owner, and António Saldanha de Oliveira, an award-winning Bacardi Legacy bartender, went to great lengths to immediately greet us and, recognizing we were new to town, shared the venue concepts and put us at ease. They showed us around and explained the intricate details of the décor and the layout of the bar, which is a stunning homage to the U.S. pre-Prohibition and uncomfortable era. The bartenders wore leather gun holsters for their mixing tools. All the bar accoutrements were carefully selected to properly represent the era.

What we found particularly magical was that, although the bar was impeccably designed to represent the days of yore, it felt modern and current at the same time; that's a talent I don't possess or understand. Somehow, it was a perfect blend of the old and the new, tied together with amazing energy. Jeni ended up holding court with a group of locals for hours while I talked global politics with a particularly smart gentleman at the bar who somehow knew more about my country than I did — just the kind of experiences we were hoping for!

To their great credit, António and Humberto understood exactly the type of experience we were looking for on this special occasion, and they delivered big time. Humberto and António wowed us with cocktail after cocktail, each as impressive as the last. So much so, we hadn't even realized that the place had been closed for about an hour when we finally checked the time. Never was there a hint of "time to go"; in fact, the guys took us on another round of bar history before we left and gave us some ornate custom muddle sticks as keepsakes of our visit.

Curfew — Copenhagen
Photo by Alexander Banck-Petersen

I'm leaving out a lot of nuances in the magic of the visit, but I'm sure you get the idea. For me, that was the trip — mission accomplished. Whatever happened after that was just fine by me. It was a stunning visit, almost overwhelming in its experiential excellence. This is the essence of what we want to try to capture for you in this chapter: how does this magic happen? Is it by accident, by chance, or by painstaking design and, if the latter, what was the journey to get there?

Dave Domzalski and I published our first book, *The Bar Shift*, with the intent of sharing some of the best bar standard operating procedures (SOPs) we knew in hopes of making the lives of operators a little better, to help drive profit, and to shed a little light on best practices from around the world of hospitality. As we surveyed the landscape of our noble profession, we couldn't help but notice what might become our next irresistible distraction: making a more strategic view of running bars and restaurants an appealing idea. It has become commonplace for people to parrot the notion of the importance of the guest experience without really defining what that means. It's akin to asking for a diet soda: it could be anything. Consider our friends the Pashtuns and what Hospitality means for them, and compare that to perhaps the experience you may find in a place like Hawaii, to which I have recently traveled to visit my son who is stationed there in the military. It's a well-known tradition to greet a traveler with a ceremonial lei as a symbol of a celebratory welcome and joy. Juxtapose that with what we may experience in Kabul with the Pashtun culture: completely different processes but both aimed at the same outcome. So, what's the point?

When we sat down and interviewed some of the world's best operators, we were prepared for, if not expecting, a very well-defined set of behaviors from each operator. A script of sorts that says, Here's what we expect from each employee, and here's what the outcome should look like every time. We were surprised by how many of our interviewees couldn't quite describe what the guest experience should look like in their venues. You could tell it was in their head — they would know it when they saw it. They know it when it's breaking down, but to formalize it wasn't necessarily readily available. So it took a lot of digging and a lot of probing and uncomfortable questions to get to a place where we landed on an answer. After hundreds of hours of interviews and pages and pages of butcher paper, we found one word that best described the venues that delivered the ultimate guest experience: immersion!

Our friend Sean Finter closes his webinars with a question: "If you and I could be sitting at a bar anywhere in the world, where would we be?" It's a fun question. When we answered for ourselves, the place that popped up for us both was Sweet Liberty. Sweet Liberty was founded by Dan Binkiewicz, John Lermayer, Michelle Bernstein, and David Martinez. Tragically, we lost John a few years back, and his loss is felt throughout our community. John was a people person. He fed off the energy of others and somehow gave mountains more than he took. We were privileged to be some of the first guests to enjoy Sweet Liberty in South Beach. Now, it wasn't that we were just a guest but we got to enjoy a VIP-level experience. What does that mean, you ask? John had built a table BEHIND the bar — a table right in the middle of all the bar warfare. Think of a chef's table, cocktail bar style. A place where you become so invested in the carnage of the night, you feel like you're literally part of the venue, part of the team ... a fully immersive experience! John was so invested in the idea of creating immersion in Hospitality that when only two people called to ask to "steal" his idea in the first year of his invention, he lamented to his partner that he couldn't understand why more people weren't doing the same.

There are many, many ways we heard people discuss this idea of immersion. It wasn't their word at the time, but when we distill all their thoughts, stories, and ideas, that's what came out. Consider our dear friend Gary Crunkleton, who owns the Crunkleton in Charlotte and Chapel Hill, North Carolina. Gary has an unquenchable passion for all things spirits, especially bourbons. On a regular basis, Gary will host bourbon tasting and spirit education for anyone wanting to come to the venue for that sort of thing, which turned out to be hundreds. Gary creates a different type of immersive experience by educating guests often before the venue actually opens. He wows people with knowledge and tasting experiences they simply can't get anywhere else. In effect he's creating a bunch of "Mini-Mes" as those he educates pass along their newfound knowledge to their friends and cohorts. He's creating an army of experts who consider his venue a "home base."

The Crunkleton, Charlotte
Photo by Alex Caterson, The Splinter Group

Another brand that exemplifies extreme immersion comes from Julio Cabrera, owner of Cafe La Trova in Miami, which we discussed at the beginning of the book — a fully immersive, authentic Santiago, Cuba, experience ... we're so in!

Now let us share with you an example of a failed immersive experience. Imagine a sports bar whose owner decides it would be a good idea to have the local sports talk channel come in and do their show from the venue. Makes a ton of sense; seems to be the right type of idea. People who are listening nearby are encouraged to come in, hang out, and have a good time. However, upon arrival they find the DJ's back in a corner the entire time, behind plexiglass and is clearly unapproachable and uninterested in being there. Yes, they are promoting the venue and their whereabouts on the airways but those they pull in only find themselves disappointed that there was zero engagement with the guests and the local celebs couldn't pack up and get out of there fast enough. It's a bit like getting the rug pulled out from under you: a buildup of excitement only to find out nobody really cared beyond you showing up. It was all part of a script.

Now imagine if afterward the sportscasters hung out, took some selfies, talked shop with the sports bar guests, acted like they cared, and gave authentic engagements. Imagine interviewed athletes hanging out for a while and becoming part of the crowd. Now that can be special and certainly immersive to people who would be thrilled by that experience. It wouldn't take long at all for the word to get out about that level of guest experience. That's a true story, by the way — one I experienced firsthand with a client — and is a perfect contradiction to the execution we read about at Sweet Liberty, Curfew, Cafe La Trova, and the Crunkleton.

So if you're seeking to become an award-winning operator with a venue that has people talking all around the world, the question for you becomes, how do you create your version of an immersive experience? It starts with authenticity, not of the concept but of true caring. You have to genuinely care about the experiences you intend to deliver, and that must be at the forefront of your ideals. One thing we have learned is, we're not in the service industry, we are in the giving industry, and that means so much more. This is an excellent juxtaposition of how giving comes from a place of "want to" and service comes more from a place of "have to" as it relates to hospitality. In our Curfew visit, they could have ushered us out as soon as the venue closed (candidly, we have no idea what time that was; I just realized we were the only people in the place at some point), but they didn't. Why? Because they didn't want to. We would have understood. There would have been absolutely no question that we needed to leave. In fact, we felt bad (only sort of) they let us stay so late. This is the stuff they are made of, so the big idea is immersive experiences are delivered through people. These people are completely committed to the idea of giving because it's in their DNA. It's not just what they do but who they are. Can this be taught? YES! That's the good news; however, in order to teach it, it has to be part of an overarching culture that is fully invested in the idea of immersion and how to create it and reward for its execution accordingly.

> A fully immersive experience contemplates all five senses in order to create a sixth, a feeling or experience we call *immersion*.

Michael Tipps, or just "Tipps" if you know him well enough, started out his career in his teenage years as well, venturing off to NYC to become an actor. Along the way, as many do, he fell into Hospitality gigs: busser, server, and bar manager, culminating in the role of manager of a bustling New York City hotel bar.

It was here where he really got his Hospitality chops. In an interesting turn of events, Tipps landed a regular role on the TV soap opera *One Life to Live*. So by day, soap actor and by night, bar manager ... very cool! The TV work eventually demanded his full attention, but after a brief dalliance with daytime TV, he felt called back to hospitality. He simply loved the industry and candidly hated the daytime TV gig. Eventually that knowledge and on-air talent paid off, landing him work on a little show at the time known as *Bar Rescue*. At this point, Tipps had left NYC for LA and joined the Bar and Restaurant scene there and opened what he describes as an upscale dive bar, Shoo Shoo, Baby, as well as the consulting firm Invictus Hospitality, where they now do full-service consulting.

Something Michael taught us that struck a chord was that a fully immersive experience contemplates all five senses in order to create a sixth, a feeling or experience we call *immersion*.

- Smell
- Sound
- Sight
- Taste
- Feel

When Tipps describes how he thinks of creating immersive experiences, he'll talk about the drive to the venue and the parking lot experience, which includes the look and feel of the door and especially the door attendant, if applicable. Every consideration is given to all five senses. In our book *The Bar Shift*, we have a chapter dedicated to "full awareness" and

Michael Tipps

seeing your venue anew each day. Tipps drives home in multiples by challenging us to deliver these exceptional sensory experiences and being completely aware of how the guest is taking in what we're offering. This is a great way to begin thinking of immersion.

When we spoke with Dave Kaplan, he discussed how immersion begins at inception! What does that even mean? Dave explains when a guest first contemplates going to the venue, say midday Friday, or perhaps plans for ladies' night or date night later in the week, that build of expectation is when full immersion begins because the mind is already working toward an expectation. How's that for consideration! So in truth, full immersion begins with branding and marketing, which sets an expectation. *When the guest arrives, we aren't at the beginning — we're already midstream in terms of an experience.* We now have to, at worst, meet expectations, and ideally we exceed what are already lofty expectations. If we stay deep here in terms of concept, the fully immersive experience remains long after the visit: exhibit A, our visit to Curfew. Upon reflection, our expectations actually began when Angus sent me the list of places to go, not when we saw the shingle or walked in the door. Hell, I nearly skipped across the street to enter the place after several mediocre experiences prior to the visit.

So are we saying every visit has to be mind-blowing to be fully immersive? No. What we've learned is that a fully immersive experience is all-encompassing. To take you outside our industry for a second, think Disney. Disney does full immersion perhaps

Death & Co

better than anyone. They don't have employees, they have cast members. You plan ahead, which sets the stage for the visit. You build excitement and anticipation. Then you go on your trip, which doesn't disappoint, and you hold on to the memories for years to come.

> When the guest arrives, we aren't at the beginning — we're already midstream in terms of an experience.

We should think of our business in the same light:

- We set the stage through branding and marketing.
- We deliver upon and exceed our value proposition.
- We create lasting memories and reputation.

You may own a simple pizza joint like our friend Tony Overall, who you'll hear about in Chapter 8. You may not be in a position to blow people's minds experientially, but don't be discouraged; you can create a product that people can't wait to enjoy, know they can rely upon, and are eager to share with friends. On Monday they are planning to buy on Friday … immersion. That's what was bothering Tony so much in our upcoming execution chapter. He knew he was getting in the way of his own success and luckily he found his way through. So, we don't want anyone to feel excluded from the idea of full immersion. Immersion is a matter of context, and we can all operate from the perspective of delivering on immersive experiences. Where our interviewees separate themselves is the spectrum of immersion. For them it starts at inception, NOT at the host stand.

In this chapter, we deliberately did not discuss in depth the role the staff plays to the extent we could have because we feel we cover this in subsequent chapters, and we want to avoid being repetitive … read on!

HELIX Sequencing

> We found varying levels of correlation between the building blocks in each chapter and the DNA points at the end of the book. The strength of the correlation is represented by 1 to 5 circles around our 5-point Hospitality DNA molecule: 1 being a lower correlation and 5 being a higher one.

Humble Nature

To create an immersive experience for the guest, you must focus on them completely, putting most of your ego aside. True immersion puts a complete focus on how guests experience your venue.

Explorer's Pursuit

Sensory exhilaration: How should it look, smell, feel, sound, and taste? We're limited here only by our imagination, which is fueled by our own experiences. As we gather unique experiences for ourselves, we can then, in turn, give them back, creating more in-depth experiences for our guests.

Lifetime of Experience

Never stop learning! The ability to create immersion comes from a glut of experiences colliding with a passion for giving and a culture of execution. It can be easy to think we know enough, especially when there's award-winning success involved. However, the exact opposite is true: atrophy and complacency can be an unfortunate by-product of success. You never want to stop gathering that which can be given to your guests.

Indomitable Spirit

Crafting an experience so complete that your guests get lost in your creation takes focused effort applied over the entire life of the business. While you can and must bake this into the culture of your business — which takes the day-to-day operational aspect of immersion off your plate — you will need measures in place to ensure that your staff always successfully applies your guest service strategy.

Xtraordinary Culture

An immersive experience that exists in perpetuity is the ultimate expression of a fully executed culture. Here, culture means a team that shares a passion for transformational experiences. The interesting thing about these fully immersive experiences is that people confuse transformation with complexity. Get your points of execution as simple as possible and your guests will get blissfully lost with you in no time.

Chapter 6

Details

> It's about carefully considering all
> five senses to create a sixth.
> —Michael Tipps

Let's go back to our sports bar from the last chapter. Yes, they struggle. A customer walks in. His mind is set on watching his favorite football team play a critically important game. There are a lot of other people there as well to enjoy watching their favorite team play. This is a big, popular spot, well known for its game days. Problem is, the gentleman doesn't know where his game is playing and doesn't know what his seating options look like. In trying to get help, the staff is running around like crazy, trying to satisfy a litany of customer demands predicated on a certain lack of preparedness. As we know, "fan" is short for "fanatics," and these people don't want to miss a single second of their game. After all, it's a sports bar, so this should be clearly understood and prepared for, yet the staff was not. What should be a wonderful problem to have — a packed bar — quickly turns into a mass of frustrated, if not angry, guests.

In our research, what we found was another very common thread among our interviewees: a certain healthy obsession with detail. We're fond of saying "The devil is in the details, but don't live in hell," which loosely translated means yes, obsess with the detail but not in a debilitating way. Teach the team the importance of the little things, put processes in place, and reward execution. We can cast a vision about the little things without drowning in them, hence the "don't live in hell" bit. In the case of our sports bar, TVs should be labeled with the game so people don't wander and wonder. There's a preprogrammed game schedule, so everything comes on in time versus someone looking through 25 remotes to find the right one. Game day guidance is written on a dry erase board or chalkboard at the venue entry point. The staff understands the urgency and sensitivity of raving fans and caters to their comfort on game day. We put detailed processes in place, which allow us to not worry about simple execution and get busy on the business of full immersion.

António Saldanha de Oliveira
Photo Courtesy Dom Cristina liqueur

If we step out of the sports bar for a second, we recall the example of how Julio Cabrera was obsessed with the details of creating a legitimate replication of a bar that could be found in Santiago, Cuba, down to the footrails. António Saldanha de

Oliveira, in his quest for the perfect cigars for his bar, made a pilgrimage to Cuba in the name of research (tough gig). Recall the painstaking detail Dave Kaplan put into every nuance of creating a "holy shit" moment at Death & Co: every sight line considered, every part of the decor, every spirit. Michael Tipps informed us about tantalizing all five senses, which requires a keen awareness of smells, sounds, textures, visuals, and tastes. Getting all five exactly right is no small effort but one that is required to create the ideal ambiance. Riz (whose story is coming up soon) opened 11 music-based venues and knew how important it is to get sound dialed in and what a massive impact that can have on full immersion. Speaking of music, make sure only the right songs are available in the jukebox so that a guest can select from a group of songs that click with the spirit of the venue, and nobody can play a mood killer at Coyote Ugly during peak trade. When we spoke with Humberto about Curfew and his vision to create a museum inside his four walls, every consideration was given, from the flower petals in the drinks to accent the olfactory senses to the napkins to portray the feeling of antiques.

When we discussed the importance of details with Salvatore Calabrese (don't miss his incredible story in Chapter 16), he was emphatic about considering everything that goes into running a bar, not just the spirits but the employee behind the bar. Salvatore plans his bar with a *three-step rule*: bartenders should never need to move more than three steps to access everything a guest requires. This allows for great service to both the internal and external customer. We owe it to our teams to make sure they are set up for success. They are the ones delivering wonderful guest experiences — that needs to be as carefully considered as the experience itself. Gary Crunkleton leads with this same ideal. When Gary opened the Crunkleton in Charlotte, despite his robust and eclectic inventory, he refused to have more than eight specialty cocktails on his menu. At that time, he believed the team couldn't execute with perfection on more than eight. That isn't to say it can't or shouldn't be done with more, but it is to say, don't let your eyes overrule your appetite. Or as Gary puts it, "You shouldn't have more cocktails than you can perfectly execute." In addition, Gary's bars have perhaps the best setup we've seen for his bartenders. As a stage should be built such that actors can maximize their performance, so should a bar be built such that bartenders have the best opportunity to execute their craft and wow their guests. This is how Gary carefully considers every aspect of his venues.

We once had a potential client call us who wanted to open up a private club featuring high-end bourbons and the like. He wanted to feature rare and antique products and solicited our help in launching his venue. I gave Gary a call, explained to him the gentleman's desire, and asked if he would mind if I sent him his way to experience his concept as it best exemplifies what I think our potential client was looking to accomplish. It's about a four-hour drive from where this gentleman lived to Gary's venue. The two of us had never met, and I gave him my first piece of advice for free. I told him to pack up the car for a long weekend and take his wife to Charlotte and visit the Crunkleton. It's the living embodiment of what he was aspiring to achieve. If he was willing to try and build something as good as that, we could move on to the next stage of consulting. My fear was, he wasn't an industry guy. He had a vison in his head, as many do, and just enough money to lose it all if he got it wrong. I had zero hesitation in sending him on a four-hour weekend trip with his wife. I had 100% confidence Gary would deliver, because that's what the great ones do: they deliver excellence with consistency because they've paid attention to the details. They build a program that can be repeated at the highest standard, no "special" effort required.

The next time I heard from my potential client (who, frankly, I was hoping to scare off because of their lack of experience and knowledge — as per Chapter 1), it was to say they had had one of the greatest nights of their lives, and they were more excited than ever to open their own place ... oops! The desired outcome not achieved; Gary's team crushed it so hard they fell further in love with their idea. But the story ends well: they are a successful couple in the insurance business and, after many failed attempts at acquiring the exact right location, they opted to open a cafe instead and are doing well, which makes me very happy. Why? Well, they severely lacked one or more of our core DNA Building Blocks that we know significantly impact the chances of success, especially with the type of concept they aspired to open — without business partners. So even though this chapter is about details, that story includes elements of execution, immersion, and professional experience all wrapped up in one.

The big idea we want you to take from this is really about paying attention to the fine details — and don't forget the ones that set your team up for success — while at the same time understanding what details matter and when to let go and delegate. Not every detail requires the same level of attention. But how to know which is which?

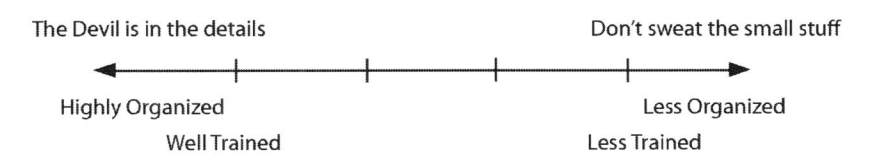

The Devil is in the details	Don't sweat the small stuff
Highly Organized	Less Organized
Well Trained	Less Trained

The Detail Paradox

It's like a heavyweight showdown of two competing well-known mantras: *The devil is in the details* versus *Don't sweat the small stuff*. What are we to believe? It's a wonderful question and candidly one we had to wrestle with. In research terms,

Hospitality DNA

the attention to details was a continuous theme found throughout the interview process. We couldn't ignore it, but it seemed to compete with the idea of working on the business, not in the business, and empowering the team to manage the little things. Nothing like a good paradox! Here's how we reconciled it. We call it the *detail paradox*. Our award-winning operators put tremendous effort into coaching and training their teams. That coaching and training almost always translates into higher levels of execution and competency. That higher level of competency lends itself to better critical thinking among staff.

For example, if we're called in to consult with a place that believes they are underperforming, and we find they have high turnover, inventory loss, guest experience issues, low profitability, and they're not sure where to begin, in this scenario we have some big things to address. If we happened to notice bottle labels are facing the wrong way at the bar, we're probably not going to mention it; we have "bigger fish to fry." Conversely, if we were to walk into, say, the Dead Rabbit, where the staff is on point, losses are negligible, guests are thrilled, and that staff is fully engaged, and we were to sit down at the bar and see four bottles facing the wrong way round, it would somehow seem completely out of place screaming for attention: "Something is amiss — let's fix it!"

A little more ... we like to use the term "draining the pond": the higher the water, the fewer small rocks we can see. As we drain the pond, we begin to see the big rocks (don't sweat the small stuff ... yet). As you continue to drain the pond, you begin to see the medium rocks until eventually the pebbles become our biggest opportunities. For our award-winning operators, their teams allow them the time and bandwidth to think about and notice the little things. You see, it's the little things that will typically propel a venue to world-class status. It's not unlike one of our favorite book, *Good to Great* by Jim Collins. To achieve a certain level of excellence, you are likely doing things fundamentally different, fundamentally better than the pack. In order to separate at a world-class level, we must have a clear view to the bottom of the pond. The only way this can be achieved is through a purposeful commitment to a culture that emphasizes training and development; otherwise, there's a real risk of an owner or manager not getting the clarity that is needed. When we have a clear view and an empowered team, they can own the details, and your opportunities will be become increasingly more obvious, no matter their size.

There's a second very important distinction to make: the difference between small and unimportant. For our industry, the little things can make all the difference. A smile is a little thing but far from unimportant. We believe the better statement is *Don't sweat the unimportant stuff.* It's not uncommon for us to find owners who struggle to know the difference between what requires their specific attention and what can be easily delegated. There's a simple process to follow to distinguish between the simple versus the unimportant:

- Am I the only one who can make this decision?
- Is this the best use of my time?
- Might someone else do it better?
- Is this a now or later issue?

Consistency is vitally important, and it also relates to details. Our interviewees don't seem to vacillate in and out of excellence. When the culture is set, it will not matter who the manager may be, who makes the drink, who serves you, or the time of day or evening of the visit. Every drink should maintain the same excellence, and every team member should deliver on the same level of experience excellence. When we sent our potential client on that weekend trip, we had our name on the line when we sent them to the Crunkleton. I never put any emphasis on the importance of the visit to Gary. I didn't need to follow up or send reminders. I had 100% trust in what our client was about to experience because that's what the great ones do: their teams are able to repeat excellence every day.

Our attention to detail is ultimately geared to exhibit a superior guest experience with seemingly effortless execution. That's the end game, the proverbial *why*. In the end, our attention to detail should manifest itself three ways, and in this case, we use the guidance of Salvatore Calabrese, "the Maestro," to illuminate the point. Here's how he teaches it:

> **The Owner** has a responsibility to create a specific environment by which they encourage a specific behavior.
>
> **The Staff** has a responsibility to execute upon a culture that is created and supported by the ownership.

When speaking with Salvatore Calabrese, he shared with us his "Three Rs" for delivering on a guest experience. Keep it simple and repeatable:

- Recommendation (Help them get comfortable)
- Re-order (So happy that they want more)
- Return (The big win)

When we are able to execute the little things with ease, that's when you begin a journey to excellence. I recall again our evening at Curfew when my wife received a cocktail that had a beautiful, perfect flower in it. It seemed too pretty to drink, almost more of a work of art than a cocktail. She began to remove the flower and was told, no, no, eat it first, it will enhance the flavor of the cocktail and improve the sensory experience. Mouth agape, I thought to myself, *No ******* way*. Imagine the work that went into that experience.

Imagine getting the perfect flowers so that they present properly. Imagine understanding the taste profile and how it might mix with certain alcohols. Imagine how you have to store the flowers to keep them presentable and edible. Imagine the care that has to go into making the drink. Imagine the work that goes into explaining it to people so that most don't throw it aside as a garnish ... imagine that for one drink, imagine that level of detail execution for your business!

In closing, I can't help but think back to Jack McGarry's advice on hiring for attitude over aptitude, which you will hear about in a forthcoming chapter. There's a strong tie-in there as well as it relates to detail: having the right kind of people who buy into the "little things matter" attitude and who show attention to detail. Find the people who get the nuance of your business, and be sure to hire for it. Let's sequence this chapter!

HELIX Sequencing

> We found varying levels of correlation between the building blocks in each chapter and the DNA points at the end of the book. The strength of the correlation is represented by 1 to 5 circles around our 5-point Hospitality DNA molecule: 1 being a lower correlation and 5 being a higher one.

Humble Nature

You're not the only person who is capable of handling decisions for your business. Free yourself up. Empower others around you, and give yourself the time and energy to distinguish between the small and unimportant and the big and transformative. Apply your best talent to your biggest opportunities, and eventually your biggest opportunities will become small.

Explorer's Pursuit

Many of the amazing details we all get to see are a product of a unique experience that our award winners found on their journey. The edible flower at Curfew doesn't happen by accident; it was the product of an exploration and discovery that was simply too good not to share. These little touches help make discovery and reinvention valuable.

Lifetime of Experience

Time is one of the best teachers. In this case, it educates on the idea of what matters most and what doesn't. The specific details our award winners thought were of critical importance early in their career changed significantly over time. With hindsight, these revelations are obvious but nonetheless poignant. Now ... if you don't have industry experience, make sure you have access to it. Someone with a lifetime of experience can help someone without it navigate through those details that require ownership attention and those that can be delegated or set aside.

Indomitable Spirit

I recall the first time I met Julio Cabrera. At the time, Julio was already very well known in the industry and working toward launching his first concept. However, he was struggling with budget constraints. His extreme clarity on the details — the Santiago experience — never left his mind's eye. This focus on the details of his vision helped get him to where he is now.

Xtraordinary Culture

You cannot sustain the details without building a foundational culture. The more we invest in our teams, the more capable they become. If we want people to execute at the highest level, they must understand all the whys around the little things that matter. Getting your team to understand the little whys is the foundation of culture. This then becomes a natural multiplier; the more people understand, the more productive they become.

Chapter 7

Training

> If you want great people, start with
> creating a great place to work!
> —Ken Burgin

People have an innate need to succeed! In the very first days of one's employment, we send a strong and serious message about our mission and commitment to performance, tone, and expectations.

Most operators will tell you they have a training program in place. Our experience is that training delivered to a new employee rarely coincides with the actual executional expectations for the bar and restaurant. Training is often done by another same-level employee as the new hire shadows their peer for a period of time until the trainer deems the trainee worthy of a solo campaign. While this concept is viable for teaching someone the skills of the job, it's rarely the ideal way to indoctrinate someone into your culture. The how and whys of the business are best taught by the owner or a member of management who has a strong grasp of the larger cultural implications of the business. You can think of this as "skip-level" training, if you like. How much time is set aside by a member of leadership to coach and train new hires on the critical aspects of things like culture and expectations? It's one thing to set standards and steps of service. It's another to coach on why that matters so much and how it's entwined with the brand and overall well-being of the organization. In our experience, the best operators are never too busy to spend quality time with new hires on items of cultural significance.

As workforces become more sophisticated and certainly more socially aware and brand savvy, pulling them into these conversations and coaching early is good for business. While having a team that can crush on steps of service is great, having a team that can do that AND be an army of brand ambassadors is multiples better. That idea of force multiplication and productivity propels success.

Too often hiring is done in times of immediate need, which is the epitome of when "not to hire." Our hiring efforts should be continuous — meaning we can properly train when we're fully staffed, with space to focus on our new hires. It also gives us the flexibility to release staff who don't live up to our brand promise and values.

Emergency hires almost assuredly damage the business in one form or another, mainly because these hires are either not an ideal fit, are undertrained, or — heaven forbid — both. As a result, we encourage people to adopt a continuous hiring model that keeps healthy pressure on staff to maintain performance. What's "healthy pressure"? Healthy pressure is simply the idea that we always maintain a slight staffing excess, which allows people to compete for the best shifts. Shifts aren't guaranteed, they are earned, and to the best employees go the best shifts. There should be a certain "healthy pressure" generated to earn these shifts. It's a meritocracy: those who take the best care of the guest and the brand get the most and the best shifts. The only way we can do that, however, is by maintaining a staffing level that allows us to promote and relegate based on performance.

Very few owners have a training program that's connected to their ethos, values, and purpose. The reality is, very few Bar and Restaurant owners have a well-defined robust training platform that's inclusive of culture, coaching, and education. Why? It typically traces back to getting caught working more in the business than on the business. It's hard if not impossible to do this sort of work when you're closing the venue at 2 a.m. and are back on-site at 9 a.m. to make sure lunch gets off the ground amid a flurry of callouts, as one of a hundred reasons why. We find that our clients rarely think long term in terms of training and development. Usually, the best training we see is during a new concept launch because there's time to think through and plan how to bring on a large group of brand-new people so that we don't bomb on Friends and Family Day. Then the business finds out that 70% of those people aren't going to make it through the first 90 days, and leadership goes into battlefield-hiring mode and rarely ever gets back to the good work that was done initially to set up the venue or it simply becomes a de-prioritized item.

Jack McGarry, whom you may recall from our Knowledge chapter, is part of a brilliant leadership team that has garnered the honor of being "The World's Most Awarded Pub," which includes a vast array of honors and awards. In order to achieve great heights like this, a very structured training program would need to be in place.

When Jack and his partner Sean Muldoon opened the Dead Rabbit, they had a specific vision for their venue. The idea was "to bring the Irish bar into the 21st century." When Jack and Sean made the trek from Belfast to New York City, they had great clarity about what they wanted to create. This covered all aspects of atmosphere, attitude, products, and cocktails clearly cemented in their minds.

When they launched their concept in 2013, they had recruited and hired some of the best bartending talent in the city to execute this new concept of a 21st-century Irish pub. As always, the best laid plans of mice and men often go awry. Sometimes superstar bartenders often possess their unique way of doing things — they've experienced a certain level of success and believe their way is the best way. It's understandable. In fact, it seems perfectly reasonable if not smart to hire successful people and get out of their way.

However, big issues can arise if their way of doing things is counter to the culture and way you want things to be done. Jack found his team was lacking a common cause, which we refer to often, in order to bring about his singular vision for the entire enterprise. This was the case at the Dead Rabbit. The big-time bartenders themselves were awesome, but as part of a team with a big vision for exactly what was to be accomplished, they didn't quite fit. It's a little like a regular army versus mercenaries: each has their place, time, and space. In fact, this isn't overly unique at all. Think about how many times we see a sports organization put together a group of free-agent superstars in hopes of guaranteeing a championship result, only to see the very expensive effort end in disappointment. As the party responsible for the bar's execution, Jack had to reconsider his hiring practices. In that, he was stuck. Despite having a smash hit on his hands, he knew he needed to make a change. He had a long-term vision for the business, and it required specific attitudes and outlooks in order to be achieved. He had to make a bold change.

Jack McGarry
Photo by Rachel Vanni

While awards and accolades came pouring in, Jack found himself challenging the status quo: How do we continue to improve upon a world-class operation without employees who have proven world-class talent? Could this level of success be achieved with different staff and if so, how?

One of Jack's great personal talents is introspection. Great leaders typically reflect upon their actions first and then consider how that may impact others when evaluating results. In this case, Jack asked a very simple question: "How do we transfer our DNA, a very specific expectation, to our team so that they are positioned to execute what we envision?" Perhaps the most incredible part of this story is, Jack was asking this in the midst of significant success. Our purpose in writing this book

> "How do we transfer our DNA, a very specific expectation, to our team so that they are positioned to execute what we envision?"

is to understand more deeply what makes for award-winning Hospitality DNA. How do people with this DNA think and operate differently? This story pulls us a big step closer! Indeed, many people at the point of achieving global accolades would immediately begin to think about expansion and certainly not a reconstruction. However, Jack was fully committed to his specific ideal and knew that in order to have the type of sustained success he needed, he had to reconsider the *who* and *how* of his team.

The answer to his dilemma wasn't necessarily readily available, so using his tools of introspection, Jack began to research how he could enhance his own understanding and not just go right at his team. Jack decided to invest in himself first and enrolled in a one-year coaching program called Acceler8 led by Sean Finter, led by Sean Finter. His intent was to learn how to build out his vision for a world-class training program.

If we pause right here for a moment, we learn that building a great program begins with the coach himself. Jack began to leverage key success components, identified as self-awareness and clarity, to challenge his own thinking. Jack realized the answers he sought didn't reside within his own four walls. And despite his understanding of what he wanted done, he didn't quite know the process of how to get there.

> "We weren't where we wanted to be, and it has to start with me." These are the traits that lead to greatness!

Imagine being the winner of the best bar in the world — most would understandably sit back and revel in that success. But here we have someone who was brave enough to admit that "We weren't where we wanted to be, and it has to start with me." These are the traits that lead to greatness! If you want to understand what drives the likes of a McGarry, it starts from within: self-awareness and introspection that can be outwardly reproduced in the form of culture. Many successful people will simply bask in the glow of their own success — that's certainly understandable.

We were blown away to find a person who was on top of the world, from an industry perspective, and said to himself:

- This isn't our vision.
- I don't have all the answers.
- Where can I find help in improving myself so that I can better impact the business?

With that, Jack spent the next year in a Hospitality leadership coaching program where he began to build out his vision for hiring and training — learning to extract his DNA and inject it directly into his team.

What Jack realized at that point was, it wasn't the technical skills or lack thereof that kept him up at night; rather, it was the character and attitude of the team and how that translated to guests. This set up the first major shift for the Dead Rabbit team, which equated to hiring for *attitude over aptitude*. Getting this simple yet critical aspect right was first a matter of ownership and management understanding and training.

Once that concept took root, there was a need to establish more definition around what type of attitude and why. If we step back for a moment and consider the type of attitude Lil was looking for in a Coyote versus what the Dead Rabbit team is looking for, we'll discover stark differences. This is because they're on the hunt for very different attitudes and personalities because they have different cultures and business strategies. There is so much nuance in our industry around concepts and the desired outcome of a guest experience. Ownership has to have great clarity in this regard, and management has to have the tools in place that enable the vision to come to life. This is what people like Jack and Lil understood: the training starts with them!

In this case, it becomes a critical step for the business to establish its own ethos and mission statement. Why do we exist, what do we stand for, and how do we go about it? Jack cascades it this way:

Ethos → Values → Purpose → SOP → Handbook → Spirits Guide

The process of an employee training program can launch once the venue and expectations are well defined, and clear criteria of who to hire, and why, are laid out.

Once a new hire is onboarded, they go through a rigorous 30-60-90-day training process. This entire process has been built into an LMS, or learning management system. We're finding that the intelligent application of technology in our industry is being more widely adopted than ever, but very few people are investing in technology from a training perspective. It's a self-fulfilling prophecy of sorts.

> For want of a nail, the shoe was lost.
> For want of a shoe, the horse was lost.
> For want of a horse, the rider was lost.
> For want of a rider, the battle was lost.

This is a real challenge many operators find themselves in. They look at their financials and believe they can't invest in training properly. It sets them up in an "I can't afford it" mentality — if only we had a nickel for every time we heard "That's what I pay my manager for." It's akin to stepping over a dollar to pick up a dime. Being mindful of how money is spent in the business is incredibly smart; however, not understanding how money is generated and then investing it accordingly can be opportunity lost.

This is where the Dead Rabbit team stands apart. They are able to track the success and progress of a self-paced program while incorporating on-site training, along with regular spot checks and biannual appraisals.

Award-winning success isn't accidental, it's deliberative and introspective. We didn't start out writing a chapter on staff training that knowingly led to ownership introspection and coaching. We also didn't expect it to be about company ethos, but that's exactly where we ended up. It's a full commitment by ownership and a crucial part of your culture.

Jack won't go so far as to break down his training program for us — can't blame him — nor should he. A training program must be specific to you, for your team and your guests, reflecting your ethos. Get clear on exactly what that looks like, and the who and how will start to fall into place.

HELIX Sequencing

> We found varying levels of correlation between the building blocks in each chapter and the DNA points at the end of the book. The strength of the correlation is represented by 1 to 5 circles around our 5-point Hospitality DNA molecule: 1 being a lower correlation and 5 being a higher one.

Humble Nature

Attitude over aptitude: Success is so much more than what someone knows, especially in hospitality. It's about who they are — their attitude.

Explorer's Pursuit

Invest in yourself so that you may invest in others. Learn-ing begins at the top. The more you know, the more you can give!

Lifetime of Experience

In order to train well, we have to be able to get what we know out of our brain and into someone else's. Once upon a time this was done with manuals and steps of service; however, we now know that training is so much more. We have to make use of new technology and the assistance of others and constantly challenge our own best practices.

Indomitable Spirit

Training isn't a sexy topic. It can be extremely easy for training to become a tedious process to be followed, but it's so much more. Training isn't simply steps of service; it's who we are and what we do, which is everything to a business. Great training requires a spirit of constant commitment and a drive to instill the understanding to everyone in the business that training is among the most important things we do. If it takes a village to raise a child, it takes an entire staff to train a new hire.

Xtraordinary Culture

Culture is instilling what is important to us into our staff. Instilling is a by-product of training. Once you have everything set, your staff will self-police, and self-policing is a great sign that you have built a strong culture. "That's not how we do it here" or "Let me show you how we do that" are the sounds of a healthy culture. Your success and scale are directly proportional to your investment in your team and the culture that you build.

Chapter 8

Execution

> We're in an industry that is incredibly hard
> to do well and very easy to do poorly.
> —Angus Winchester

Tony Overall was walking home, frustrated, from a particularly challenging Friday night in Sydney, Australia. Tony ran a busy pizza joint that specialized in take-away, high-quality pizza. The venues were small by design, with a simple bar that could serve all your basic needs but nothing more. Our story begins years into the operation of his first store. Business was increasing month by month, with more and more shifts feeling like the sheer volume of guests was pushing control out of Tony's hands — a great problem to have, in a way.

One particularly tough Friday night, Tony had been smash busy and knew he had disappointed his loyal customers. Order completion times were too slow and, in the hassle of trying to keep up, quality suffered and service times at the bar declined. For more of the evening than not, his guests were being vocal about their disapproval with their experience. At the end of the night, the evening had taken a terrible toll on Tony mentally as well as on the reputation of his pizza shop.

On his walk home, he found himself angry with his customers — they were being unreasonable and self-centered. Didn't they know that Friday nights were the prime eat-out evenings for bustling crowds? Service times were bound to be much slower on Fridays. It should have been no surprise to anyone that word had spread, demand had increased, and now it was a longer wait to get a slice of the best pizza in town. Such was the price they had to pay for his success.

Through the wash of the warm evening air, Tony's head began to clear. Why was he so surprised about how busy it was? Wasn't this what he wanted?

Outside of that frantic shift, he knew he needed more throughput. He knew better than anyone that he was pushing the limits of his business. Yet he hadn't followed through on what was needed to deliver on his promise to hungry customers.

> Sometimes you just need to look in the mirror to find your biggest obstacle.

Through our interview with Tony, he waxed fretful on the hard truth before him: the business had bottlenecked, demand had exceeded his capacity to deliver, and he was slow to invest in a new oven he desperately needed to keep up.

"Sometimes you just need to look in the mirror to find your biggest obstacle," he quipped. He figured out how to get unstuck by walking himself through the "Five Whys," which were originally made known by Taiichi Ohno of the Toyota Motor Company. If it's good enough for Toyota manufacturing, it's good enough for Tony!

Tony walked us through his "Five Whys," which was a simple process of asking himself very basic questions to get to the root cause of his problem. The essence of this process is simple. When you identify an issue, you ask "Why?" Then ... you ask it again ... and again. It is not usually until we get to the fifth "Why?" that we get to the root cause of the problem.

Tony's "Five Whys" to fixing his capacity issue:

1. **Why** *did I fail my customers?* The ovens are over capacity; I need more.
2. **Why** *don't I have enough ovens?* I have been too slow to reinvest in the business.
3. **Why** *have I been too slow to reinvest in the business?* I became too busy working in the business instead of working on the business.
4. **Why** *aren't I working on the business?* I'm playing scared, trying to save money, working shifts, and thinking short term.
5. **Why** *am I playing scared?* I stopped believing in my model: using data to verify outcomes, and trusting and adjusting accordingly.

What would be very easy to do is to say the problem was that Tony didn't have enough ovens, and to some extent that would be true. Upon further reflection, the real problem was Tony ignoring his original solid business planning and understanding of the financial gateways to growth.

Plan your work and work your plan is a core concept we discussed in *The Bar Shift*, which is both elementary and effective. Fortunately for Tony, it didn't take more than a couple of nights for him to get his mind around what he needed to do to rectify the issue.

When it comes to execution, this is often where we find most of our guest experience and quality-of-life issues. Most Bar

> They're not trying to do a great many things okay; they're trying to do something specific exceptionally well — so well, in fact, that they are the best in the world at it.

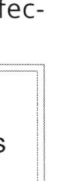

and Restaurant operators have great ideas and good intentions, but execution is the crossroads of opportunity and preparation. When we look at many of these award-winning venues, they are stark in their simplicity, and we mean that in the best possible way. They're not trying to do a great many things okay; they're trying to do something specific exceptionally well — so well, in fact, that they are the best in the world at it. Guests rather enjoy excellence, and people by nature enjoy being associated, even if only via patronage, with excellence.

One thing we know for sure is that complexity makes excellence in execution much more difficult. There's an old scientific principle known as Occam's razor that is attributed to a medieval Franciscan friar, William of Ockham. In a very simple concept, he submits that the more layers of complexity, the less likely a positive outcome. It's also used in the reverse where you'd say the simplest answer is usually the best answer. This idea is very much at play for the Hospitality industry, and we'll find clear evidence of it in this chapter as well as how it affects our ability to scale, in Chapter 13.

For this purpose, we'll set up our very own fictitious venue that may feel familiar. Let's imagine for a moment we've come up with a concept where we have a unique mix of American football and a BBQ smokehouse. Imagine it's a well-adorned sports pub where the ladies wear cheerleading outfits and the gentlemen wear uniform tops, for effect. Let's throw in some pool tables and DJs to drive late revenues. This is a purely fictitious venue, mind you, so any similarities to an actual venue of this type are purely coincidental. On the surface, it seems simple enough: good BBQ, cold beer, sports, flirtatious servers, late nights, and some entertainment. We'll call it Pom-Poms. Sure, it could work.

> The multiples of complexity drive volatility, and volatility puts your brand at risk.

Through a purely operating lens, what William of Ockham continues to teach us from the medieval ages is that the easier something is to replicate, the easier it is to execute. Far from state of the art but as true today as it's ever been. We'll examine this concept a little further through this lens. So what's the challenge here? Singularly, it's not the beer or the food. It's not running a sports bar, or late nights — all that is being successfully done all over the world. The larger issue becomes the overarching value proposition.

In order to create repetitive excellence, we must have a well-defined value proposition. In the case of Pom-Poms, is it a BBQ joint, a sports bar, a "breastaurant," a late-night destination, or all the above? It's hard enough to be great at one of those things, let alone all the above. The multiples of complexity drive volatility, and volatility puts your brand at risk. What's more, it's already a huge challenge to get great servers and even more to get great servers and bartenders to stay with your business long enough to deliver on superior guest experiences.

That's under the best of times when we have access to skilled staff. Now we must limit our field of view to only those who can don the uniform in a way that is suitable and becoming to the brand and be willing to deal with everything that comes along with that, night in and night out. Let's flip the idea on its head for a second. What if we simply ran the best BBQ joint in the world? How would that do? Or the best sports pub in the world. Will that attract people? You bet! Time and time again we see people confuse complexity with delivering a great guest experience. That's just not how it works or at least it doesn't have to, as an independent. Now if you get massive funding and support systems, could you open a behemoth restaurant with a 10-page menu someday? Sure — but by the numbers, successful award-winning venues simply don't operate that way. Let's keep digging even deeper ...

Returning to Chapter 4, branding starts with identifying our tribe. Who will this attract, and in what quantity? How will they become our greatest advocates and spread the word about their experiences with us? That's a critical question every single Bar and Restaurant owner must be asking themselves all the time. When you market to everyone, you are effectively marketing to no one. This leads to the question of identity: who are we, what do we do, and how do we do it? The easier it is to answer that question, the easier it is to execute a strategy. Perhaps if we opened up this place in Las Vegas, which draws a ton of sports enthusiasts and guy trips, it would be easy to see it working well: bachelor parties, golf, beer, gambling, late nights, and all the trappings of a "good time." That could make sense. Take that same concept to a suburban city anywhere in the world and you're quickly faced with a whole new set of challenges with tough questions to answer.

- Who is our ideal guest?
- How do we attract and retain talent?
- How will the community respond?

These questions, if unanswered, become an existential threat to the business. Matt Plapp, author and CEO of America's Best Restaurants, suggests creating what he calls an "avatar for your marketing": knowing exactly who you're marketing to and how you will reach them and then relentlessly delivering on your brand promise. Keep in mind, this is an industry with tough success rates already. When we interviewed our world-class operators, a striking commonality was simplicity. They typically hone in on a concept and do it better than anyone in the world. If you aspire to execute your promise at the highest level, here's what the best operators understand:

- What is our concept?
    - Ideally, one great thing. It could be more, but each addition is a layer of complexity you will have to execute on.
    - Create great clarity (per the previous chapter) on what you are and how you will execute.
- Who is our ideal guest?
    - Who is your target demographic?
    - Do they exist in the market you intend to occupy?
- How do we regularly "wow" our ideal guest?
    - Explain, train, and maintain excellence!
- How do we monetize the process?
    - Can it make money? There are a lot of ideas out there that simply can't be monetized in a way that generates meaningful financial and emotional health for owners.
- Can success be replicated?
    - A very interesting fact: many extremely successful operators, even award winners, find themselves stuck in one venue. Why? Because their success is largely predicated on their specific personal involvement. This issue led to a dedicated chapter on Scalability, Chapter 13.

Perhaps our favorite example of honing in on the exact nature of their business is the Dead Rabbit, which we discussed last chapter: winner of the World's Most Awarded Pub, the 2016 winner of World's 50 Best Bars, winner of "best bar in the world," four-time winner of Best Bar in North America, and winner of 10 other prestigious awards from Tales of the Cocktail, Time Out, and much more. They are famous for simply being a total kick-ass Irish pub, most well known for their Irish coffee. In an ordinary week, they sell thousands upon thousands of Irish coffees.

Now, I don't want to diminish just how hard it is to run the best bar in the world as Jack McGarry and Sean Muldoon have done, but what they haven't done is take an already challenging situation and figure out a way to make it even harder. They keep it super simple. *Bringing the Irish pub into the 21st century* is their specific vision for the business, and everything they do is pointed toward that ideal. The concept is easy for the consumer to imagine and understand, and it is very reasonable to execute.

Here's a very interesting caveat. We would naturally advocate, by way of simplicity, that you should focus simply on scaling one concept. That is to say, master a single concept and repeat it over and over until full-scale potential is achieved. That would seem perfectly logical. However, we've interviewed and worked with many super-successful operators who have scaled multiple concepts. How is this possible? In every case of super-successful operators with multiple concepts, they have established a repeatable *culture*.

Yes, each concept is unique, but they all have interchangeable parts. Essentially, the group has a well-established way of doing things that is understood throughout the organization. So the concept is merely a facade for the true operating culture of the business. It's still a plug-and-play operation that may look different to the guest on the outside, but internally it runs in a way that is familiar to the operators. This continues to allow for economies of scale and cultural alignment. We have included a perfect example of this in our scalability chapter and the commitment to training and culture it requires. So sadly, we're going to eighty-six Pom-Poms. Goodbye, friend. It was good while it lasted.

Execution

HELIX Sequencing

> We found varying levels of correlation between the building blocks in each chapter and the DNA points at the end of the book. The strength of the correlation is represented by 1 to 5 circles around our 5-point Hospitality DNA molecule: 1 being a lower correlation and 5 being a higher one.

Humble Nature

To expertly execute, you must ask yourself the tough questions. Sometimes the hardest person to be honest with is ourselves. Our interviewees typically had systems and cultures in place that afforded productive feedback. This is both part of the culture we build and in this case, it's about being humble enough to admit when we're wrong and being able to accept feedback. It's easy to point the finger at surface issues, but it almost always rings true that the issue presented to us is a product of many other factors coming to a head. Whether you use the Five Whys or another method, be sure to have a process in place that allows you to receive and analyze productive feedback.

Explorer's Pursuit

Once you have a great process in place for solving problems, be open to the different possibilities and solutions. It can be easy to fall back upon what we've always done or what's worked in the past, but the business world evolves quickly and relentlessly. Keep an open mind to the art of what's possible.

Lifetime of Experience

Keep it simple and start with the end in mind. Build a mental Rolodex of best practices and situation management strategies to apply instantly or over time, depending on the situation. The longer you are dialed in to the industry, actively paying attention to what is going on around you, the more examples of what works and what does not work you will collect, and in turn, be able to apply.

Indomitable Spirit

Interviewing these award-winning talents taught us that inspiration triumphs over desperation. That isn't to say there weren't low points or even moments of crisis, but in every case their indomitable spirit would help drive them through. This industry faces innumerable operational challenges. We must not just be up to the task of facing down whatever comes our way but be able to do so with enthusiasm.

Xtraordinary Culture

What would it mean to say "we have a culture of execution"? It means we know the specific operational intricacies that matter most to us. We measure them, and we promote, reward, and terminate based on the execution of these processes and concepts. These things are very clearly defined in the venues of our interviewees, and there is very little doubt about the hows and whys of the business. When we build a lasting and highly productive culture, we attract the right people to the business who are aligned with our values and outcomes.

Chapter 9

Community

> Alone, we can do so little; together, we can do so much.
> —Helen Keller

The independent Bar and Restaurant community is not only one of the largest business communities in the world, it is also the most disparate. Tens, if not hundreds, of thousands of independent owners across the world are facing similar challenges with business models akin to one another. Venues may seem outwardly different — whether they be a Cuban cafe, an upscale dive bar, a cowboy bar, a steakhouse, a lounge, or a nightclub — but on the inside, they're operating basically the same business model with many of the same challenges. Most independent bars and restaurants lack the benefit of shared learnings and resources, such that you may find in businesses comparable in size and scope. They are left searching for success in their isolated silos.

Bringing independent Hospitality businesses together by sharing best practices is one way to contribute to shared learning and community, which is why we write our books. There are also some colossal events where our community can rally that lend themselves to community, sharing, education, and good times. Nothing exemplifies this as much as the the annual Tales of the Cocktail conference in New Orleans.

When Tales was facing a financial crisis in 2017, Neal Bodenheimer recognized the critical need for industry events and took it upon himself to save this event. But before we dive into that, let's explore Neal's ability to tackle something so audacious. Neal stayed true to the notion that experience matters and that time on the job is critical to success. He began his adventures in Hospitality at the ripe old age of 18 where, despite his size, he worked as a bouncer at a New Orleans bar. As it turned out, Neal wasn't hired for his physical prowess as much as it was a promotional idea to drive more young people into the bar. In those days, the drinking age was 18.

With a formal education and passion for history, Neal Bodenheimer told us that he viewed spirits as "history in a glass." When people can find a connection or a blend between a personal passion and the allure of spirits, powerful connections tend to form. Neal eventually went off to college and upon graduation found himself in a position to start his education-based career. But what was he to do with a history degree?

Neal Bodenheimer
Photo by Denny Culbert

Before he took the lifelong career plunge, he aspired to travel the world and soak in as many cultural experiences as possible. He invited his brother to join him on his journey. He too was just starting his career and had the freedom to partake in a massive one-year adventure spanning the globe!

So the two set off, making stops throughout Europe, as well as in Turkey (partially in Europe), Bali, Nepal, Indonesia, and ultimately, Malaysia. Neal and his brother fell in love with the area and decided to not only stay a while but to run a small coastal restaurant during their stay in Malaysia. It was a two-man operation that favored food prep in the morning and scuba diving in the afternoon. The island was run by a generator, so food was kept in a freezer overnight — not state-of-the-art food safety protocols — but they made do with what they had. The tandem just needed enough money to cover rent, food, and to maintain a daily scuba habit!

During their sun-kissed sabbatical, 9/11 happened. It was an intensely sobering moment that called the pair home to the United States. Neal felt compelled to go back to New York specifically to help in any way he could. This unimaginable crisis called for a rebuilding and healing process for the people of the city, and Neal was dead set on being a part of that.

Once arriving in the Big Apple, Neal credits two meaningful mentorships with shaping the next phase of his career in Hospitality — one with Steve Hanson's group, who owned 21 bars and restaurants in NYC, and the venerable Danny Meyer of the Atlantic Grill. Danny has since become a household name with his well-known Shake Shack venture and his book *Setting the Table*, which we strongly recommend as well! During his time at the Atlantic Grill, Neal gives great credit to Eben

> You should appreciate the past while challenging the status quo.

Klemm for introducing him to the art and science of mixology. Eben served as the corporate mixologist for Danny Meyer's group and has a great gift for not only the creation of specialty cocktails but also coaching people on how to think about creating them for themselves.

Neal has a real passion for history and stories — he sees classic cocktails as "history in a glass." It was during this time that he started to craft a vision for "Looking back on history to gain insight into the future of craft cocktails." Neal wholeheartedly believes you should appreciate the past while challenging the status quo. We find that there's a certain commonality between several of our cocktail enthusiasts where the attention to detail and passion for understanding the history of the cocktail is important to them. That desire to understand allows them to take something that is considered a classic and then put their modern spin on it. Not only does this allow for product evolution, but it also inspires stimulating conversation at the bar — the guest wins twice! Neal is the embodiment of this idea. We also see a similar effect with the modern craft beer market, where all the beer options not only create a wide variety of choices for the consumer but allow for a wide variety of conversation as well.

After spending several years in New York City learning and mentoring among industry giants, Hurricane Katrina hit New Orleans. Just as the events of 9/11 had called Neal back from Malaysia, Katrina called Neal home to New Orleans. He believes Katrina was a call to Cajuns everywhere to help rebuild and save this one-of-a-kind community.

We noticed Neal was engaging in a personal trend to help humanity that seems intrinsically duty-bound — a call to act. Neal gathered his newfound knowledge of classic cocktails and restaurant operations with a vision for New Orleans that would not only survive but thrive. Neal decided he wanted to open a world-class restaurant in his town and in 2009 Neal founded Cure with his partners, Matthew Kohnke and Kirk Estopinal. Nine years later, they would win the coveted James Beard Award for Outstanding Bar Program!

Neal immersed himself in both his local community and the larger Hospitality community as an active member of Tales of the Cocktail. Tales was founded by Ann Tuennerman in 2002, and in 2017, they fell upon hard times, putting it at significant risk of folding.

Neal had concerns about the future of Tales and its possible extinction. From his point of view, the event was an incredibly important part of the global Hospitality community; it had to be saved. And saved it would be. Neal pitched the idea to his friend Gary Solomon Jr. of the Solomon family. For those of you who don't know, the Solomon family is a somewhat famous philanthropic family of New Orleans. Moving to New Orleans in 1969, Gary's father, Theodore "Teddy" Solomon, built a movie theater empire across seven states and then began donating a large amount of his wealth to the people and city of New Orleans. Philanthropy is in the Solomons' blood, and they definitely had the means to support and revitalize Tales, keeping it viable while it went through a rebuild and new capital infusion; however, there was a catch: they wouldn't do it without Neal. Neal originally had no intention of getting involved; he had pitched his idea to save and reshape an institution in which he saw much potential for good. The problem, such as it was for Neal, was that he did much too good a job of painting the picture of what Tales could be: an organization based on education and doing good works in the industry. A decision was made to convert the business to a not-for-profit organization. At the same time, much effort was put forth to emphasize education and well-being, on an equal

Hospitality DNA

wavelength with products and services. A bit less emphasis was put on the parties, though they are still majestic.

Tales has rebounded with overwhelming success as it continues to evolve on the culture and content scene. There are also wonderful events like the Nightclub & Bar Show and Bar Convent, which we also participate in, respect, and strongly encourage people to attend — these are wonderful forms of education offered in the industry. Let us say now as well, we apologize to the many we didn't mention here. Globally, it's just way too much to list; we appreciate you all!

We felt it was so important to share Neal's story because it highlights — better than most — the importance of building up your community. Where Neal is operating on a massive platform, the same is true for any business — especially local bars and restaurants.

Tales of the Cocktail — New Orleans
Photo by TOTC

Community comes in many different forms. We just highlighted a group working with the Bar and Restaurant industry, but you don't need to tackle such a large-scale project to impact a community. For most of us, our local communities — our neighborhoods, if you will — provide ample opportunity for impact. The health and well-being of our local communities allows us to thrive and build our brands in the heart of where we live and work. Bars and restaurants are often cornerstones of our neighborhood communities, which provide an opportunity that shouldn't be ignored. It should also be mentioned that being an active, positive influence in your community is also great for business. Many will say, "We don't do good works with the idea of personal benefit," and that's 100% true! However, the reality is a grateful and appreciative community will reward in kind the generosity and good works of others. Whether your venue sponsors youth sport teams or local events, or you make your space available for use by charitable organizations and fundraisers, we are uniquely positioned in our communities to make a measurable difference, and people typically will show their appreciation for the effort.

Some may see this simply as extra work or as a zero-sum game. Nothing could be further from the truth. Neal, who runs four world-class venues, Cure, Cane & Table, Peychaud's, and Val's, found time to rejuvenate Tales and thrive. In fact, Neal will tell you Tales doesn't create any drag for him or his team. As a co-chair, he leans heavily on a board of directors and a team of highly motivated volunteers, who make up the heart of the organization.

The industry has responded in a very appreciative and positive way, many eager to not only attend but

> It's hard for any business to be healthier than the industry or community it serves.

partake in the event if called upon. Let's draw you back to how this parallels your business.

It's hard for any business to be healthier than the industry or community it serves. Neal would be quick to tell you the story of Cafe Henri, a venue that he and his partners jumped into, post-Katrina — a seemingly *slam dunk* opportunity that turned sour.

Cafe Henri had for years been at the heart of a thriving community whose backbone was the movie industry, known as Hollywood South. During the launch of Cafe Henri, New Orleans changed certain tax incentives that were afforded to the film industry, and the business along with its employees began to migrate elsewhere.

It didn't matter that the cafe had a world-class menu or carefully crafted cocktails: the community suffered and down with it went Cafe Henri. The closing of the cafe left an indelible mark on Neal and emphasized the vast importance of community to him. It might seem obvious, but community, it turns out, is not an option for us — it is the primary Building Block of our businesses. If there is no one to serve, there's no business to be had. Opening our doors and hoping or assuming the community will be there because they always have been can work, but it can also get us into trouble when there is a shift, usually out of our control, like the one Neal experienced. It is when we focus on building and serving our local communities that we create a sort of protection for our business that will see us survive, and even thrive, when times get tough. As we explore here the idea of human DNA, if restaurants and bars had DNA of their own, community would be at its core.

The Tight Community of Peers

We have to believe that there are more examples of bar owners finding amazing success by creating a strong community around their establishment than not. The very nature and definition of Hospitality makes this particular aspect of bars second nature. For those of you who read this and don't find that part of the journey to be so natural, we would like to tell the story of OKRA. As an award-winning operator who owns venues that regularly occupy "best of the best" lists and have been nominated for six James Beard awards, Bobby Heugel has built a tidy empire through hard work and tenacity. However, it was Bobby's studying to earn his master's degree in intercultural communication that I believe exemplified his most valuable skill and passion: the ability to build a community. While he had already gained great success and notoriety with Anvil Bar & Refuge, it was Bobby's third venture that made his mastery of building a community undeniable — in this case, starting with creating a special community of his peers. In 2011, Bobby gathered 12 trusted friends in the industry to launch OKRA, or Organized Kollaboration on Restaurant Affairs. Originally meeting to discuss a proposed parking ordinance that could have a negative impact on their immediate community — independent restaurant operators — it later blossomed into much more. This original meeting had the singular intention to help Bobby's local restaurant community with a specific problem. The proposed ordinance essentially stated that all bars and restaurants in Houston were directly responsible for providing a certain amount of parking for their business. Because of the preexisting build-out of the land around Houston, this new proposal was designed in such a way that many smaller operators would be faced with financial and logistical burdens that could easily put them out of business.

Using their combined skills and connections, the original OKRA team succeeded in their endeavor, and OKRA soon blossomed into a group striving for the good of all Houstonians through many collaborative efforts. One of these was the OKRA Charity Saloon.

The concept was simple. This would be a regular bar out front; however, on the back end, 100% of all profits would be donated to charity. Further engaging the community, guests receive one vote for one of four locally based charities selected by OKRA's members every time they purchase a drink, further cementing this as a fundamental part of who Bobby is. The idea of the charity saloon predated all of his others; he just needed a few successful ventures first to make it a reality.

The closing of OKRA in 2021 might look like the tearful end of a great community-focused idea — another casualty of the COVID-19 pandemic. However, this is less an end of a wonderful charity vehicle and more an evolution. Rather than being closed, it was purchased by Mary Ellen Angel. OKRA will be renamed and revamped and will continue to share a portion of its profits with local charities. As a last act of charity, OKRA's members sold the bar to Mary Ellen for $10. After 10 years with the Charity Bar being an integral part of who they are, the 24 members of OKRA will go on to focus on other charity efforts. Bobby's original restaurant idea, the Charity Bar, will live on and the lives of 24 people, infused and invigorated with continued purpose of community, will further spread this idea of a connected community.

One could argue that as much as anything else, Bobby's acumen as an operator, creative builder of cocktails, curator of interesting spirits, or designer of engaging experiences are what led to his success. However, I posit that it is his dedication to all of his professional and personal communities, his neighborhood customers, the city of Houston, and further, that has drawn amazing partners, and then dedicated customers, to each of Bobby's new ventures.

Starting with a single meeting of 12 people and a focus on those around him, Bobby touched countless lives. At the time of sale, OKRA had given a total of $1,303,630.07 to its community. The return on investment seems incalculable.

Whether you are building a special group of locals who love your specific brand of neighborhood haunt, or you are working to unite a network of like-minded operators to help change the face of the industry in your town, building a community starts with getting clear on what it is you are looking to achieve. No matter which level you want to focus on, it proves time and again that building a community around your business always pays off.

As a final thought, keep in mind that building a community does not require you to get involved in charitable works; it is just common that they do. Starting a softball league for your customers who love sports has simple brilliance in it as it gives some guests a reason to be further connected to you, your team, and your business. The number of ways to build communities is as varied as the type of people who frequent restaurants. Find the need in your community and fill it. If giving back is a part of your goal or you are on the fence, there are two detailed stories about how two incredible people achieved their visions in our next chapter, The Power of Giving.

HELIX Sequencing

> We found varying levels of correlation between the building blocks in each chapter and the DNA points at the end of the book. The strength of the correlation is represented by 1 to 5 circles around our 5-point Hospitality DNA molecule: 1 being a lower correlation and 5 being a higher one.

Humble Nature

We do good works for the sake of the work and not for the credit. This goes without saying, of course. Don't worry so much about specific returns that come from building your community; focus instead on the good that building your particular community will achieve. Recipients typically have great appreciation for the effort and opportunity good works afford them.

Explorer's Pursuit

There are immeasurable ways we can help in our communities, big and small. We've seen people use their space for chili cook-offs, political rallies, cancer-awareness rallies, emergency fundraisers, disaster relief sites, industry events, and much more … All of our award winners were engaged in some form of community building or another, though each at different stages in their own processes. For some, it was executing a lifelong dream, and for others, it was something that they stumbled into along their journey that just felt right. Regardless of how it starts, community building is never a flash-in-the-pan experience; rather, it is something that grows with us as we travel through this industry.

Lifetime of Experience

Perspective is a critical tool of creation. The more perspective we have, the more creative we can become, and the more comfortable we get with our place in our community, the easier it becomes to dive in. It is much easier to rally your community when they have had time to get to know and trust you. For the most ambitious in this arena, involvement is something you can become known for. Becoming a cornerstone of your community pays off in many, often unexpected, ways.

Indomitable Spirit

Sacrificing for others may be the ultimate gesture of indomitable spirit. When we relentlessly put ourselves out there for others (while still taking care of ourselves), we exude the best of the human spirit. There's nothing more worthy than lifting others up.

Xtraordinary Culture

Good works beget good works and garner great appreciation. When we create a culture of giving and helping, beautiful things happen. Too often operators don't think in terms of culture when it comes to attracting the best talent, but talent is always seeking out culture. Our award-winning operators seem to understand this better than most and make sure that community building is a part of their business culture.

Chapter 10

The Power of Giving

> Anything long-lasting or worthwhile
> takes time and complete surrender.
> —Ryan Hidinger

Some stories are simply too impactful to not be shared, and here we bring you two of those. These good people exemplify what it means to put others before themselves and to use the power of giving. At the core of Hospitality is taking care of others, and those who do it best derive incredible satisfaction from doing so. Indeed, they thrive in the process of being there for others, especially in times of need. Stephanie Simbo's story exemplifies this ideal.

Stephanie found herself in a nightmare when her brother was wrongfully imprisoned as a young man. During his time in jail, the machine that is the penal system crushed who he was, transitioning him from a bright young man — your stereotypical "good kid," involved in sports, who was always trying to get those around him to laugh and feel good, the "big brother" of their tough neighborhood — to a fundamentally different person, one mired in darkness. For any sibling, this would be difficult to witness, but for Stephanie, who was incredibly close to and often inspired by her brother, seeing his light extinguished was heartbreaking. After a suicide attempt that she witnessed, which was brought on by his time in prison, she made him a solemn promise: make it through this and I will dedicate my life to helping others lift themselves from darkness and toward an inspired new life. And so, an oath made, Stephanie began her work to help change the lives of those in desperate need of a hand up and a way out.

Although a Parisian, she decided she would take her talents to South Africa to help women who were imprisoned. Stephanie didn't know anything about the country, except that they had some of the most dangerous prisons in the world and the recidivism rates were upward of 80%. So she thought, *Perfect — those are people I can help!*

Stephanie's goal was to be permitted to work inside the prison, teaching women a trade or craft so that they would be able to support themselves upon their release. It was her time as a bartender that would lead to her decision to start her job training program as a bartending school. Interestingly, it was also her 12-hour bartending shifts in London that allowed her to hone her skills of active listening and an ability to perceive body language — skills that would become part of the foundation that allowed her to navigate the complexities of creating a school from scratch.

Her program was called Beyond Bars, and it quickly became a huge hit! Her trials quickly went from struggling to find a prison who would let her in to help to the demand for Stephanie's program being so high that it became too large to continue on-site. At the time, the South African prison system was overpopulated by more than 300%, led by gangs, and in utter chaos. And yes, she was here to help!

When Stephanie first met the women she worked with, she would tell them her brother's story. She made it clear that she was there because of an oath she had made to him and was bound and determined to honor it. She was there to help those who wanted more for their lives, with the potential to have a career when they got out.

As quickly as her program outgrew the prison facilities, she also realized that she could better serve the women she was helping by offering classes on additional trades outside of bartending, as well as basic life skills classes. She rented out a former hostel, serving as both a school and a halfway house. She brought in more coaches to teach these women complementary skills to serve them at work and beyond.

A wide array of classes were offered, including carpentry, wine knowledge, math, theater, coding, and much more. It was clear on these women's faces how much excitement and joy the classes brought them. After spending their own time in darkness, they were finally in an environment that was infused with energy and hope, something they hadn't felt in a long time. They began to see the possibility that lay ahead for a brighter future.

Learning new crafts and life skills was a great start, but Stephanie also recognized that more would be needed to help ensure their long-term success. Through her conversations with these women, Stephanie came to learn that many of them had endured horrific abuse — one of them ending up in prison after killing the man who had been beating and sexually abusing her for years — so counseling began to be offered along with things like yoga classes, "circle of truth" sessions, where they could say whatever they wanted without repercussion, and sex education. In this way, the women could begin to heal emotionally from the trauma they endured while also building skills to allow them to successfully provide for themselves. To hear Stephanie tell it, when she first started, she wasn't ready or equipped for the logistics of teaching these women en masse and supporting them mentally. The requirements and needs were so extreme, from an emotional perspective, that she couldn't do it all on her own, no matter how well intentioned. While she hired teachers and administrative staff, some of the most important people she brought into her school were the psychologists — some for her students, and one specifically to help her and her staff navigate the mental stress of growing such an ambitious undertaking.

All of these additions and changes paid off in spades. After about a year into the program, Stephanie was pleased to already be placing new bartenders. She later received funding from organizations, like a grant from Tales of the Cocktail in 2018, that allowed for even more training, more healing, and getting more women into the program.

By 2019 Stephanie found herself running a full-blown school on a proper campus, complete with dorms, a true commissary kitchen, and multiple classrooms. With this success, there also came a larger student body: women who were no longer being hand selected and for whom the original program was not providing the same cultivation. The women who were initially chosen for the program were "butterflies trapped in a cocoon." They had it inside of them already to transition from someone who had been incarcerated back to a human being who could thrive in the outside world again, becoming "who they were supposed to be all along." The new mix of personalities and backgrounds brought new challenges that were overcome through a mixture of self-awareness, selflessness, and the determined application of drive and purpose.

Interestingly enough, after graduating from the program, many of the women didn't choose to stay in hospitality long, but that's not what's important here. What was life changing for these women was being given confidence, the tools they lacked, a newly found sense of hope and possibility, and then taking their newfound powers into the world to create lives for themselves that may not have ever been possible without Stephanie's help. Hospitality was the healing tool that allowed them to take back the power they had lost.

In looking back on her time building and running Beyond Bars Akademia, Stephanie realized that the school was a reflection of who she was. If she wanted these women to open up, she needed to open up herself. As the CEO, she had thought she needed to be closed off and strong, keeping a gap between herself and them as a way to protect herself. It was opening up to them in their "circle of truth" sessions, letting them know how difficult and frustrating this was for her, that built their trust. She was no longer just the director of the school. She was the captain of a boat that they were all in. They explained to her that they didn't just stay at the school because of how nice she had made it or the valuable skills they were learning; they stayed because of the relationship she had created with them.

Sadly, Beyond Bars Akademia now finds itself closed — with the COVID-19 pandemic, the vast majority of their funding dried up. Stephanie, however, is continuing to fulfill her promise to her brother by pursuing her education in psychology so that she can take her ability to help women in need to the next level. We're confident Stephanie will be a force for good, for years to come!

A Massive Blessing

Giving Kitchen in Atlanta, Georgia, a story of both great hope and great heartbreak. Co-founder and Senior Director of Community Engagement, Jen Hidinger-Kendrick, was born to a Spanish mother from Andalusia, Spain, and a father from Indianapolis, Indiana. Jen grew up in Indiana and met her first love at

17 years old, a young man named Ryan Hidinger. Jen describes meeting Ryan as love at first sight.

Jen and Ryan were married in 2005. Shortly, before they married, they decided to embark on an adventure, experiencing new sights and communities before finding a place to call home in Atlanta. In 1997, Ryan attended the Culinary School at the Art Institute of Atlanta. At that juncture in his life, Ryan felt somewhat overwhelmed by the big city and after his southern education decided to head back to Indiana to begin his career. This time it would be different; Ryan now had a few years of experience under his belt and his secret weapon by his side: Jen!

In August of 2008, Ryan was involved in a bad car accident that landed him out of commission for eight weeks. In the U.S., it's not uncommon for people who work in hospitality, especially for independent operators, to find themselves uninsured. Fortunately, this wasn't the case for Ryan. He did have insurance, which was a blessing, yet that still didn't pay 100% of the medical bills. So, Ryan faced his share of the hospital bills, but what about income and ordinary bills?

Fortunately, Ryan's career was on the rise and he had a great network around him. Family, colleagues, and friends all rallied around the cause to help emotionally, financially, and frankly, in any way they could. This experience transformed Ryan and Jen. Their good fortune wasn't lost on them and eventually would become a source of great inspiration.

Post-recovery, as a thank-you, Ryan and Jen decided to start an underground "supper club," where they would take reservations for paying guests into their home and treat them to a formal five-course meal, one day per week, in hopes of raising funds for their vision of opening a restaurant of the same concept. It also served as a thank-you to all those who did so right by them in their time of need. It was simply a beautiful concept.

The continued feedback from people was tremendous, which only led to confirm that they were onto something special, and with perseverance and continued help from family and friends, eventually Staplehouse Restaurant came to fruition: a fine-dining restaurant in downtown Atlanta — an old two-story, stand-alone brick building that could easily be mistaken for an apartment if one didn't know what they were looking for, exactly. A meal here would feel home-cooked, with multiple courses and bountiful portions, promoting conversation and memories. A very rare concept in today's day and age. Ryan, Jen, and founding members of Giving Kitchen created a for-profit subsidiary that would donate portions of its profits back to the non-profit parent that owned them. That non-profit parent was Giving Kitchen. This is very similar to what Bobby Heugel had done at OKRA (Chapter 9).

Before the creation of Giving Kitchen and Staplehouse Restaurant, this intrepid couple received grave news. Ryan suddenly fell ill. After a series of tests, he was diagnosed with an aggressive form of gallbladder cancer and given six months to live. It was devastating news to everyone who knew him. He was too young, too smart, too successful — how could this be? As you would expect, Ryan began extremely aggressive chemotherapy treatments in the hope that perhaps he could prove the odds wrong and fend off such a dire prognosis.

Once again, the community rose to the occasion, hosting all sorts of fundraisers to help support Ryan and Jen through the process. The outpouring of help and support was simply astounding. These efforts plus the experiences from his earlier accident were the impetus for the launch of their concept in 2013, which became known as Giving Kitchen. Its mission couldn't be clearer, or more personal: helping food service industry workers in dire need with financial assistance and connections to community resources through their Stability Network program. Good works beget good works.

Tragically, Ryan passed on January 9, 2014.

Jen has never forgotten how much the community rose to help them during Ryan's car accident and yet again during Ryan's battle against cancer. While Ryan's life was cut short way too soon, it didn't lack impact. He left behind an indelible legacy that perseveres and thrives to this day under Jen's leadership and guidance.

With the support of her business partners at Staplehouse Restaurant, Jen continued to develop and grow both ventures. At one point, both grew to such a level she felt she had to choose a path or risk failing to meet the lofty standards she and Ryan had set for themselves. In 2019, Jen decided to sell Staplehouse Restaurant to her business partners — who later renamed it Staplehouse Market — and focus.

From its website, thegivingkitchen.org: "Giving Kitchen provides emergency assistance for food service workers through financial support and a network of community resources."

Jen has found purpose in Ryan's passing and puts it to work helping others in need every day — just as she was called to do. As you might imagine, Giving Kitchen was at the forefront of importance during 2020, a time when our industry bore the brunt of the COVID-19 pandemic safety protocols. Untold numbers of industry workers were fed and supported during unimaginable strife.

On behalf of everyone in our community, Jen, you have our sincerest gratitude. Thank you!

Giving Kitchen helps food service workers in crisis. As a growing regional agency, they will not turn away any qualifying client who comes their way throughout all 50 states, and they are building a model for national expansion. Giving Kitchen features two core programs: financial support and a stability network. Since inception (2013), Giving Kitchen has surpassed $7.5 million in financial assistance to those in need and has served over 11,000 clients — plus over 3,000 children in the homes of food service workers! At the time of our interview, Jen explained that the total assistance was roughly the same as paying 43,000 gas bills, 130,000 water bills, or 65,000 power bills for food service workers in crisis.

Jen Hidinger of Giving Kitchen
Photo by Audra Melton

Giving Kitchen accolades include:

- Fast Company: Brands That Matter, 2022
- James Beard Foundation: Humanitarian of the Year, 2019
- Center for Civic Innovation: Civic Impact Award, 2019
- Georgia Restaurant Association: Industry Partner of the Year, 2015
- Charity Navigator: Encompass rating — 100 out of 100

Powerful Desire

There's simply no other industry quite like ours, in our opinion. These two examples serve to show us there's rarely a traditional business case for giving back; it's something that comes from within and is always worthwhile. How and why we give back can vary, and there's no rule for exactly how we should go about the business of good works, but we all should.

A very common thread we found through our interviews was a powerful desire to help and lift up others in all sorts of unique ways. Many would describe it as a calling. We were wildly inspired by the stories of Stephanie and Jen, but not all giving may be at the extreme. You may not be able to travel the world and start a school like Stephanie or generate $6.5 million in support like Jen, but there are opportunities all around us to help, especially within our communities. We found more often than not that our award winners were dialed in to opportunities where they were able to impact the welfare of others on both a global and local scale.

There's an indelible spirit to be found here. These two set the bar, pardon the pun, for what extraordinary giving looks like. We will also experience it in Chapter 14, with Ivy Mix and her massive charitable organization Speed Rack, where you will see her willingness to give and seek mentorship with others. We see it with the Neal Bodenheimer-led Tales of the Cocktail Foundation, which seeks to support causes exactly like these, including Speed Rack and Stephanie's organization, Beyond Bars Akademia! But what does it mean from a success perspective? Why give back that which was so hard-fought and rightfully earned? Our interviewees, without exception, gained a certain energy and enthusiasm in these good works; they all seemed to have some sort of higher calling that motivated their continued success.

Winning just for winning's sake seems to become a short-sided endeavor for them, and the idea of striving to a higher calling seems to provide meaning and motivation beyond what we might call "regular business." This energy then seemingly provides personal fuel for whatever additional challenges they decide to take on. Our conclusion here is, people do good works for all the right reasons. At the same time, there is an unintended benefit for our award winners: an awesome multiplying effect on energy, well-being, and their personal brand. The best part of this story is, there's no downside for them; everybody wins in the effort to make our world a better place!

HELIX Sequencing

> We found varying levels of correlation between the building blocks in each chapter and the DNA points at the end of the book. The strength of the correlation is represented by 1 to 5 circles around our 5-point Hospitality DNA molecule: 1 being a lower correlation and 5 being a higher one.

Humble Nature

The willingness to put one's life aside in the pursuit of helping others advance their own is the ultimate gift and highest example of a humble nature.

Explorer's Pursuit

Seek out the opportunity no matter where it may lie. When Stephanie told us she sought out where women were the worst off and she decided to take a brand new idea with absolutely no support to the toughest place she could find ... I mean, what more can we say? It's crazy, it's brave, and it's an otherworldly example of an Explorer's Pursuit.

Lifetime of Experience

It was hard to not tear up while interviewing Jen. Her story is both heart-wrenching and heartwarming. A lifetime of experience has taught these award winners about the highs life can afford us and the tragedies of remarkable loss, but that you do not need your own lifetime to start to help others.

Indomitable Spirit

If there was ever a good excuse to quit, they had it. Who would blame either of them? Jen and Stephanie teach us to never give up the fight. Yes, they were down — devastated even. How could they not be? But they were never out. They chose, over and over again, to rise above, and through that, they managed to build something bigger than themselves. They made beauty out of tragedy in ways that are nothing short of heroic.

Xtraordinary Culture

The world needs aspirational figures — people we can aspire to become, even if just a little. Being someone who gives is one of the few cultural pillars where simply showing others what you are doing engrains it into your culture. We need examples of people who have overcome the greatest obstacles. It can make our day-to-day challenges seem very manageable by affording us both context for our problems and targets for personal growth, which all then makes it easier to give of ourselves. We thank you!

Chapter 11

Information Systems

> The tighter you hold on to information,
> the more decisions you'll have to make.
> —Gaurav Patel

Until very recently, our industry has lagged far behind other industries when it comes to the use of technology. In 2007, while visiting Chicago bars with a group of friends, I was watching how the venues we went to ran. Out of all of the idiosyncrasies I observed, one struck me as so odd as to be crazy. In 2007, 20 years after the invention of the touch screen point-of-service (POS) system, many of these bars were using old-school cash registers, and even the most high-end venue we went to — a gorgeous bar on the 94th floor of the very tall building — was using an old-school, green screen POS system where you needed a full keyboard to enter codes to run it. The Micros 3700 touch screen POS system for restaurants had been around for 11 years at this point, for God's sake! I could probably write a whole book on how and why the culture of the restaurant industry shied away from tech for so long, but looking back, what seems infinitely more interesting is how rapidly and intensely that trend has shifted over the years and what that means to us, the restaurant operators.

Hospitality DNA

We could have called this chapter "Navigating the Fog of War." In our day-to-day business, it very common for us to see one of two scenarios:

1. Businesses running with little or no actionable data
2. Businesses with many disparate systems running independent of each other, creating as much confusion as they do actionable information

Rather than providing clarity, many people use information in ways that further cloud the decisions that need to be made. When used correctly, the decision process becomes both easy and impactful.

We're firmly grounded in a couple of core philosophies in this regard:

1. Great information allows people at different talent levels to perform at above-average levels
2. Exceptionally talented people will underperform in an environment operating with no or incorrect information

It can be hard to get people excited about great information because, let's face it, it's not a sexy topic. It's ho-hum stuff! Full disclosure: both Dave and I live in a data-based world. Every single day, we're working through data to impact bars and restaurants to great effect. There are two critical data attributes you need in order for it to positively impact your business — yes, just two very simple things we call *AA: accurate* and *actionable*. Can I trust it, and do I know what to do with it to make my business better?

Operators we know do not lack access to numbers — data, in effect. But as we

> The more we can get done, the more we can get done.

Information Systems

discuss in *The Bar Shift* as well, data must convert to information, and information to action. If that process isn't in place, all you have is a bunch of numbers that you will quickly learn to ignore and despise. The fog of war for us is no info or bad info combined with the demands of the daily grind, which leads to a fog or uncertainty in terms of what the most pressing actions and focuses are in the business to effect meaningful change.

When we embrace technology and properly apply it to the day-to-day operations and issues that arise in our businesses, we become more productive in ways that seem like magic to outsiders. Productivity is rarely discussed when it comes to the benefits of technology, but it lends itself to reason that the more we can get done, the more we can get done. It's a matter of momentum, which we call *The Propeller Effect*. So why haven't we figured all this out? One of the main reasons is that we didn't have the ability to collect certain types of data that we needed, as they were not readily available to us until recently.

At this point in the history of our industry, there have never been more tools available to help us manage our decision-making processes. In 2004, both Facebook and Yelp launched, which for better or worse, gave us unprecedented access to the thoughts and feelings of our guests. As these two platforms quickly gained popularity, many others followed suit and something really cool happened.

Where there was once a sparse wasteland of secondhand tech for the smaller operators (1 to 25 units), there has sprung up a verdant and sprawling valley of options for every metric imaginable, all custom made for bars and restaurants. This has presented a new problem that we discuss frequently with our clients. Where once, only the giants of our industry had the capital (financial and human) to create the invaluable information systems needed to speed up decision-making, there is now a gluttony of options available — so much so that deciding what to use and why can be daunting — and they fill every area imaginable.

- POS
- Human resources
- Scheduling
- Communication
- Accounting
- Customer service
- Product order consolidation
- Cost tracking
- Loss tracking
- and so on ...

Of course, you are told that each one of these is mission critical — "You can't run your business without my newest widget!" — making where to start an even more difficult proposition.

The title of this chapter is "Information Systems" and, ultimately, this is not a "technology" conversation. What I will say is this: technology is an important tool that we need to use to make decision-making easier and faster. If any given tech creates additional bottlenecks in the business, it is either not the right solution for you or it has not been implemented or managed properly.

What tech works for you might not work for the guy across the street. You might have the budget to hire the full-time database manager you need to make your comprehensive F&B supply chain, cost, and inventory software provide you with the timely actionable information you need. The gal down the street might need to outsource that to another company.

One way or another, the industry greats have turned the intimidating number of options and configurations into a robust productivity machine, but before you get started, you need to answer a question for yourself:

Do I need more time to work on my business?

For most, this journey is not a short one, and it requires dedication over time to accomplish, but even partway through, it tends to have payoffs in multiples. The outcome of a well-run information cycle is to increase productivity — for you, for every member of your staff, and for the business as a whole. In addition to increased productivity, if you have these running well in all the areas of your business where you need them, your managers will spend less time in the back office and more time on the floor with guests.

Gaurav and Julie Patel
Photo by Eschelon Experiences

While we have talked to some of the most impressive and successful people in our industry for this book, none achieved the level of success that Gaurav "G" Patel did as early in life or as quickly, building a company of eight hundred employees by the age of 25. While he had the talent and drive necessary to achieve such a feat, it was implementing robust information systems and cycles in his business that pulled him and his team together to accomplish this feat. For G, the owner of a management group with several highly successful locations, this journey started with a single meeting.

At the time, his company was more a loose group of individuals managing their restaurants than it was a structured company. Being a rather young group, they had embraced technology in useful ways that allowed them to find success where others had struggled. However, "Initially, all the shit was rolled uphill." G could not walk away for any length of time; most decisions had to go through him. If he wasn't there to manage the data, everyone got stuck. The first step was to figure out who they were.

After pulling every manager and chef together in a long meeting to define what kind of company they were — asking, "If we were a car, what car would we be?" — they had a starting point to begin to figure out what they needed to focus on. Six months and many meetings later, they turned this idea of a car into their four pillars of operation.

- Passion
- Integrity
- Innovation
- Quality

These concepts defined who they were as an organization and allowed them to start identifying what aspects of the business they needed to focus on by giving them a universal, common language to use to discuss any aspect of the business — including their information systems. However, until they did, G was still a bottleneck of decision-making, the only one who knew how to interpret the data they had in front of them.

Information Systems

This is an inherent problem with data that many people get stuck in. If you do not have a data-reduction process in place — something that allows you to take many numbers and convert them into a singular actionable figure — then one or two people get stuck as the sole decision-makers in the business.

There are 100 decisions to be made in even a single restaurant. The power of getting your information cycle right is in the ability to empower your staff to make many of those decisions on their own. They cannot do this in a vacuum or alone; they need guidance: a structure with fail-safes built in to allow them to make the decisions you don't have the time for while protecting the business from "bad" decisions. A good example of this is giving them a budget to work within.

After working out the "pillars" with his team, G saw another critical gap in his current operating structure: a business plan. He didn't have one. You can certainly start a business without a business plan, but I wouldn't recommend it. At some point in the growth of your company, you will get stuck — bogged down by the lack of a common language and singular vision to bind the team together. Some people see business plans as a nice-to-have or even as unnecessary — something that is just making it take longer to get started. For G the thought was "I was in the practical world actually doing it." Running the business or even part of it can make the prospect of stopping to write a solid business plan feel like "a rubbish waste of time," as it did for him. For G, the realization that "A decent business plan … it's amazing how powerful that can be … that's your roadmap" allowed him to take his business to the next level.

Hospitality DNA

> **A note on business plans:** The business plan actually fits into the last part of the information system cycle, but it is one of the first things that should be done when, or really before, you launch a new business. On the surface, this might feel contradictory. Understanding that a good business plan actually fulfills a slew of requirements for the business helps this make sense. While it is invaluable during the planning phase, it also happens to provide much of the framework for the end of your information cycle process, though not 100% of it. If you do not have a business plan, we would highly recommend getting one together as a top priority. Even if you are years in, you will quickly see the massive value this brings to your business on multiple levels.

If you are not sure where to start when building a business plan, check out the Small Business Administration (SBA) tools. This link takes you to a quick guide on business plans along with a few examples.

https://www.sba.gov/business-guide/plan-your-business/write-your-business-plan

While this is a U.S. government tool, it is a generic business plan template that will work for you no matter where you live. If you cannot access U.S. .gov websites, you should be able to find something useful by performing an internet search for "Business Plan Template."

The humble business plan can fill in the last step of the information cycle, but there are three distinct parts to every one of these cycles in your business that have to be completed.

- Capture **Data**
- Convert that data into **Information**
- Use that information to take meaningful **Action**

$$\text{Data} \rightarrow \text{Information} \rightarrow \text{Action}$$

There is a review process of each of these cycles that will need to happen at regular intervals as well; however, the longer your cycles are running, and so the more you have tweaked them to get them right, the fewer and further in-between reviews there need to be.

Data: Data collection has been the most tedious and time-consuming part of the information cycle. While technology has definitely made this much less painful, there is also a multitude of outsourcing options, from online bookkeepers to third-party inventory companies. Making it all even easier, finding out which data you need for any given opportunity is both readily available on the internet as well as in the minds of eager companies ready to educate you on what you should be looking at and how they can help; educational salesmanship has almost become the norm.

Information: Converting our data into actionable information is actually where technology has provided the biggest leap. Gone are the days of hand calculations or even a complicated spreadsheet to crunch your numbers into a usable nugget of info. Accounting software calculates your labor cost after pulling the relevant data in from your POS system and payroll company, summing it up and doing the relevant math. Once set up, you don't even have to consider where it is coming from; you just have one beautiful metric to work with.

Action: There is one and only one tool that has ever made the process of making decisions on the information in your business efficient: the humble dashboard. This has become somewhat of a buzzword, but dashboards have been around for the better part of a century. Even when I got into the restaurant industry in the early aughts, I could find whiteboards showing the current weekly revenue, cost of goods, and labor targets along with the previous week's performance. Technology just makes that easier. Whatever tools you choose to use, make sure that they dashboard the information you need to look at in a way that makes sense to you.

A proper dashboard consists of two major values that interact with each other; one is a simple reality, and the other is a measure that you may have to tweak over time: a target. A great example of this is the simple budget. You may start by telling your head bartender that they have $5,000 a week to spend on alcohol. You feel this number is correct because you know what your sales are and you have a target cost of goods in mind. Each week, they spend an amount of money that you will compare to that budget. If they go over or under that figure on a regular basis, you will need to discuss it and dig in on that metric.

Are your sales lower or higher than you expected?

Have costs gone up so much that you have to revisit your expectation on your cost of goods sold (COGS)?

Is there a potential loss issue that will require a new "Data ⟶ Information ⟶ Action" process to be implemented?

No matter the question and the answer to it, having that initial information cycle in place allows you to tweak your business operations, your targets, and your processes.

Information Systems

It is not always possible to get this right on the first attempt; do not get discouraged. It is rare that people get this right the first time. A classic example is the assumption that 20% blended alcohol costs is "good" in our industry. This simply isn't true for most operators. Of all the venues we have worked with internationally, the "right" target can be anywhere from 10% to 25% and depends on many different factors: location, clientele, product sales blend, and so on. However, having that target as a starting point and initiating an information cycle around it allows you to begin discovering for yourself and your business what the true correct figure is.

If you consider your business, you will probably realize that you are likely already running a solid information cycle in a few areas. If you look at your cost of goods at least once a month and have a measure to compare them to and then hold meetings to determine action to take when they are off, that is a Data → Information → Action cycle. You know you have this right when the meetings are short and the actions decisive and quickly effective. If you are in a place where you feel you are constantly discussing "why the numbers are bad" but see no improvement over time, then it is time to re-evaluate your process, starting with a set of good questions.

Explaining the Terms

Data: Raw numbers and statistics gathered, usually in large quantity, for the purpose of conversion into useful figures with which to make rapid decisions

Information: Sums of data parsed down into as few useful and meaningful figures as possible

Action: The process of doing something to achieve an aim

- Are we looking at the right metric?
- Are the data we are starting with reliable and accurate?
- Are we using the right tool?
- Is the right person in place at each step of the process?

For example, if your food costs always seem high to you and you have an exhausted cook auditing a kitchen, walk-in coolers and freezers, dry storage, and so on at 9:00 a.m. when he left the restaurant at 2:00 a.m. earlier that day after entering a stack of invoices for three hours, you might want to consider discussing a food cost-tracking tool with your largest food provider (most offer a tool like this). If they don't have one, there are many solid third-party options out there today that can automate much of the food cost-tracking process and give you much more timely information you can use to determine effective action.

Getting everything set up to start follows a different flow, but once you have each one set, the Data ⟶ Information ⟶ Action process is the same for all. The first step is to identify where the biggest opportunity in the business is. As the ultimate goal of information cycles is to increase productivity, it is easy to start with "Where do you feel you are spending too much time?" However, sometimes the financials are a bigger concern, so "What area of the business seems like revenue or costs make the least sense?" may be a better opportunity-seeking question.

Once we've identified our biggest opportunities, we should bias our best talent and resources toward them. In this scenario, we are going to look at one of the most frequent issues we see with our clients: difficulty in attracting and then keeping talented staff.

> **A note on style:** There are many ways you can run a strong information cycle. G Patel feels most comfortable with Open Book Management (a leadership model pioneered by Jack Stack, author of *The Great Game of Business*), which is also how I run my business. However, showing your books to every employee might feel too exposed to you. If you are more comfortable launching your team into the information cycle with the exact information they need to make those decisions, that can work well too. You will find that the cycle is more important than the style. The one required element, however, is that you must allow your team to make decisions for you, based on the framework you have created.

Before we get started we need to

A. Put our most talented people on the issue. That may be you, the owner; it may be a manager who just seems to get people; or it may need to be a third party.
B. Apply enough resources to solve the issue. You can't prep a 100-guest dinner with one cook in an hour.
C. Get the information right so that we can start the relevant conversations. If you're not sure where to start, research online, with your colleagues, or with other industry experts. Most people like helping.

The initial question "How do we go about solving our staffing issue?" feels like a tough one to answer. People are messy, fickle things, so what data can we start mining to get on the path of turning this problem into an opportunity?

We can break "not enough people" into two questions, both of which we can answer with an information cycle:

Are we able to hire enough people fast enough?

Are we losing people too fast?

As they are at the opposite ends of a singular issue, there are two information cycles we will want to start, to answer each of those questions. There are targets and metrics that you can apply to answer both of these questions as well as technology you can use to help.

Are we able to hire people fast enough?

Target: How many new hires a week do we need to be fully staffed by X time, and when should we be able to stop hiring?

Measure: Number of hires per week over time

Tech: Payroll software and hiring software

Are we losing people too fast?

Target: Desired staff turnover (per position)

Measure: Actual staff turnover (per position)

Tech: Payroll software

The information that comes out of your tracking systems will determine where your conversation goes, and every restaurant will have its own set of issues that need to be resolved. Additionally, seemingly disparate problems might actually have the same cause. If you are not seeing a lot of applicants come through the front door and you find you have a high turnover rate, these could both be caused by an internal culture issue that causes staff to leave and which they in turn talk about with other industry people who then stay away.

Let's say that you find you have high staff turnover, like most operators in our industry. Why would you want to try to fix it? Staff turnover in our industry runs at an average of 73%, which is obscenely high, and we have seen it as high as 175% in some locations. According to Center for Hospitality Research at Cornell University, losing a single frontline employee will cost you around $5,864. If you are tracking staff turnover, you can easily multiply this figure by each employee lost; if you only lose ten people a year, that is $58,640 a year that could be recaptured.

So once you have your turnover information on your dashboard each week and you want to reduce it from 70% to 35% to start, what do you do? There are two easy sources of information that you have right in front of you.

Find out what your staff thinks about working for you: The answers you need to the question "Do people like working here?" are easy to get. Gaurav created his own employee survey to determine if his staff happy working on his team. The Q12 survey from Gallup is a great place to start if you don't have anything in mind. Keep it anonymous for honest answers and, if possible, digital (you can use Google Forms to do this for free). You might find you have a cancerous employee everyone was afraid to tell you about to your face, or maybe they all just want a little more growth and education in the industry. Maybe they just want a better sense of camaraderie. All of these would be solvable issues that would create further opportunity for your business. However, until you have the information from the staff, you can't start working to address whatever issues there may be.

Find out why staff is leaving: Exit interviews are ubiquitous in the corporate world for a reason: the big, successful companies understand that knowing why people leave is incredibly valuable. Ask both closed- and open-ended questions, and do not be afraid of the answers. If you find conversations like these to be confrontational and uncomfortable, treat them as a simple need to get clarity for yourself from someone who can provide it. Again, no matter the information you get from these people, they provide you with the opportunity to close any gaps you have in your business and then to get people to stop leaving.

My clients who do track it generally have very low staff turnover; we tend to do well at what we spend our time and attention on.

This is part of an example of one possible outcome of one of many different paths you could take to start using information to save you serious time and money and multiply your productivity, but when should you start?

Now.

Toward the end of our conversation, Gaurav lamented that when he started correcting his lack of these systems and cycles in his business, he was "building a plane and flying it at the same time." If he had to do it all over again, he would have started implementing and refining these systems in his business when he had one or two simple, single locations. No matter how hard and fast you feel you are flying when you open your first location, if you go to expand, you will miss the days when life was so simple. Even if you stay at one location, you can minimize the time needed

> Gaurav lamented that when he started correcting his lack of these systems and cycles in his business, he was "building a plane and flying it at the same time."

to make all the small decisions in your business by getting these into place. With the advent of these new technologies and the number of companies competing for your business, there has never been a better or easier time to get a dashboard in front of you that previously only the likes of OSI or Yum! Brands had access to.

G's accomplishments and input on information is all valuable; however, it becomes all the more impressive after learning even more about his journey.

Gaurav "G" Patel's story[2] begins in the small farming village of Zervavra, in the Northern Indian state of Gujarat. As a child, he was given a plot of land and was told to grow small crops — choosing spinach due to its aggressive growth cycle — so he could make money for school supplies. This was his first of many successful business ventures.

At ten years old, G moved with his family to Morehead City, North Carolina. Upon his arrival in the United States, G spoke zero English, becoming fluent through the U.S. education system. Twenty-one years later, G has become a staple name in the dining scene in "the Triangle," three distinct cities in North Carolina — Raleigh, Durham, and Chapel Hill — owning six top-ranking Triangle restaurants and employing more than three hundred people in the area.

His journey as an entrepreneur began when G moved to Raleigh to pursue a degree in business at North Carolina State University. Throughout his education, G directed his attention to the area's potential for business opportunities and decided to begin the foundation of Eschelon Experiences in Raleigh.

---

[2] From interview with Gaurav Patel by Dave Nitzel and Dave Domzalski conducted on 11/3/2020.

Since his business's conception in 2006, G has grown his company at a staggering rate and has set the standard for the restaurant industry in the Triangle area. His vision for Eschelon is to encompass a business model that focuses on the importance of people.

In addition to his business ventures, the president of Eschelon demonstrates the importance of community and civic responsibility by working closely with nonprofit groups. These include the Tammy Lynn Center for Developmental Disabilities, Raleigh City Farm, Band Together, and Hope for Haiti Foundation.

In 2015, G was presented with a 40 Under 40 Award from the *Triangle Business Journal*. This award recognizes 40 individuals under the age of 40 who have provided phenomenal contributions to their own organization and wider community.

G's work endeavors would not be possible without the support of his loving wife, Julie, their daughter, Zara, and son, Azil. Being the hospitality guru that he is, G also enjoys traveling and mentoring young minds.

HELIX Sequencing

> We found varying levels of correlation between the building blocks in each chapter and the DNA points at the end of the book. The strength of the correlation is represented by 1 to 5 circles around our 5-point Hospitality DNA molecule: 1 being a lower correlation and 5 being a higher one.

Humble Nature

In our lives, there are Known Unknowns and Unknown Unknowns. Those of us who embrace the idea that there is more that we don't know than what we do know tend to be the most successful in our industry. When we get cocky or complacent around harvesting and using the information available to us, our ability to make valuable decisions and our likelihood of making bad or even disastrous ones increases.

Explorer's Pursuit

Information opens up the exploration of the inner and hidden workings of our businesses. Just as we scour the world to learn about the ways that different cultures around the world approach and execute hospitality, we need to set up information systems that allow us to easily explore the insides of our own businesses.

Lifetime of Experience

This is a rare case where it is easy to learn from others so that you don't have to learn the hard way. Though you will need to shift what you measure from time to time based on the state of your business, once you put a strong process around processing and discussing information in your business, the day-to-day work on these systems becomes routine.

Indomitable Spirit

The application of well-mined and curated information built into the systems of the business does nothing but make the entire operation run more smoothly and make it easier to manage. When times get tough, while the greats don't quit, it is still easy to turn away from critical yet mundane aspects of the operation. Make sure they do not require significant effort to maintain, and your information systems will be an asset, helping to identify and resolve issues in times of crisis.

Xtraordinary Culture

We've all heard *what gets measured gets done*. Very few operators have measurable indices around their business culture. Award-winning operators understand the vital nature of measuring culture. Because measurements drive behaviors and behaviors drive performance, we must have data and targets readily available to everyone involved. If we aspire to having a world class culture, we must have the information available that clearly and succinctly shows us how we are performing. Anything short of this lends itself to hope, and hope is not a strategy.

Chapter 12

Discipline

> For a man to conquer himself is the
> first and noblest of all victories.
> —Plato

Our story so far has been told from the perspective of industry leaders, giants, and visionaries. If we are doing what we set out to do, you are feeling inspired, energized, or both. You are currently mentally reliving the experiences you have gathered in your life, furiously searching for gaps you will drive to fill over the next few years. You are looking through your Rolodex of relationships, poring over whom among those you have crossed paths with might partner with you to supercharge your vision for the perfect venue. You are revisiting your plan, pondering every detail to ensure they are all clearly worked out and ready to be realized.

We have to hope that we have been doing pretty well at keeping it positive to this point. We have been laying out in front of you the bright and clear paths of where some amazing individuals have tread. These paths have helped guide these leaders to achieve greatness in their own right, and we hope these have started to give you new and wonderful insights into your own journey to date.

As we begin to work out this next chapter, we have to be clear with you: this will not be a well-laid-out plan — your guide, if you will — to disciplined enlightenment. The beauty is that it does not have to be. There are countless books written by better authors (better people, too, I would wager) than us about how to inspire, create, or drive discipline in yourself and your team. They will lay out the paths, goals, tips, and tricks you need to help you and your team be more productive than you could ever imagine. Why would we stomp on the toes of those whose obsessive genius lies in routine, regime, and regulation?

This set of tales that so far have been inspiring stories of achievement will, for a few pages only, take a turn. This next section is a story of the "almost was," a cautionary tale of what happens when you lose sight of your end goal when you do not have the discipline to see your vision through to the end. This also happens to be our own story. This is a story of how detrimental a lack of discipline can, and likely will, be to all best-laid plans.

One last, probably obvious point of information before I get started: as there are some less-than-flattering points to this story, all names other than Dave and Dave have been changed.

When $150,000 in three days is a failure.

In 2017, we were asked to design the beverage program and staff training for a pop-up restaurant and bar at one of the coolest events in the world. We had months to put together everything that was needed, from spirits and equipment lists to an operations guide for the event. About one week out, the project ballooned slightly from simply designing what was needed to managing and running the entire operation over the three-day event. At about 3 p.m. on a Saturday afternoon, there were twenty-eight bartenders, four cocktail waitresses, and six barbacks in our main tent, along with another five bartenders in the major tequila brand-sponsored tent, and we were cranking at full peak capacity.

Discipline

With no more than a few seconds between finishing one order and starting the next, our team was fluidly taking care of one guest after the next, producing $140 per minute and climbing. We were thrilled about finishing strong above all measures for a typical Saturday.

The afternoon rain had cooled off the grounds. There were 200,000 race fans who had been camping out for the last 72 hours and finally, after hours of well-executed service and a months-long marketing effort, word had gotten around about what we had created. They were hungry for something new, and we had it!

We were headed into an evening with high expectations of it being one of the best events of our careers. This was our perfect opportunity to bring home the full $250,000 we had signed up to haul in over three days at this major race event.

Six months before we had turned this 3,000-square-foot concrete slab into a full bar and restaurant with entertainment, one of the biggest auto racing organizations on the planet had finished negotiations with a man we shall call Bob, who brought us in to consult. Bob is a rather brilliant and highly capable man. He not only conceptualized and brought to life this unique restaurant pop-up, he also spent a year convincing multiple corporate executives that he, the owner of a modest family entertainment complex with five bartenders and two managers behind a simple bar, was the right man to turn said slab into a high-volume bar and restaurant. As part of his process, he worked out three ground rules with the host of the event.

1. **Make It Big:** We want something that has never been done here before — something big and bold.
CHECK!

2. **Make It Profitable:** We want you to prove that we can sustain a similar pop-up-style venue for years to come. DOUBLE CHECK!
3. **Make It Family:** This was the time to take racing to the moms and the kiddies. Let them feel safe, and make it somewhere they want to be.

Up to this point, we had this pretty much locked in, but this is also where the wheels started to come off, if you can pardon the pun.

One month after negotiations and five months before the event, I received a call from Bob. Bob is a marketing and strategy prodigy! I learned so much from him on these two fronts.

He explained the deal he negotiated with the top people in racing to install a pop-up restaurant on the local racetrack grounds for its biggest event of the year. If he got this right, there was a handshake deal in place for him to replicate this strategy at racing events around the country nearly every weekend!

Bob was from a completely different field outside of the large format bar and restaurant. An engineer by training, he was a genius when it came to mechanicals. He holds a patent for the exact manufacturing process of a specialized type of robot. His father was the inventor and patent holder for the robot itself; intelligence runs in the family.

Bob was not green when it came to Hospitality either. Five years before the event, Bob created a fantastic family entertainment complex that also had a small bar and a kitchen that produced high-quality food, ranging from house-smoked pit beef to a premium steak.

One last important piece to this puzzle: Bob is not your typical engineer. Bob is charming. Bob understands how to create the allure of a great spectacle. Bob can sell. If you have ever spent serious time with engineers, you know that this is a somewhat unusual combination.

What Bob didn't have was all the necessary skills to execute an ambitious and spectacular pop-up restaurant. He had no idea how to create a bar program on that scale. He also wasn't well versed in designing a training program, getting thirty-three bartenders trained and aligned within eight hours after they arrived on-site, and then to manage that staff throughout the entire event, which was designed to produce $250,000 over three days.

With all that in mind, his continual and strong ability to create amazing relationships would get him over some of those hurdles.

So, my phone rang, and we talked.

Bob asked me to design an event-appropriate beverage program for him and to manage his inventory for the event. No problem for us — it's all in a day's work!

Three weeks later, Bob needed a job ad created to hire thirty-three bartenders, bringing them into his town. There was not enough local talent to staff the bar, so Bob wanted to gather bartenders from around the country to make this happen. I knocked out a targeted job ad that would attract the right kind of people for the event. An enticing ad was created that ended up pulling in solid talent from across six states. Mission accomplished, right on schedule; all systems go, as this was tagged as the toughest part of the operation ... or, so we thought.

Two more weeks swept by, and Bob needed a full beverage program with simple-to-execute cocktails specced out.

By the time all the requirements Bob needed from me were laid out, the opportunity had gone from "his" deal to replicate around the country to "our" deal to replicate around the country. I was now building and executing his training program, sourcing the product and bar tools, managing the team, closing all drawers, and reporting the financials. I had become the "go-to guy for operations," and I was excited!

There remained one, significant operational conundrum to solve, and the two former engineers were keen to tackle it.

The bar we were designing was a 100-foot-long U configuration. There was a central island where the call liquor would live, and you could only enter from the end of one very long bar. Because of the requirements of the space, the interior would be tight. Even with a narrow central island, our barbacks would barely be able to squeeze by the bartenders as they moved up and down the bar.

So here we are ... two engineers with a dream of solving an old bar-restocking problem. When we got down to the solution, we designed a rail cart pulley system that would restock the booze and ice in one direction and remove trash in the other. We had to cut a path down the middle of the islands, and while this made the bartenders' space tighter, it allowed us to easily move product where it needed to be.

Of course, the guys using our creation during the busiest hours of the race figured out how to make it work even better. They found a guy just the right size to ride the cart up and down the center of the bar, restocking each station as he went.

All of this would have to be pre-built and designed for quick and easy assembly over a 48-hour period on-site.

For his last trick, Bob pulled together his full kitchen, reproducing the same scrumptious roast beef, steak, and burgers he offered at his primary location.

As we were designing the build-out of this ambitious temporary bar and restaurant, Bob also launched a marketing machine. The moment he was given a green light, he was on every racing broadcast, podcast, and webcast. He worked the locals, person by person — some of whom he didn't know personally — and created an online network.

All this was done to get the word out on the street: a one-of-a-kind, fantastical bar/club/restaurant and live music event open to the public! This venue was unlike any other, located on the vacant lot of a storied 67-year-old racetrack.

If you haven't figured this out yet, there was serious gravity to the tasks Bob had set up for himself. There were two vastly different, long-entrenched institutions, the constituents of which were fighting decade-old habits of two disparate populations. On one side, you had wealthy race fans who showed up every year to attend posh invite-only events held in white, three-story event tents, decorated with supercars, filled with ephemera, and catered by top French chefs.

Then there were the other hard-core race fans. For 50 years, they had built an honest-to-goodness fiefdom — reproduced year after year. According to Bob, complete with "mayors, bizarre rules, impromptu bars, intense booze- and drug-fueled parties, and hillbilly elevators." From a very young age, Bob had been a big part of this intense shanty town for every year of his life and loved every crazy second of it.

Side note: For those of you wondering what a hillbilly elevator is, like I was, it is a scissor lift that they set up around the track in order to get a better view of the race. Yes I got on one, and yes it was awesome!

To recap, Bob had

- Decided that a pop-up should exist at an event that hadn't had one for 66 years
- Created a venue in a converted warehouse so that he could court the right people in auto racing to agree to his concept

- Courted world-traveled multimillionaires in said warehouse entertainment center
- Convinced one of the most powerful sports institutions in the world to allow him to be a part of their rebranding effort
- Launched a multi-platform marketing campaign effort designed to shift an entire event from debauchery and rich excess to a new "for the people" paradigm
- Reached out to me to take up the operational parts he did not have the skills or team to handle

At this point, I realized that I could not mess this up. The planning portion was easy. I pulled out some simple-to-train-and-execute cocktails, cash-handling, and reconciling procedures. I also negotiated a few supplier deals, and worked with his POS company to set up the platform to handle what we needed.

What I did not have was the management team in place to handle 33 people who were strangers to one another but had to work like a well-oiled machine. All of this was needed over the span of a four-day, fast-paced environment.

Thankfully, my dear friend and co-author Dave N is a huge racing guy. I want to ask you: do you like racing? Nitzel races a Dodge Viper as a hobby — pretty cool, huh? I don't know anyone who has more of a true passion for auto sports than Dave.

Dave graciously offered to come help me with the event — for free, if necessary (he welcomed having an excuse for just being at the track). He brought in two other players who would prove to be key to the operation.

Bright and early on day one of the event, which was a Thursday, I was drowning in what I call "employee relations." Before I had arrived on-site, I told my man Nitzel that I wouldn't need him until the middle of day two. "Fans will just be getting here. Why would I need you to help me then?" I foolishly asked.

Day one was warm-up time with day two slowly ramping up. I was wrong, and I admit to that. The staff of 33 women from around the country and multiple different industries whom Bob had hired were clashing, and I was the one and only manager on a site that spanned a 3,000-square-foot bar, an additional 300-square-foot bar, and 40,000 square feet of grounds space.

Nitzel, who arrived none too soon, strode in at hour 32, when hundreds of thousands of people were learning that this new space existed. It took him only 45 minutes to rearrange the staff, repurpose the security team, and bring a strong sense of order to the group. Harmony happened. This was my personal penultimate moment of partnerships coming together!

A day later, I discovered that Dave's wife, Jeni, had been brought in to help manage the event. Jeni had been working with, talking to, coaching, and mentoring the all-woman bar team to strengthen their working relationships and their individual strengths. Later, I learned that Jeni had been training her entire life to support young women in their professional careers. So, it all came together at the right place and the right time! While that is a compelling lesson about getting exactly the right people together in a partnership, that is not the story we are here to tell.

> **Experience** — Our combined experience was more than adequate for the task at hand.
>
> **Clarity** — Bob had spent years working on a clarity of purpose that we all were able to align with.
>
> **Training** — We spent a short but intense amount of time to build a strong and executable training program.

Information — I created an impeccable cash-and-inventory-auditing program to make sure we had all the information anyone would need to ensure success.

Partnerships — This was the ultimate key and fabric to the sum of all parts we scrambled to achieve. Bob had assembled the exact team of people he needed to achieve success.

Details — We had worked out every granular tidbit of what needed to happen to make this magnificent event work.

> By the time the lunch rush came on Friday, we were well on our way to $250,000 in three days.

Whenever we discuss the four-day ordeal, we generally leave Thursday out of the conversation. We knew it would be a warmup day that would allow us to work out issues before things really heated up for the weekend. After Thursday was over, there were several indicators that we had this in the bag!

There is enough to this story to fill a whole different book, but for this lesson, the key is this: By the time the lunch rush came on Friday, we were well on our way to $250,000 in three days (again, Thursday didn't really count). All we had to do was keep doing what we were doing.

The moment our first guest walked through the door, Bob had one job and one job only: direct person-to-person marketing throughout the fairgrounds. This was a job he assigned to himself, and he was well suited to it. He theorized that to break through the decades-old traditions of partying where you camped, he would need to constantly convince people to move over to our spot. He did this by working his way through the temporary camps. Through Thursday, he had executed this task to an exceptional degree.

He had this cool four-wheel Gator and was driving around the grounds, personally marketing our concept. We could see the impact on-site with the steady flow of new guests, all of whom we made sure left both satisfied and happy, with good food, good drink, a place to sit in the shade away from the pounding sun, and a live TV simulcast on 12 big-screen TVs. This, to our knowledge, was an unprecedented setup for the "average" fan. Thursday night ended up exceeding our expectations, leaving us very confident that we would hit our $250,000 goal with ease.

In the four years after our pop-up club ran and closed, I have pored over the entirety of the event, from planning through execution, as well as the final hurrah: the conclusion. Looking back at it now, the fantastic outcome was destined to be. Even when we factored in the knowledge we had had when it all began, it still turned out to be a grand slam achievement, despite not making our target profit!

What we learned since that long weekend is that the man who brought us all together had displayed immense effort, energy, and applied willpower. Bob had showcased his solid self-mastery over nearly a year before the event started. He would not carry that same pigheaded discipline once operations began. The downfall began on day two.

Friday morning started slow, but as lunch approached, guests started arriving in larger and larger numbers. We were preparing for a lunch crowd that we predicted would stretch our crew to their limits.

At almost exactly 11:30 a.m., Dave and I were both on the floor managing the ever-growing crowds when Bob walked in. It was clear that he was drunk from the night before or had woken up drinking, or both. It was hard for him not to feel like he had done the hard work and that celebrating on the slowest night seemed like a well-earned reward. The only request we made was that he stay away from the tent until he sobered up. He agreed, and we didn't see him until later that afternoon.

It was right around 3:00 p.m. when Bob showed up again, with a woman he had met while tooling about in his 4-wheeler. He found Nitzel. While we were originally surprised at how slow business was after our lunch, Nitzel quickly realized that Bob was no longer keeping up his critical end of the bargain.

Bob had spent most of the day hanging out with this woman whom he now wanted Nitzel, who was our head of staff, to put behind the bar, picking someone at random to fire to make space for her.

Of course, doing this would have done irreparable harm to morale and our ability to manage the team, so Nitzel, incredibly busy getting ready for the evening rush, had no choice but to sideline her. He let her know he had nowhere to put her currently but that if someone didn't show for the evening, he would slot her in.

The idea that most of this team had traveled across country for this gig and up to that point had behaved exactly the way we had asked them to, despite their desire to join in on the fun, demanded we show commitment in kind. Bob's friend eventually went on her way. I think Dave made it reasonably clear, in the kindest way, that she wasn't a priority. As time wore on, perhaps after an hour or two, the "Bob effect" wore off. I think her better judgement kicked in, and she realized work wasn't going to happen on this day.

It would be several hours before we understood just how far Bob was straying from our initial, meticulously detailed plan and the singularly most important mandate the owners of the event had made: a "family-friendly" oasis.

Discipline

From the very beginning, it was made repeatedly clear by the owners of the grounds that they were working hard to shift their sporting event from its reputation of a den of debauchery to a family-oriented, safe place for anyone to come spend a weekend.

Our pop-up was going to be critical in that effort. With that in mind, there was one mini-show planned by Bob that he and I had argued about. Bob had rented a large stage for a few live shows that set up in an open field that I would say was about the same size as a football field, for reference. We even had a Jumbotron to simulcast the events and show racing movies by day! The lineup of seven acts was mostly made up of beloved local bands — well suited to the organizers' good taste.

For some reason I still cannot wrap my head around, Bob insisted on having a bikini contest at the tail end of the day on Saturday. Nitzel and I knew this lay somewhere between a really bad idea and an epically bad one, for several reasons. I did my best to convince Bob to scratch it in the months leading up to the big show, but his stubbornness made him dead set on it — he would not be swayed. Some of Bob's hidden motivations were coming to the surface, at exactly the worst time!

Unfortunately, due to more last-minute decisions, the impact would be more detrimental than we could have imagined. It would be the final nail in the coffin of our initial goal. Between this and what had happened on Friday night, we quickly realized that there was no way Bob would ever be invited back to run this pop-up again.

Hours after the "last-minute bartender" had wandered off on Friday afternoon, Bob showed back up again. The lady's existence was apparently forgotten. He had a plastic kiddie pool in hand and a few of the security guys behind him were hauling bags of what he called "wrestling mud." We'd known of his plans to do mud wrestling on one of the nights. And we assumed we had talked him out of that horrible idea the day before — boy, were we wrong!

Bob decided Friday was the night to do it. He spread the word to everyone, inviting them to come check out the mud wrestling. In a bold set of moves, he quickly guaranteed a sharp end to the night with no hope of extending our earning hours past the end of this high school boy's dream.

As the hour of raunch approached, every single woman in our tent left, and most of their significant others followed. By 9:00 p.m., we were left with 30 hooting and hollering guys drooling. There were two bartenders whom Bob had convinced to writhe around in a pool of mud, with only a thin piece of plastic between them and the hard, unfinished asphalt beneath them. It was so poorly thought out that no one had considered that when the women tipped over during the mud wrestling, they would be falling directly onto a rock-hard concrete floor. Fortunately, Nitzel was measuring the risks and insisted that the security guards surround the ridiculous mud bath and catch the women from falling ... they hardly needed encouragement. The only good news here is that no one got hurt ... physically.

Utter chaos ensued. Numerous drunken arguments with higher-ups at the grounds were building. Bob also received many public, angry warnings from security for drunk driving his four-wheeler in off-limits areas.

We knew the prospect of getting a return invite the following year was very slim. A lucrative contract to have another pop-up of ours at their other parks was dead. Dave and I still hoped that we would get close to our grand total goal, but hopes were dwindling.

Saturday started off perfectly — well enough that we thought we could make up for the Friday night disaster. The lunch rush started early and after it was over, the party didn't stop. Every single one of our bartenders was three-deep from lunch on — our barbacks were moving nonstop, with our waitresses swarming around like bees, serving the endless flow to our tables.

We had been working with our staff round the clock over the last few days to prepare them for this money-making machine that was up-coming — each and every staff member rose to the occasion.

We were starting to push into our dinner rush when, at 4:30 p.m., Nitzel came frantically running up to me asking where the hell his bartenders were. I had been working with the back-of-house team to keep the flow of fresh-squeezed lime juice steady for the tequila tent. We had bought out every supplier, grocery store, and convenience store in a 10-mile radius of the pre-squeezed stuff. I had no idea what he was talking about.

After Nitzel had been in the tequila tent for 30 minutes resolving a minor conflict, he returned to the main bar to find 5 of our top bartenders missing.

What we did know was that Bob had been setting up the bikini contest for the last two hours, and we quickly figured out what had happened. While both Dave and I were off the floor of the main tent, he had quietly recruited our bartenders to come walk across the stage. There was about a football field-sized space between the restaurant and the concert stage, which was also part of the big plan — did I mention the concerts? Anyway, at a time when we were the busiest since we had opened, we lost five bartenders. Losing 18% of the main tent staff devastated our ability to serve our guests.

Within 30 minutes, lines had backed up out of control and the guys left to view the contest and the women just left. Any hope of recovering the project was pretty much dashed. What's more, an hour later when the five bartenders returned, too drunk or otherwise impaired from "show prep" to perform their jobs, we found ourselves limping to the finish line. Just one hour after they had initially been stolen from the bar, the entirety of our momentum was completely gone. Any hopes of achieving our goal vanished into thin air!

Sunday was, unsurprisingly, dead. We made under $1,000 for the entire day as it was a post-race day, and everyone was packing up and heading home — the party was over.

Over the four-day event, we cashed in $150,000. It is hard to consider this a loss as it was our first attempt. But it clearly was a loss when taking the bigger picture into account. It was easy to see the failure when we accepted the fact that two prime selling periods were artificially cut short — both victims of undisciplined efforts.

It's extremely easy in our business to lose our good discipline — there's temptation at every turn! It's critical to remember:

- Discipline takes you from proper planning to excellent execution.
- Discipline to let your team do their jobs: if you have the right team, having the self-control to let them do their jobs will lead you to success.
- Discipline to focus on the job: when we don't control destructive impulses, all the planning and clarity in the world will not save our plans from falling apart.
- Discipline to stick to your core principles: make your decisions guided by the key principles you have set.

I think the moral of the story here is clear: you must have self-discipline. Don't be your own biggest problem. Unfortunately, this is somewhat common to our industry. What's your motivation? What we came to learn about Bob was, his motivations had nothing to do with running an epic event and growing it to scale. His motivations were impure, to say it kindly, and there was no planning that would allow us to overcome the owner's total and complete disregard for his own ideas and the help he employed.

HELIX Sequencing

> We found varying levels of correlation between the building blocks in each chapter and the DNA points at the end of the book. The strength of the correlation is represented by 1 to 5 circles around our 5-point Hospitality DNA molecule: 1 being a lower correlation and 5 being a higher one.

Humble Nature

Check your motivation. Hospitality is a combination of the art and science of providing for others. Our success is a product of the execution of this concept. Our personal goals matter — they matter a lot — however, we must understand the path to achieving those goals is by focusing on others and how they will lead us to our targets, over self-serving, ulterior motives.

Explorer's Pursuit

Aim true to your purpose — don't be your own dream crusher! Discipline is almost the opposite of Exploration; stick hard to where you plan.

Lifetime of Experience

If you have not figured out the key principles that you will use to guide your business, get them locked in. If you still aren't sure, don't hesitate to bring in experts who can help. It's extremely easy to feel like we need to have all the answers in positions of leadership. The gift of a lifetime of experience is knowing that's impossible.

Indomitable Spirit

There will be distractions, failures, and successes all throughout your path. Constantly self-assess and follow your plans while adjusting as necessary; discipline is a trait you can never put aside for long. As they say, "If at first you don't succeed, try, try again!" Never stop dreaming!

Xtraordinary Culture

Have an accountability partner in your business who has the ability to call you on your BS without repercussions. It can be hard to hear that you're wrong and even harder to hear character issues. You have to be willing and able to take that feedback and use it to improve upon yourself. The more successful one becomes, the less willing one is open to the idea that they have certain flaws. It's especially important to remember that we are either on an improvement trajectory or in decline; there is never really a time when we are truly flat. We need new ideas and new interactions to keep us in a constant improvement mode. In this way, the accountability partner acts like external discipline.

Chapter 13

Scaling

> If you want to build a ship, don't drum
> up people together to collect wood
> and don't assign them tasks and work,
> but rather teach them to long for the
> endless immensity of the sea.
> —Antoine de Saint-Exupéry

This chapter is where things for many great independent operators go full stop. So much of what we have learned is the product of an individual, most typically an owner, and a direct output of their personality and creativity. That can become challenging when it comes time to scale. On one hand it means giving up an element of control upon which their personal brand has been built and resides. If the venue slips, they've slipped. However, you can't scale and micromanage at the same time, not well anyway.

There are different ways to scale a business. Some people try to keep it in a tight geography. Others believe they should only have one venue in a major market, and those markets are carefully selected based on demographics. Some owners opt out of trying to manage multiple venues and opt into franchising models. All of these are valid ways to think about scalability and growth. It's important to know your brand and how it may thrive in a different part of town, city, or even country, depending on where you live.

It's a natural trajectory to want to multiply and scale a successful concept — why not? Let's just replicate what we've done here and do it again over there and reap the reward. The benefit of scaling is obvious: financial multiplication, cost leverage, brand awareness, and more. The challenge, however, is one and the same. As we've discussed, culture has a disproportionate impact on success, meaning in a long list of things that really matter, it's the king of kings. And as we've discussed before, very often, the culture created in a venue is a product of the owner's/owners' personality and vision, and as we know, personality does not scale. In this chapter, we'll take you through a process of how to scale your business in an effective way. We'll give you a process along with case studies from people who have done it at an award-winning level. Throughout our interviews, to a person, every one of them agreed on the importance of culture building. At the same time, they acknowledge that in many ways, it's their greatest difficulty. Here are a few key points to review from our previous chapters:

- Great leaders focus on a specific culture versus a cult of personality
- Leadership attitude and competency will become your business culture
- Empowered staff becomes a massive force multiplier
- Self-awareness drives personal growth
- Culture is found in your actions, not your words
- It takes a total commitment to get it right

To describe the biggest issue our Hospitality award winners share in better detail, it is how to bottle their ideas, vision, expectations, and execution and then hand it off to others to execute with the same veracity. It's no small thing. We heard often how hard it was to let go. It's a matter of great trust. Trust is hard-earned and is rarely simply given. After all, as you now know, much of this success is a product of a lifetime of experience. This is where we find one of the first conundrums in scalability.

> It's no small thing. We heard often how hard it was to let go. It's a matter of great trust.

In order to trust, we must build a culture that allows people to learn and grow. It must allow for mistakes to be made and for people to own their issues and self-accountability. That means from the outset owners/leaders must learn how to give away certain aspects of responsibility that they are not comfortable giving up. It's normal but necessary, as culture building begins on day one. For the long run, it's much more productive to build a culture with the end in mind than it is to build a culture of right now because those "right now" habits stick. In our consulting practice, we get to see a lot of less-than-optimal cultures and it's very rare to see someone completely change their culture without completely changing their personal habits and the habits of their staff, which is extraordinarily difficult to do once established. It becomes vitally important that if scaling is something you aspire to, you must factor this into your culture building on day one.

When we went through our interviews, there was one that clearly stood out among the rest as it relates to scaling: the interview with Riz Shaikh. Riz had a certain clarity around what powered his success. It took him no time to define how and why his venues became elite. Riz and his team at the Columbo Group operate eleven venues throughout Greater

> Culture is total bullshit unless you totally buy in.

London. His venues offer a classic blend of music, food, and drinks that create perfect harmony and a holistic experience. For many, this would be challenging in one venue, let alone eleven.

Seven of the concepts are unique unto themselves, which makes scaling even more challenging. Within minutes of conversation, Riz dove directly into the importance of culture and not in the typical clichéd way but in a brutally honest manner. He bluntly put it this way: "Culture is total bullshit unless you totally buy in."

For Riz, he had a watershed moment when he was asked to speak at a small business owners' event. He's a confident guy and a natural speaker, and admittedly he hadn't prepared well for the talk, which was a TED Talk-style event. When he arrived, he was a bit taken aback when he saw a full audience and a large-scale production. In that moment, he realized the immense gravity of the event, as people had traveled from around the world just to hear the experts speak — to hear him speak!

Riz is successful by any measure, and he felt like he knew his content well and was self-assured about his ability to discuss their company culture and management philosophies. That is, until the lights came on and Riz froze. As he tells it, his mouth turned into the Sahara desert, and he realized in one fell swoop, he didn't really know his content, or more specifically his culture, at all. They had been very effectively "winging" their culture without a formal, demonstrable structure or strategy. How does he explain that?

The Columbo Group boasts multiple unique locations, including:

- The Parakeet
- The Blues Kitchen

- Phonox
- The Old Queens Head
- The Jazz Cafe
- Eastern Electrics
- Metropolis
- Maiden Voyage Festival

Ultimately, Riz survived the experience but left with a certain sense of foreboding. He realized they were playing with fire and really needed to dig deep into the idea of culture: what it really means and how to build it. As such, he and his team made a full commitment to building what is now called the Columbo Academy, an intracompany coaching/training program. It's a full-course platform that all members of current and future management must attend and features four stages of growth:

- Supervisor > Manager
- Manager > Assistant manager
- AGM > GM
- GM > Partner

The academy focuses each progression on five principles relevant to the role in areas of:

- Development
- Recruitment
- Culture
- Operations
- Finance

In the beginning of building the academy, much of the content was outsourced but needed to be taken back in house. The reason for this, as Riz described it, was a matter of translation. "Much of the material simply didn't translate to the roles of the people specific to our industry and our organization." The way the Bar and Restaurant industry operates is unique and not quite like what you may call a typical business. Point being, make sure your content is specific and relevant to your business so that people understand precisely how the material they're learning impacts their role directly and that it has real-life application.

> We were living a lie at first and had to fix it.

Riz believes that what makes him a good entrepreneur also makes him a poor manager. This makes sense, as many creative types are more solution driven versus organizationally driven. We were impressed by Riz and his emphasis on self-awareness, which is also one of our core tenets of scalability.

If we go back to the TED-like talk, he explained, "It took us a while to understand first, who we were, and second, who we wanted to be." In other words, "We were living a lie at first and had to fix it." The academy and a full commitment to change was that fix. "We had to build an environment that facilitates personal growth, simply arousing excitement in people to deliver great customer experiences — and we had to remove ourselves from the equation." Essentially, many operators have a concept in mind when they launch their business and they can effectively cast a vision; however, amazing culture is about building a common cause through common actions and purpose. When Riz says they were "living a lie," this is what he means. They lacked a common cause, which could only be brought about through common learning experiences that emphasized team building and unity. They wanted to build a vibrant *company* culture.

When Riz speaks of a full commitment, he emphasizes two things: time and money. There are no half measures on either side of this equation, as far as he's concerned. As an owner, you must be fully committed to your culture — this in and of itself will be evaluated by your team every day, meaning your actions will speak louder than words.

> We had to build an environment that facilitates personal growth, simply arousing excitement in people to deliver great customer experiences — and we had to remove ourselves from the equation.

Culture is about our everyday behaviors. We find many leaders, even those in the biggest, best companies in the world, can make the mistake of thinking their culture is what they say it is. That's simply not the case. Culture starts at the very top of an organization, and it's about how we "live" within the company. You can't "memo" your way to a great culture. It requires hard work, dedication, and a full commitment to those specific behaviors in which you believe.

That's exactly what Riz discussed. He realized that he was, in fact, the best culture coach for his organization — and not outside experts. So, he took the reins on cascading his specific vision of what he wanted their culture to be. He learned it had to be his responsibility to coach and enforce his expectations to the leadership team. The how and why of behavioral coaching within the organization had to be a reflection of his values.

> You can't "memo" your way to a great culture.

That isn't to say you should isolate your training programs either; bringing in outside experts to augment your training, as long as they are culturally aligned, can be invaluable. For instance, Riz will bring in experts to coach segments to the team. Actors may come in and lead a class about being "onstage" for a shift and getting into character. They may also bring in the likes of a former SAS soldier (British Special Forces) to coach on how to do a proper shift debrief. This really engages and entertains the team!

This level of expertise is electrifying to learn from, and the team not only gets incredibly impactful content, but it's memorable as hell. People will recognize the commitment from the top and respect the investment being made in each team member. This motivates teams immensely, leading to great enthusiasm on delivering the brand promise. A successful culture creates front-line culture champions, which takes us back to our earlier conversation. Culture is how we behave, not what we say. Culture comes alive in the kitchen, at the bar, and on the floor, and it reveals its strength when we're pressed — when the chips are down. That's when we find out about culture.

Now of course we can't share the Columbo Group's Academy platform in its entirety. But we can share with you one of our coaching concepts to help you get started that aligns very well with what Riz shared. By no means is this an end-all model, but we believe you will find these concepts very helpful as you work toward scalability.

Below is our "COST" model for scalability. We hope you find it to be a start to how you might think differently about scaling, or perhaps it's simply additive to something you already have in place. We have found it very useful to our clients, and we're happy to share it with you as part of our Hospitality DNA.

No, it's not a financial model, as the acronym may imply; rather, it's a way to go about building a scalable culture, which is the core of multiplication. We find most independent Bar and Restaurant owners who are living differently from both a well-being and a financial perspective have often scaled to three or more venues. This affords a lifestyle that's not chained to one venue and financial flexibility that allows people to do what they want to do versus what they have to do. The ingredients are:

Consistency — In our interview process of staff and team members over the years, one of the primary reasons people leave jobs has to do with volatility, especially emotional volatility. If, in our industry, we can provide predictable emotionally mature leadership, reliable income, and predictable expectations, people tend to stay longer and enjoy their job. In fact, people will become advocates of the leadership team. These are the types of people who allow for scalable teams.

Order — Simply stated, talented people seek out order as it allows them to compete and set themselves apart from the competition. Order creates a framework for success. Meanwhile, chaos has the opposite effect: it attracts exactly the types that put the business at risk. It's also important to note that order doesn't mean inflexibility, it means process, and within good processes, there is always a mechanism for process improvement. That's an important point that we can't emphasize enough. If we are too strict, we can stifle creativity and input, so be sure to *have a process for improving the process* and cultivate the creative nature of the team.

Self-awareness — In our estimation, this is the most crucial attribute any leader can possess. If you have the ability to understand how your attitude and actions impact yourself and others, then you are laps ahead of the field. When we understand our effect on others and we have the ability to self-reflect, we can make constant improvements. As the leader goes, as goes the business. One nemesis to self-awareness is ego or hubris. Most driven, successful people have a healthy ego; in fact, in many ways, having a healthy ego is a prerequisite to success. Beware, however, our strengths and weaknesses are often one and the same, and when ego runs unchecked or unchallenged, those attitudes will be absorbed into the bloodstream of the organization itself. Successful people are used to being correct, so it can be hard to humble oneself and be open to new and different ideas. When it comes to matters of scalability, this can be a massive impediment to growth, as the business model will be ever-evolving. How we run five venues is significantly different than how we run one venue. We must manage through influence rather than presence.

Trust — You might think this one needs no explanation. People know what it means to be trustworthy, on the surface. If we break it down more on the business level, you can find many examples of otherwise trustworthy people who exercise many untrustworthy business practices. Here are a few examples:

- Can I trust you to be on time for meetings?
- Can I trust you'll take care of the payroll issue we discussed?
- You said I could have next weekend off. I made plans and had to cancel.
- You said I wouldn't have to work more than 50 hours per week, yet I always do …
- We agreed I have kids and can't work doubles, yet you always schedule me on doubles.
- I'm supposed to get a raise every year, and I've been here two years with no raise.
- I've been understaffed for a month, and I'm getting no help …

You get the idea: trust can be the obvious big lapses, or it can simply erode over time. As a person, you may think, "I'm extremely trustworthy; people like me and I'm a good person."

As it relates to scalability, this is inconsequential. You can be a great, trustworthy person and have a very untrustworthy culture. Consider those examples above. If people are having those types of experiences, your culture will be deemed untrustworthy, which then makes scalability extremely difficult.

> You can be a great, trustworthy person and have a very untrustworthy culture.

The bigger you become, the more trust you must build. If you think about larger companies, when they get to scale, they put fail-safes in place to try to ensure trust is maintained. Notice we say "try" because plenty of large companies still fail here as well. Imagine a company that employs 50,000 people with 50% turnover each year. It would be a completely untenable model. Many bars and restaurants we work with experience 100% annualized turnover. In one venue, it may be manageable — perhaps even two venues — but when you begin to reach critical mass, if you don't get your arms around matters of turnover, your restaurant organization will quickly turn into a temp agency.

So hopefully you're asking something along the lines of, "How do I measure this?" If so, we've gotcha right where we wantcha. You simply ask your team. The best process we found is anonymous surveys where people know they can give their untraceable opinions. We have found paper surveys or outsourced surveys to be the best option because people don't fully trust (there's that word again) in-house trackable tools. It must be truly anonymous.

First, define what each category means as described above, then simply ask your team to rate, on a scale of 1 to 10, where they think the organization falls in terms of achievement, with 9 to 10 being strongly agree, 6 to 8 being somewhat neutral, and 1 to 5 being an opportunity to improve.

Hospitality DNA

This is a simple survey you can take yourself first, then deploy to your team to get you started. It serves as a good check on your level of self-awareness and engagement.

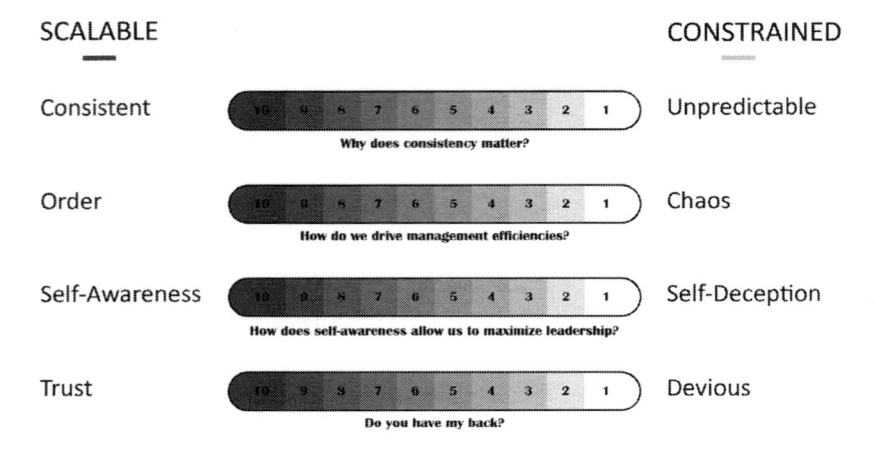

SCALABLE — CONSTRAINED

Scalable	Scale (10 → 1)	Constrained
Consistent	10 9 8 7 6 5 4 3 2 1 — *Why does consistency matter?*	Unpredictable
Order	10 9 8 7 6 5 4 3 2 1 — *How do we drive management efficiencies?*	Chaos
Self-Awareness	10 9 8 7 6 5 4 3 2 1 — *How does self-awareness allow us to maximize leadership?*	Self-Deception
Trust	10 9 8 7 6 5 4 3 2 1 — *Do you have my back?*	Devious

Scalable versus Constrained

Be sure to make use of tools and make them part of your *Order* initiatives. In fact, regular feedback and the use of tools promotes both *Order* and *Trust*. Do not start a program you can't commit to or make it very clear what the goals and objectives of any survey initiative are. And be 100% certain that the feedback stays anonymous, or the *Trust* hit will be insurmountable.

Culture-building tools to consider:

- 360 surveys
- NPS scores
- Gallup Q12 surveys
- Peer-to-peer awards
- Skip-level meetings
- Personality assessments
- Company outings and conferences
- Technology such as apps to facilitate employee feedback
- Culture-based bonus programs

HELIX Sequencing

> We found varying levels of correlation between the building blocks in each chapter and the DNA points at the end of the book. The strength of the correlation is represented by 1 to 5 circles around our 5-point Hospitality DNA molecule: 1 being a lower correlation and 5 being a higher one.

Humble Nature

Though the things that matter to the owner is where culture comes from, culture is scalable; personality is not. Once you have it set, keep your ego in check. Eliminate ego-driven attitudes from the business: we first over me first! Practice self-awareness.

Explorer's Pursuit

Exploration isn't just about the physical pursuit of experiences but the mental as well. We have to deliver unique experiences to our teams so that they can learn and grow, all the while wowing guests with our immersive concepts. People have a deep appreciation of and loyalty to those who have helped elevate their careers.

Lifetime of Experience

Cultivate talent around you that shares your aspirations and beliefs. Part of what makes people great leaders is how they develop those around them who bring the leaders' vision into form. A lifetime of experience is wasted if isolated in your own head. Build programs and processes around what you know and how you want your business to run, then trust (and verify through information) in those who know how to do it best!

Indomitable Spirit

The spirit of leadership cascades throughout our interviewees' organizations, by design. Scalability and success will not happen by accident. Our interviewees have a genuine passion for their people and the brands they've built, and they never stop investing in it, personally and financially.

Xtraordinary Culture

Talent seeks out order and consistency; chaotic people are drawn to chaotic cultures. Measure your culture and leadership, promote honest and open feedback, and activate on that feedback. Be predictable, while encouraging creativity. You cannot scale properly until you have a rock-solid culture in place.

Chapter 14

Mentorship

> Bartending is a craft you can't learn in school. It's a skill that gets handed down through mentorship. I want to know who you learned from.
> —Ivy Mix

When people own an ability with complete mastery, it often seems like a superpower to those who are lacking that skill. During our interview, Ivy Mix downplayed her natural perception and command of the mentorship process when she told us that mentorship "is just a different type of learning." She was not wrong, but she has turned this particular type of learning into a mechanism that has supercharged her career. We found this downplaying of her abilities quite normal as it is exactly the kind of language nearly all our interviewees used when we started talking about their areas of extreme, natural proficiency.

Before the age of 19, Ivy was unknown to the professional bar industry. After a trip to Guatemala at that age ignited a passion in her for "the industry," she began a journey that put her on the Wine Enthusiast 40 under 40 list only 10 years later at the age of 29 and racking up accomplishments and awards at a breakneck pace. To give you an idea of some of her accomplishments, here's a short list:

- Started Speed Rack in 2011
- Opened the award winning Leyenda in 2015
- Won Tales of the Cocktail American Bartender of the Year 2015
- Won Wine Enthusiast Mixologist of the Year in 2016
- Won Tales of the Cocktail award for Philanthropy (Speed Rack) in 2019
- Won the Tales of the Cocktail award for World's Best Bar Mentors in 2019
- Published *"Spirits of Latin America"* in 2020, which won the AICP award for Best Book in Wine, Beer and Spirits, and Tales of the Cocktail Best New Book on Drinks Culture, History, or Spirits
- Opened Fiasco! Wine + Spirits in 2021

In addition to all of that personal accomplishment, Ivy Mix is a rising force for good in our industry as evidenced by her creation of Speed Rack. Speed Rack works to elevate female bartenders through competition and, in parallel, raise money for breast cancer awareness and research. At the time of writing, Ivy had taken Speed Rack international and raised over $1 million after only nine seasons of operation. That alone would be enough to wow any reasonable person, but if we told you Ivy is still merely in her mid-thirties, her story becomes only more phenomenal.

Our interview process tends to meander a bit as we hear about people's careers, and in some cases, life stories. Often the two are inseparable. As Ivy was sharing her story, she humbly proposed that she really did not have any "super-traits" and really wasn't special in any way.

Perhaps very productive, maybe stubbornly relentless, but otherwise not special. We said to Ivy, "There is simply no way you can achieve all that you have and not possess something extraordinary that makes you unique."

We noticed in short order that Ivy routinely made reference to her mentor and eventual business partner, Julie Reiner. Ivy describes Julie as the "Matriarch of Cocktails" in the New York scene and as a super-influential person. Ivy would say, "She's someone you want to know."

Julie played a critical role throughout Ivy's career, first as a boss, who became a mentor, and then as a business partner. It should be mentioned that Lynnette Marrero, Ivy's partner in Speed Rack, also got her start working for Julie as a busser. Julie's role was influential and important in the eventual success of both Ivy and Lynnette, as Julie served as an accelerant that really fueled their professional growth.

Ivy and Lynnette
Photo by Gabi Porter

Before we get too far ahead of ourselves, it is important to understand where Ivy truly got bit by the hospitality bug. Part of her undergraduate program required her to spend time each year "not on campus" studying in her field. During her first year in college when that "go get worldly experience" time came, she had no field of study so she set one condition for herself. Wherever she went, she wanted it to be a place where she could immerse herself in learning another language. It was this desire to further experience the world that brought her to Guatemala; which coincidentally, is where is where she fell in love with being on the other side of the bar. Her first six months in Guatemala were so transformative for her that she ended up going back every chance she got, spending half the year, every year, for the next four years bartending in Guatemala. Clearly, it wasn't just being behind the bar that drew her back there. Just as much as she was becoming enamored with learning hospitality, she was falling in love with Latin culture via Guatemala.

What if she were able to mix (pun intended) her passion for Latin America with the love she had developed for the NYC cocktail scene? In order to make this dream come true, she took advantage of an offer from her now friend and mentor Julie, owner of Flatiron Lounge and Clover Club, to become a business partner and help bring this dream to life. That's when Leyenda was born: a neighborhood cocktail joint in NYC featuring exquisite Latin-inspired cocktails and experiences.

It occurred to us that we were starting to find a hint of one of her Building Block talents, perhaps one that had been handed down generationally, so to speak.

Julie served as an extremely influential figure in Ivy's professional development, from when Ivy started out as an employee

> A successful mentorship has defined rules and two willing participants ready to play by those rules, or else it just doesn't work.

with much to learn to becoming an eventual business partner at Leyenda. While it is clear there were many ways that Julie invested in Ivy's growth, it was when Ivy was 29, starting the next phase of her career, that what I have found to be one of the most unexpected powers of mentorship came into play. Ivy had been the rising star, working hard to make a name for herself and racking up awards and accomplishments, becoming a paid judge of prestigious cocktail competitions and making the Wine Enthusiast 40 under 40 list. At this point Ivy had been working at Clover Club for Julie for three years while also taking Speed Rack international and earning accolades. During what would be her fourth and final year at Clover Club, Ivy was also working on opening her own spot. It was here that a harsh reality of the financial world that many of us aspiring business owners have learned stopped her in her tracks. In Ivy's words: "Banks do not care about accolades." We all have our own versions of this truth; my version was that it wasn't until I already had money that any banks were interested in lending me any. Ivy had been shut down, and it was disheartening.

Mentorships start as a relationship between someone who has some combination of experience, connections, power, and money agreeing to invest their time and energy in someone they believe is worth the spend. When the mentee proves to be worth that investment, the relationship often grows into much more. In this case, Julie was able to get a very close look at who Ivy was as a mentee, an employee, and as a professional completely outside of their relationship. When a space became available across the street from the Clover Club, Julie asked Ivy if she wanted to become her business partner and open her concept. It was only a matter of time before Ivy found a path to open her own place. However without this relationship, it would not have happened at that moment, adding another accomplishment to an already impressive life: opening a concept before the age of 30.

Julie saw the potential in Ivy and curated it accordingly. At the same time, Ivy had to be a willing learner, open to the possibilities of doing both more and better. A successful mentorship must have defined rules and two willing participants who are ready to play by those rules, or else it just doesn't work. When it works, as is the case here, beautiful things can spawn and success begets success. The process of paying it back began as Ivy eventually launched Speed Rack with her longtime friend Lynnette.

In sports, when a successful coach creates other successful coaches, it's known as a coaching tree. In this case, two members of Julie's coach- ing tree teamed up to create Speed Rack. Now, Ivy and Lynnette team up, traveling the world, hosting competitions, and in effect coaching, training, and challenging countless numbers of women bartenders who aspire to higher ground.

As we continued to listen to Ivy's story, we could see that coaching and mentorship was revealing itself as her clear Building Block. There was a point she was making that solidified this idea, as we delved into learning more about her past relationships. She said, "Mentorship is a cyclical relationship. I've been both. You learn as both the mentee and the mentor. It's just a different type of learning. So it's not just purely selfless. Both people benefit." As with most things Ivy has tackled in her life, she went at becoming a mentor full bore winning the Tales of the Cocktail "Mentor of the Year Award" in 2019 with her Speed Rack partner, Lynnette.

It is worth making the point that this is the most powerful possible outcome of starting a mentorship relationship. When you are able to learn enough about how the process works as a mentee, becoming the mentor and creating these relationships from the other direction creates a cycle of learning and teaching.

Mentoring naturally builds uncommonly strong bonds with everyone involved. The ability to do this in both directions acts as a dynamic accelerator of relationships. If you subscribe to the "It's not what you know but who you know" adage, this cycle can create a formidable network of peers who can assist in advancing your career, whatever that looks like for you, in stunning ways as it has for Ivy.

In terms of the benefits to her professional life, her success in business speaks for itself. As Ivy's career has boundless off-site demands, it's critical she develops the team around her to handle the business while upholding her vision while she's away.

> "Mentorship is a cyclical relationship. I've been both. You learn as both the mentee and the mentor. It's just a different type of learning. So it's not just purely selfless. Both people benefit."

That's when it occurred to us that, while Ivy had made an accurate point in explaining that she is intensely productive, we did not yet understand why. Does she simply out-hustle everyone? Perhaps. Or is she part of a larger construct that involves a learning curve that allows for constant growth and attainment? As Ivy mentions, it's cyclical. All the attributes and processes she learned from Julie became her own, with her now passing those lessons on to her team. This allows her to delegate so that she can meet the new demands attained as she continues on to the next stage of her career.

Ivy's knowledge and productivity is an outcome of a life-altering mentor-ship cycle, which led us to look deeper into that concept. Beautifully, we found them right here among our very own Hospitality DNA interviewees. Salvatore Calabrese mentored Angus Winchester, Humberto Saraiva Marques mentored António Saldanha de Oliveira and Costin Gache mentored Katalin

Bene. All of these people, mentors and mentees alike, have Hospitality skills that we hold in the highest regard. When it comes down to it, this is all as simple as "success begets success." The mentorship relationship ends up being one critical part of the traditional educational framework of our industry.

Mentorship is a critical component of productivity and competence in any field, enabling growth both professionally and financially. It's also not uncommon to find very strong mentorship relations that eventually become more of a peer-to-peer relationship or even a friendship. This, in full candor, can be awkward at first but rarely in a bad way as it should become a source of great pride for both the mentor and the mentee.

I hope to avoid sounding arrogant here, but I feel that I (David Domzalski) am supremely qualified to speak on this matter. For the remainder of this chapter, I must apologize as I break our inside joke of informing you which Dave is which as both of us are key to this story.

While it was not until I was well into my 30s that I realized it, my life has been defined by mentorships. When I was 8 years old, my mother moved us to Columbia, Maryland. My parents had divorced when I was 3 years old, and I was missing a father figure. Living just up the street from the house we moved into was a kind, giving, insightful social work professor named Stanley Wenocur. Through his beautiful Doberman with a floppy left ear named Daisy, I, an 8-year-old child who needed some unknown set of perspective and guidance, connected to a man who had exactly what I needed.

A mentorship is a relationship wherein a more knowledgeable or experienced individual invests in the professional or personal growth of another. In this exact sense, Stan helped guide me through the uncomfortable and unknown space of being a troubled 8-year-old boy to a confident and stable young man of 18. This particular mentorship relationship was one of learning how to face the world, with lessons around peer relationships, professionalism, love, and many other areas of life that a young mind needs to grow. While mentorships can come from the most unexpected places and cover literally anything one can experience in life, it is knowing how to properly define and pursue them for a specific purpose that allows you to turn them into an unstoppable force of growth and productivity on your own terms.

As I look back on my life, it was between my late 20s and early 30s where I switched from lucking into mentorships, most of which were useful and enriching, to being taught how to effectively seek them out and define them. Oddly, it was a boss of mine, someone who by definition cannot be a mentor, who taught me how to go about finding and connecting with the people I needed to learn from rather than hoping they would serendipitously cross my path in my hour of need.

Getting started — that is, finding the right mentor — takes effort to get the right fit. Once you determine where in life you currently need this type of relationship, it can take multiple attempts with different people to identify the person who both has the knowledge and experience you need and is a good fit for you to work with.

One more word on the nature of mentorships before we get into the process of finding the right one; they come free of charge. As soon as you begin to pay for advice, it's no longer a mentor relationship and becomes paid consulting—an entirely different relationship. For the same reason, neither bosses nor employees can ever truly be a mentor for one another; the very boss/subordinate nature of that relationship prevents it from attaining the open communication a strong mentorship requires.

There are any number of ways you can start this process, but I was taught this one, which I found to be the best. Ask yourself these three questions.

- Where are you?
- Where do you want to be?
- Who could help you get there?

When I made the decision to stop being an employee and open a Barmetrix franchise in Miami, Florida, I thought I had everything figured out. I had been working for the company for 10 years and had spent the last 4 training and coaching every new franchisee they brought on. I literally wrote the book on the process of launching a new office. I had written not one but three business plans outlining my first three years based on varying growth rates, researched the first 200 venues I wanted to approach as potential clients, and had a short list of both preexisting and desired relationships that I knew would help me grow my business. There is more, but the point is that I was well educated and prepared to launch my first business and was preeminently suited for the task at hand.

It was about one year in when I identified that there were gaps in a few aspects of owning a business that I had not anticipated and in fact could not quite identify what I was missing. I knew it had something to do with transitioning from an employee mentality to being an owner. Ultimately, my productivity was off and what was clear to me was that I was not going to figure this out on my own. Of all the possible solutions available to me, I felt that finding the right mentor would be the quickest path to getting me "unstuck." This person would need to both help me define where I was struggling and what I would need to do to course correct.

I knew where I was, and I had clearly defined where I wanted to be; all I needed to do was identify the right person to mentor me and make the ask.

The next step I took was to slyly interview three people I knew who might be the right fit. Unbeknownst to these three, I created casual conversations that were actually interviews that allowed me to figure out which of them would be the best fit to mentor me in this current situation; your method to find a mentor may start differently. I presented each of them with my known as well with as my unknown parameters. One set of parameters, for example, that I presented them with was this issue: "I know that I have a list of tasks that does not seem to stop growing. So far, I have not been able to figure out what is preventing me from stopping these tasks from stacking up."

With each of my three interviewees, I started a discussion by explaining what I had already tried, what had helped, and what had not. Those conversations lasted anywhere from 30 minutes to 2 hours and involved a bit of discourse around their initial thoughts about what I was going through, some of their relevant experience, and a few beginning pieces of advice they had for me. I quickly decided which of the three would be best suited for the specific problem I needed to solve. Any one of them would have been highly qualified to guide me through to success, but the deciding factor for me happened to be more about a soft skill that had nothing to do with my situation than anything else. There is a shopping list of reasons why you might choose or reject any given potential mentor or why they might choose to not work with you.

- Not enough time/bad timing
- Bad ethical or moral fit
- Dislike for one another (in either direction or both)

- They didn't have the experience you thought they did
- They do not think you are ready
- You realize you are not ready

Whatever the reason and no matter who says "No," keep any decisions to not work with someone exceedingly civil. Specifically, if someone rejects you, do not take it personally. Keep a relationship with them. One way to think about this is that it was you who decided they were a valuable resource and you likely had good reason to do so. To this end, I chose to not tell any of my prospects why I was talking to them about my issues and only told the "winner" of my true intentions after our initial conversation. In fact, I would later be mentored by one of the two I "rejected" for a separate need.

It may surprise you to learn here that Dave Nitzel was the mentor who would help me get back to my path of productivity.

This certainly was a bit of a surprise for us. The beginning of our relationship was that of a trainer-trainee configuration when he purchased multiple franchise territories, and I was the one who taught him how we do what we do. Our relationship began with me as his teacher.

After engaging in and working through a purely mentor/mentee relationship for over a year, our relationship has since evolved into a mix of peer, partner, friend, and coauthor relationship. From time to time we also fall back to a mentorship relationship. This is not always the way things work out, but the complexity of this relationship is a more common path than I anticipated.

Regarding what I needed from Mr. Nitzel, it turned out that many of the reasons I was struggling were due to some deficiencies in soft skills that found me mentally stuck. While I am a strong extrovert and am exceptionally skilled at navigating broad social situations, my ability to navigate the intricacies of individual professional relationships, and more specifically those relationships I was forming as an owner, were lacking. Until I was in the thick of it, I had no concept of how different it was to work in a business as an owner and I did not have the personal insight to even figure out that this was the overarching reason as to why I was stuck. I could not see the forest for the trees, as they say. Something I had learned about Dave in the few years leading up to this change in our relationship was that he has a skill with people that I see as pure magic. It was this skill that drew me to him as a mentor.

If you were to meet Dave in a professional setting, and you're inclined to have a business conversation with him, he would likely casually chat with you for 15 to 20 minutes in a seemingly arbitrary way. In that conversation about "whatever," he will derive a strong understanding of how you think and process information as well as how you conduct yourself in business. This leads him to freakishly accurate insights that he's always willing to share with any interested party. It is his ability to listen and ask the right questions that is a core tenet of a mentorship relationship.

Early in ours there would be long periods of time in our phone conversations where I would hear nothing on the other end of the line. Often I would ask "did I lose you?" and he would say "no, I'm just listening" or "no, I'm just thinking." This reflects what I enjoyed the most in my mentorship with Dave is he didn't come with preconceived ideas of what the right answer is. This is still true; he is always processing what the best answer is for me and my specific situation.

His ability to listen and ask the right questions defines a core tenant of every successful mentorship relationship. This is something he is keenly aware of. Dave will be the first to tell you that the ability to listen, to truly listen, is both a gift and a skill; most call this "Active listening". To listen is to understand, understanding is the gateway to learning, and learning about the true needs of your mentee is everything. Dave Nitzel has a set of skills that make him a natural at this.

I now try to emulate this approach when I find myself in a mentor role because I know the impact it has on the relationship.

While the majority of this chapter is about finding mentors, Dave and I would be remiss if we did not give you a few points on being a mentor.

1. Be an excellent active listener (google "active listener" if you are not sure what that is).
2. Apply your knowledge dynamically. Never assume your mentee thinks the way you do.
3. Define your parameters. You must let your mentee know what your expectations are.

We can all learn active listening (I have been told this many times and am still working on learning this skill — no matter what year you read this book, I am probably still working on it). People like Nitzel exhibit this skill as a natural trait. I witnessed his abilities on a large scale at the event discussed in Chapter 12: Discipline, when he magically shifted 33 young women from being discordant to harmonious within 45 minutes of quick one-on-one conversations. This skill is what made him the perfect fit for me in that moment.

Over the next year, he coached me on how I interacted with employees and clients. He changed the way I approached leadership, mainly from an emotional maturity perspective. While the conversations were many and the topics vast, the main lesson he had to give was that anger was a completely unproductive use of my energy. This was a lesson I wish I had learned much earlier in life: "You do not have time to be angry." I was getting rightfully upset about various interactions and, after a particularly rough one, I called my mentor Dave and ranted to him for the better part of 30 minutes, at the end of which he said something to the effect of "What an amazing waste of time that was," followed by the most important lesson of my adult life. The amount of time I have saved in my personal and professional life with that mantra in the back of my head is boundless.

What is most interesting to me about this lesson is that it is one that my mother, who I have the utmost respect for, tried to teach me when I was a young man. This is exactly why we need mentors. Sometimes, if we are talking with those who are the closest to us, for many complex reasons, it can be too easy to ignore or too hard to listen. That is why it is so critical to have these outside voices to whom we have given intellectual authority to teach us.

All of this said, understand that this was my trial. Yours will be different.

Here are some of my ground rules when seeking out a mentor and beginning a mentorship relationship:

1. Be bold but respectful in asking people to become your mentor. Do not assume they do or do not have the time; they will let you know with their response.
2. If you are not sure where to start, look for those who have experience with what you are looking to accomplish. In that, be very clear with what you are hoping to learn from them.
3. Seek out people who have similar moral and ethical alignment. (Note: Do not confuse this with political, religious, social, or other ideals.)

4. They need to be able to tell you the brutal, honest truth; you're seeking out wisdom in ways that are impactful.
5. Keep an eye on the relationship. If it lasts more than a year, it's likely becoming more of a friendship than a mentorship. This is fine, but it may be time to shift gears and/or find a new mentor.
6. Make it easy for them. This isn't a paid-for gig, so be super respectful of their time and the effort they need to spend. You will repay them by listening and growing.
7. Don't expect paint-by-numbers instruction. Many will offer their experiences and anecdotes over specific advice.
8. In person is the most impactful format, but it can be done by phone or video call as well.
9. In terms of frequency of interactions, monthly is typical, but bimonthly or even quarterly can work, depending on the circumstances.

It's also important to note that not all mentor relationships are good ones. How do you know when you perhaps have the wrong mentor?

1. You are constantly getting advice that isn't relevant to your situation.
2. You are getting advice or feedback that is in conflict with your values.
3. You are only being told what you want to hear or what you already know.

If you find yourself in a mentor relationship with one of those issues, find a better mentor for yourself. It's not unusual to cycle through different potential mentors until you find the one that resonates. With some practice, you will learn to better identify the traits in a mentor that work for you.

Once you have connected with someone and confirmed that they are the right person at the right time, know that there are as many ways to mentor and be mentored as there are to teach and learn. Even your own individual mentorship relationships will likely be different from one to the next. You can work out a very structured process or one that is more on the loose side. What is not negotiable is that you need to work out those terms at the very outset with your mentor. Do not get started until you have both shared and ensured understanding of your expectations with each other. As much as you need to know what they expect of you, you need to be clear with them as to what your goals and expectations are. Whatever you agree to, aggressively apply yourself to it. Outside of honoring their time and this process, the only thing you owe them is to give your absolute top effort to apply the advice they are giving you. As a mentor myself, I can tell you that it feels incredibly insulting when someone asks you for this free help and then ignores it.

At this point in my life, I have one or two people actively mentoring me and at the same time I counsel a number of people myself. While being mentored has pushed my professional development in ways I have never experienced before, the satisfaction and reward I get out of mentoring others brings the experience full circle.

To those who invest in this process, we found this trend of eventually giving back to be quite common. Ivy seems to effortlessly slide in and out of both mentor and mentee relationships; the benefit of this amazing skill of hers is clearly written in the story of her many achievements. For the vast majority of us, the process of finding a mentor is one that feels ambiguous and elusive or reliant on luck and circumstance. For my part, I am hoping that this passage demystifies the process of finding and working with a mentor. While you will face rejection from prospective mentors who are uncomfortable with the idea, don't like you, or simply are too overloaded for such a relationship, keep at it and you will find mentors who will have multiplying impacts on your personal and professional development.

As a testament to their power, if not for mentorships, you would not be holding this book in your hand.

HELIX Sequencing

> We found varying levels of correlation between the building blocks in each chapter and the DNA points at the end of the book. The strength of the correlation is represented by 1 to 5 circles around our 5-point Hospitality DNA molecule: 1 being a lower correlation and 5 being a higher one.

Humble Nature

Seeking out both mentor and mentee relationships is a wonderful way to constantly learn and grow! It's sadly common for us to meet people who are very prideful and have convinced them-selves they know all the answers; they believe they have nothing left to learn. It's to some degree understandable in the world of very hard knocks that we live in, but it's none the less personally and professionally limiting. No matter what stage of your career you are in, you should always seek to give and gain wisdom.

Explorer's Pursuit

It's not only about the exploration for experiences but for knowledge as well. Discovery can be found in many ways, not the least of which is in mentorships. What's more, it doesn't need to be someone from within the industry; sometimes an outside voice is better. If you find yourself at the pinnacle of your industry, perhaps getting an outside voice is the only way to continue to grow at the rate you require. There's no requirement as to the source of knowledge—just that the exchanges happen.

Lifetime of Experience

Mentors often learn as much as the mentee. There's a ton of personal growth found in teaching. Our award winners are eager and willing to share their knowledge with others. For them, they don't fear being replicated or "stolen from." They are confident and understand that success begets success. There's a certain reciprocity that can only be found in sharing.

Indomitable Spirit

As we discussed in the introduction to the book, we aren't in the service industry, we are in the giving industry. We give to our guests openly and willingly the gift of great experiences. Wonder-fully, giving openly and willingly to those who want and can benefit from our growth does not take much effort. The spirit of giving is alive and well in those we interviewed, and to watch the multiplying effect they have on others is delightful.

Xtraordinary Culture

The culture we create is a reflection of ourselves. Our award winners create cultures of teaching and knowledge, giving of themselves in many ways that are replicated throughout the organization. Including mentorship in that teaching tool set is a no-brainer. The growth gained in a mentorship relationship is unlike anything a "normal" training program provides. As we say, increased productivity comes from strong culture, and adding a mentorship program into your culture will act as a turbo boost to both.

Chapter 15

Partnerships

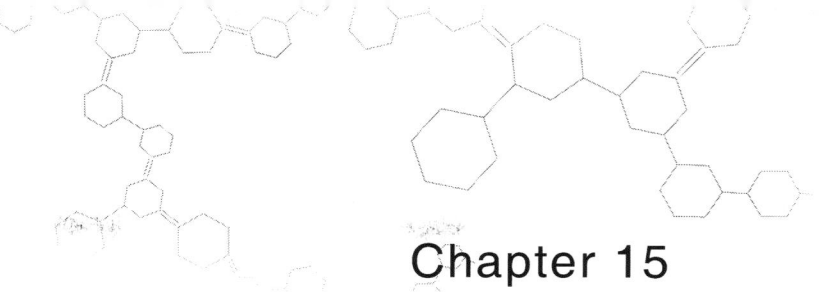

> Teamwork is the ability to work together toward a common vision. The ability to direct individual accomplishments toward organizational objectives. It is the fuel that allows common people to attain uncommon results.
> —Andrew Carnegie

As we started to flesh out the traits and abilities that are paramount to the leaders in the award-winning businesses we were investigating, it became clear that discussing partnerships—and more so, how these extraordinary individuals approach partnerships—would be a vital undertaking and one that we would need to take great care to get right. On the surface, partnerships are not a "trait" in the traditional definition of the term. However the ability to seek out, set up, and maintain successful partnerships is a confluence of skills that you must at least be aware of, if not strive to master.

Amazing partnerships work in a way similar to elite military teams. Much like a highly functioning special ops team has people trained for specific functions and an unprecedented level of trust to execute those functions, great partnerships thrive on knowing the guy next to you has your back, no matter what hell rains down on you.

While there is cross-training, the true value each member on a Delta team brings cannot be quickly or easily replaced. In addition to this, the team members do not step on the toes of the specialists who have strengths in particular traits that they have trained heavily around to complete a set of tasks better than anyone else on the team. Similarly, every partner in one of these teams must rely on their teammates without hesitation. Once in a combat situation, the ability or need to rely on each other is a foregone conclusion. The right people must have been selected with exacting perfection and then allowed to complete their functions at a level surpassing excellence.

In any given firefight, the forward observer is the eyes and ears of the platoon, responsible for locating targets and calling for adjusting indirect fire support. This person has studied operational terrain, has specialized knowledge of the tactical situation of any given mission, knows how the unit needs to maneuver, and has been well informed of the priority targets. Medics, on the other hand, have trained in the complex task of keeping everyone alive while under direct fire, and in constant, combat-ready shape.

Both of these people need to have an ability to see a bigger picture. They have the same overarching set of goals. They need to be highly intelligent and have a knack for understanding strategy and executing tactics. However, if, in the middle of a mission, the medic decides to stop focusing on keeping people alive and instead diverts a squad to a different path through a battle zone because he thinks he knows better than the forward observer, everyone is going to have a bad time ... a very bad time.

Creating and running successful restaurants might not be quite as "life and death" as getting shot at for a living; however, it often feels like a battle zone and certainly can have a similar level of chaos. It is the method by which each finds operational efficiency and exception inside of this chaotic structure where the similarities between elite strike teams and hyper-successful partnerships overlap.

For our partnership system, the steps you need to follow look like this.

1. Select the right partner, one with complementary skills and traits to yours
2. Create a clear, written understanding of accountability, authority, and responsibility
3. Trust them to do their job well/stay out of their way/rely on them
4. Communicate about "missions" regularly and effectively

The Delta Construct

We call this partnership setup The Delta Construct.

Through our years of coaching operators, we have had the opportunity to meet hundreds of these amazing people. Among these are those who own and those who aspire to own. Though we get asked hundreds of questions, one of the most frequent questions is "How do I find the right partner?" Though we have encountered many solid partnerships, it is difficult to find people who have a good answer to that question. Most of those we do know who can answer that question well tend to be in their own silo; if you don't know them, and further, don't know to ask them that specific question, you will never know their answer.

In 2016, after spending a lifetime studying and experiencing bars and restaurants, Julio Cabrera had found the moment in his life when he was ready to open his first restaurant. Those 30 years spent traveling the world had afforded him connections to countless, incredibly successful owners whom he now called on to help him fill the few remaining gaps in the knowledge he felt he needed to transform his meticulous plan into a reality. One of his questions was whether or not he should engage with a partner. While it may seem obvious that those he talked to who had found success in a strong partnership would encourage him to seek out his own, there was a major surprise for us in his experience. There were a few owners he spoke with who had such a command of the industry that they did not need to bring anyone else into their business; they could keep 100% of the control and 100% of the profits. To the last, each and every one told Julio ...

Julio Cabrera
Photo by Anthony Nader

"Don't do it by yourself."

The main line or reasoning we continually ran into was that, without a partner, everything will be on you, all the time. At their most basic level, partners help divide out the various types of labor only an owner can perform. For example, if your general manager disappears for a month for whatever reason, forcing you back into running the business, your partner can split shifts with you, take over the critical task you were supposed to be working on, but now can't, and at the very least, provide emotional and motivational support. Without them, the burden will be incredibly heavy. It will be entirely on you all the time, and you will not sleep when anything goes sideways.

Partnerships

The decision of whether or not to bring on a partner will be the second biggest you ever make. The magnitude of the question "Should I?" will only be eclipsed by exactly who you decide to go into battle with. On the surface, creating a partnership can seem quite simple: find someone you get along with—probably a friend—who has a set of qualifications that you lack, come to an understanding, and get started. In fact, it is that simple to create a partnership. Creating a strong, lasting, and effective partnership, on the other hand, is an involved and complex process.

The things that go wrong in partnerships can mostly be traced back to the very beginning. That said, in our experience, fully failed partnerships are not the norm. The majority of the partnerships we run across work, one way or another, for better or for worse. Some of these hit all of the points we lay out below and some barely hit a few.

Those relationships that miss more than one or two of the points that define multiplying partnerships tend to have some level of dysfunction that holds both the partnership, and therefore the business, back in a significant way. What we want to challenge anyone who is reading this to do is to take the Delta Construct partnership test at the end of this chapter. Be open to the possibility that there may be ways to strengthen your partnership, wherever it currently stands.

Many of the issues we see tend to come down to assumptions made at the outset of these unions.

- Assumptions destroy friendships
- Assumptions destroy partnerships
- Assumptions destroy businesses

Not everyone needs or wants a partner in their business. However, for those of you who answer "yes" to that question posed throughout this chapter, the goal here will be to give you a perspective and framework with which to get this critical step in your business correct. Of course, if you are against partnerships, it is also possible that after you finish reading what we learned on the subject, you might change your mind.

There are three simple steps to a partnership broken up by its natural life cycle.

- Finding or selecting a partner
- Creating your partnership agreement
- Working in the partnership

The success of the last step in the life of a partnership will likely be completely determined by your approach to and execution of the first two. If you find the right fit and work out all the details necessary for a smooth relationship, the last piece tends to just work.

Before we get into the process of how to select a good partner, it is important to be thorough in your deliberations regarding the prospect of bringing in one at all. The main reason the owners we spoke with brought in a partner was to complement their skill sets. After 30-plus years of gathering knowledge and experience, Julio knew he only had a fraction of what he needed to open his restaurant and had two options: hire talent for the missing pieces or bring on a partner. There are benefits to both options, but the value of having partners in his business easily won out.

When looked at over time, bringing on a partner and giving them a percentage of your profits can be more expensive than hiring someone who has a similar skill set or sets of traits. That lost income is compensated for by vastly empowering gains.

- **They are locked into the business:** You don't need to worry about them looking to leave for another job or being poached by a competitor.

- **They have a vested interest in the success of the business:** No one will ever care for nor work as hard for your business than another owner.
- **They share time and responsibilities with you:** This one cannot be overstated and was stressed heavily by everyone we spoke with. If you are a sole owner, you will spend nearly every waking hour in your business; many burn out in one or two years. You are 100% time committed. You get no vacations. You can't call out sick. Having a partner to share the load from day one doesn't just make long-term ownership easier; for many it makes it possible.
- **They can bring a vastness of experience:** If you select well, you can get someone with knowledge and experience you will likely never find in an employee.
- **You get a built-in board of directors:** Whether you have one or four partners, you have someone built into your business who you can bounce ideas off when the need arises.

Part 1: Selection

In 2005, Julio left Cuba to work for a hotel bar in Cancun. Unbeknownst to him, a seemingly simple decision to move for work would lead him to meet two people who would fundamentally change his life. Husband and wife team David Martinez and Michelle Bernstein were opening a restaurant nearby where Julio was working. One year later, Michelle and David made the decision to close shop in Mexico to relocate to Miami, Florida, to launch their ultimately incredibly successful restaurants. It was clear to Julio that he needed to follow.

Something to understand about Julio is that he is a deeply introspective person who has a strong understanding of both his abilities and shortcomings. At the age of 42, Julio was intimately aware that he was not ready to open a restaurant in the U.S. He had significant gaps in his knowledge to fill and a plan that was not clear enough for him yet.

> It is important that your partners not just be your friends, but your close friends. More specifically, it is vital that you believe in them as human beings.

For the following 10 years, in addition to earning awards, ending up on the cover of *GQ*, filling in all his gaps— knowledge and otherwise—and adding an extreme level of detail to his plan, Julio had found the two people who would be the first he asked to join him in his venture. He had also clearly identified for himself the first of our rules for a strong partnership. This rule has since been echoed by every owner whom we have talked to since, no matter if they learned it the easy or the hard way.

#1 — They have to be your friend. This is one of those points that came directly from our interviews that we were not expecting; frankly, even after coming upon the possibility of this as a need for a partnership, we heavily debated whether or not we should include it. The way it was explained to us was that it is important that your partners not just be your friends, but your close friends. More specifically, *it is vital that you believe in them as human beings.* As we dug into this, we started to understand that this has a lot to do with cultural and value alignments. You are going to be spending a lot of time together, and both your life and business will be better for it if you select someone with whom you have a strong relationship. All that said, it is important to note that not every best friend will be a suitable business partner, but the best business partners tend to be very good friends.

Partnerships

You'd better truly know the person you decide to let into what will be your closest inner circle. You will likely spend more time with this person than you do with your own family. Running a business will feel like a battle at times; is this person someone you would want in your foxhole with you when the bullets start flying?

It is not enough to know this person in passing or to only know them when hanging out and drinking. It is best to have worked with them in a business for a year or more to see how they operate under pressure and when things are slow. We have watched and even mediated partnership breakups between people who knew each other as business acquaintances and thought they were aligned, only to find out after working together directly in their new business that they had too many hopelessly differing points of view.

Julio had known David and Michelle both as friends and in business operations for 16 years before he asked them to join him as a partner in his business. His next choice was a *cantinero* he had worked with in Cuba for 20 years. While he did not know his fourth partner nearly as well, he was a longtime friend of Michelle and David.

Of course, not any friend will end up being a strong partner in your business. There are some questions to help you get yourself on the right path of determining whether or not someone would be a good fit for you to join you on your journey.

- What are their personal ethics?
- What is their work ethic like?
- How is their sense of morality?
- Are they as passionate as you about your vision?
- Do you like spending time with them?
- Would you have them over for dinner with your family?

#2 — You must trust this person explicitly. They are going to have more power to help or harm you professionally than anyone you have ever known. I know people who have friends who they don't necessarily trust; this cannot be one of those people.

#3 — Make sure they complement you and your knowledge and skills. Bringing a copy of yourself into the business will gain you nothing. You want to look for partners who bring something to the table that you do not have. Most commonly, I have found that one partner will be a creative type and the other a more rigid operational type. This is an amazing pairing that can have a multiplying effect on the overall productivity of the business. While it might be obvious that you should find someone with a set of skills you do not have, there is an added bonus when they have a very different demeanor than you as well. Where you may be the quiet one at the table, having someone who is more boisterous and outgoing can allow you to pick and choose which outside relationships each of you manage by matching your personalities to theirs.

Do they complement your skill set?

Do they complement your demeanor and personality?

#4 — You must be aligned to the same clearly defined purpose. In the most general sense, this purpose should be the same for every partnership: to drive our business to success. However, the specifics tend to be vastly different for each partnership. For the Dead Rabbit team, it is "Bringing the Irish bar into the 21st century." For the team at Cafe La Trova, it is "Creating a faithful Santiago, Cuba, experience in Miami."

Each person in the partnership is going to have their own interpretation as to how this purpose is accomplished. Alignment of purpose does not mean you will or should agree on everything. Sometimes, on any given topic, everyone will be in perfect alignment, and at others, they will disagree to the bitter conclusion on whatever process they feel differently about. The key to getting through any disagreements is to remember that everyone on the team does indeed have the best interests of the business in mind, respects diverse perspectives, and is ultimately aligned with the same overall purpose.

#5 — They should be someone you can have constructive arguments with. Arguments that are a discourse of disagreement are transformative when embraced between people who respect each other. On the other side of that thought, yes-men have no place in a partnership and, in time, will likely damage the business. You are not always right, and it is best to have someone who thinks differently than you and who is not afraid to make their case when they think you are wrong.

#6 — There should be a healthy ego of competition and embracing one's willpower to release that ego when necessary. Unfettered hubris and ego tears more partnerships apart than any other issue we've observed. We have mediated multiple partnership dissolutions within the Hospitality industry. From each one, we unearthed two compounding issues. First, the ego of one or more parties had created serious friction and they could not resolve their conflicting beliefs. This was exacerbated by the second issue, which is a lack of sufficient language in their operating agreement to iron out clashing disputes or define clear-cut roles in the business.

A strong and healthy ego creates productive partnerships. In contrast, an overbearing ego can cast a wide shadow. We learned that healthy competition between partners is the driving force to help propel you, your partner, and your business forward. The golden ticket is to navigate partnerships in a healthy manner. So, the million-dollar question is this: how?

You'll also want a partner who counters your weaknesses and is an open communicator. To illustrate the point, the following is a real-life example.

One day we had received a call from an ownership team that was interested in our services. We have a diverse offering, from inventory solutions and management coaching to speaking engagements and content creation. In this case, we were asked to have an exploratory conversation about inventory services. As per usual, we asked to meet them at one of their venues for a meet and greet.

In a situation like this, we prefer to arrive early and spend time in the venue. The reason we do this is to immerse ourselves in the surroundings. We want to enhance our understanding of the vibe and culture of a place before meeting with ownership.

In this case, we were scheduled to meet with Drew Schenck and Kevin Barrett of Dram & Draught in Raleigh, North Carolina. Kevin and Drew have three very successful cocktail bars known for their award-winning craft cocktails and outdoor urban settings. They have aspirations for a fourth bar and are launching an exciting, brand-new cola-flavored vodka called Coladka.

The ambience at Dram & Draught was both vibrant and chic. It was a reimagined old gas station, extremely well appointed with exposed brick accents. The bottles of spirits shone from ceiling to floor, showcased on back-lit shelves. The interior was cozy, with plenty of old wood and leather, capturing an air of classic chic without a hint of being pretentious.

As we sat and enjoyed a hand-crafted cocktail at a bar-side table, two guys walked through the door. They could have been straight out of casting for an Indiana Jones sequel. One was wearing a brown fedora with a white button-down shirt, carrying an old leather briefcase. The other sported a well-groomed beard that only a man of significance could carry. He walked with a cadence of purpose. They walked to the table where we were sitting and sat down right next to us, opposite one another. The man in the fedora plopped his briefcase on the table.

We weren't sure what to make of these guys. On one hand, they seemed poised to conduct some serious business. On the other hand, if that were the case, wouldn't they want more privacy? Why sit right next to us?

The briefcase was opened, and out came ... a chess set! Admittedly, we looked very cool sitting next to these chess enthusiasts. Then it dawned on us that we were likely sitting in their usual seats. We thought perhaps we should move, but they insisted we stay and that they weren't bothered in the least.

The man whose name we later found out was Drew spoke first, not knowing who we were. He asked, "How do you like your cocktail?"

I replied, "It's tasty. I have a bit of a sweet tooth, so I tend to savor things an eight-year-old would find interesting."

Drew hopped up from the table while Kevin set up the chess game and went behind the bar to eloquently whip up a sweet summer concoction for me to enjoy. With great pride, Drew hand-delivered the splendor to my table. I was impressed by the orange peel twist that dangled with a burst of color at the top of the glass. Make no mistake, this was the place for unique cocktails!

As I took my first sip of this cocktail specifically crafted for me, I was experiencing firsthand what all customers raved about regarding the drinks here — the care, the attention to detail, the taste! I felt like the most important person in the room! It was at that very moment we realized our meeting had arrived. We introduced ourselves and shared a laugh.

Drew and Kevin began their game as we began our conversation. They explained to us that they have a running game of chess, and they always keep score. They are very happy to crow about who has the lead or who has won the most recent game. It's clear they take their games seriously. Chess continues providing them with a unique outlet for banter and rivalry in a healthy and productive way. It also allows them to enjoy one another's company doing something completely unrelated to work.

Kevin Barrett and Drew Schenck
Photo by Edie Alexander

As someone who understands just enough about chess to know what's happening — but never actually plays — I was blown away at their speed. As we watched two entertaining games during our meeting, we were enthralled — incredibly impressed by what we saw!

I've never seen anything quite like their partnership. They banter. They compete with each other. They don't hold their opinions back. And it's all done from a place of deep mutual respect.

There's so much we can learn from these two admirable business partners as it relates to healthy partnerships. Relationships come in all different forms and fashions, but Drew and Kevin's embodies the ideals we have set forth in this chapter:

- Friendship

- Trust
- Complementary skills
- Alignment
- Healthy competition
- Ego
- Honesty

All the above play a role in their wildly productive partnership. Although this relationship is obviously unique, allow it to serve as a standard to aspire to. It's a wonderful example in a quick vignette of how a relationship can fuel competition, agreement, disagreement, honesty, and more, while retaining a strong sense of trust and respect.

Part 2: The Agreement

When starting your own business, it is essential to take time and care to put as much detail into the operating agreement as possible.

Before we get into any details, we must be clear. We are not lawyers, and none of what we are saying here is legal advice. The absolute best advice we can give you here is this: GET A LAWYER! Do not try to create your own agreement. Do not use a "boilerplate" agreement; we have been told by our lawyers that there is no such thing. Find a lawyer who has experience with operating agreements, who is knowledgeable in your local laws, who is admitted to the bar in your state of operation, and — if your business is incorporated in a different state than the one you operate in — they should be admitted there as well or have a partner who is admitted there.

It is possible you will need two separate lawyers to create this document — one to do the majority of the work writing the agreement and another to make sure it passes muster in the other state. In addition to this, each partner should have their own, separate lawyer look over the agreement on their behalf. If you skimp on this part of the process, you could pay for it dearly in the future, as many have before you.

Operating agreements have little to do with any current relationship you might have with someone. No matter how long you have known someone you are intending on partnering with, you must understand that this process will change that relationship forever. If approached correctly and well, whatever bond you previously had with that person will find a richness and depth you will achieve with few others. A proper operating agreement will go very far in protecting that relationship and helping you keep it as a friendship.

At the start of any new relationship, things tend to be light and cheery. In marriages, we call this the honeymoon phase, and it is little different for starting new business relationships. As you look to have your operating agreement written, keep in mind that it is designed to protect you and your partner from issues in the future. When serious money gets involved, years have been poured into a project, and maybe you are talking about scaling the business further, attitudes, feelings, and perceptions can change. A well-written operating agreement is designed to make or heavily guide any large future decisions for you and your team.

One of the best examples of what this looks like when it is working comes from the Dead Rabbit in New York City.

In 2020, Jack McGarry and his partner, Sean Muldoon, came to an impasse about spending during the COVID-19 pandemic shutdown. Money was tight and the future uncertain. Both knew that they needed to make multiple shifts in their operation to allow the Dead Rabbit to make it through the crisis. Their game plan was to come out stronger on the other end of this uphill battle.

Sean brought forth a new branding idea with an expanded line of merchandise. Jack, on the other hand, thought spending money this way would be a risky move, as the industry was 100% shut down in New York at the time. These were strange times in the history of the world! The restaurant/bar scene felt like a ghost town — completely unheard of in a city like the Big Apple!

Jack even prepared a cost-benefit analysis based on previous years' sales of products to prove the financial risk involved. They debated and argued, but the one guy could not convince the other.

Years before, when forming their business, a strongly written agreement was developed. This included a clause on breaking stalemates in larger operational decisions. There are three other partners in their business who are more of the silent variety. If Jack and Sean ever encounter dissent over the direction of any project, they loop in one of their other trusted partners. Jack and Sean each make their case, and a binding decision is made by the third partner.

A well-written partnership agreement works in harmony with the previously discussed criteria of selection for any partner. The resolution of disagreements is one of several circumstances that should be clearly defined by an operating agreement. This protects the friendship from serious discord dissolving into fights. Jack and Sean's disagreement clause works by making space to set aside ego, allowing the strength of their friendship and their mutual commitment to the Dead Rabbit's success to shine through.

Jack lost that particular disagreement. The decision to move forward with the marketing effort was made. At that point, Jack put aside his feelings and fully invested in the program's success, and why wouldn't he? It felt empowering to do this for the sake of the business, and now Jack could put all of his efforts into proving his friend and partner right! In the end, they both experienced a strengthened and further unbreakable partnership.

While an agreement can be structured in a variety of ways, every successful operator we met insists that you absolutely must have one; there are no exceptions to this golden rule! In its totality, an operating, or partnership, agreement is a legal document. When you are looking at the bigger picture of what it can accomplish in your business, there's more to it than just the standard legal nitty-gritty.

Below is a list of some of the basics. We see these broken into two main categories.

- Financial and major legal decision-making capabilities
- Operational structure

DISCLAIMER: We are not lawyers, and the following content should in no way be considered legal advice. The only legal advice we give is to get a lawyer to draft your operating agreement.

Financial and Major Legal Decision-Making Capabilities

On the surface, there are two basic questions everyone asks when entering into a partnership.

- Who gets what?
- What are any shares conditional on?

Those are simple questions with complex answers. Determining who gets what is generally an involved process with quite a few steps and considerations.

First, you need to answer the question of how each partner is contributing to the business. There are three ways that each partner can be "operating" in the business.

- Solely working in the business, no financial contribution
- Solely funding a portion of the business; an investor
- Both working in and funding the business

There is no one way to determine how many of what kind of shares any individual partner should get. Much of this comes down to the personal feelings of each person involved in the negotiation.

For your first property, valuing the "idea" of what you want to create when talking to investors or partners can be a tricky proposition, and your emotional connection to your baby can easily get in the way. Of course, you have to assign a fair value to the worth of your idea as well as the fact that you will be the one putting your blood, sweat, and tears into the business, day and night.

The best piece of advice I have ever gotten on this process was from my lawyer when Dave and I set up our partnership for writing the first book. Do not let your ego get in the way of making a ton of money.

Further compounding the complexity of determining who gets what is the different ways that you can design the shares in the business.

There are two main types of units or shares that can be sold or shared in business: financial units and management units. Many agreements will lock these into a single economic and management unit; however, it can be very handy to assign or sell them separately. For example, if you have a financial backer who has little to no industry experience and whom you do not want to have decision-making power in the operation of your business, you can sell them economic units only. In other cases, a particular partner may want to have a 100% veto right in the business and you can use management units to give them a larger say in how the business is operated and grown.

After you figure out who gets what kind of shares, there is a part that many people skip, and it can bite you in the ass. What are any shares conditional on? Here are two examples of questions around conditions that can be placed on shares:

- Do you require a certain level or type of participation in the business for the shares to remain in that person's possession?
- Should there be a morality clause defining how shares can be taken away from a member?

Finally, you should decide when and under what conditions distributions will be made to partners. Will they be available once a year, quarterly, monthly, or by some other time metric? What financial markers on the business must be met before you will distribute any profits, such as a certain amount of liquid capital in the main business account? Will you allow distributions in the first year or do you want to wait three years before allowing them? The list of questions you can ask yourself here is vast. For us, it all came down to protecting the business first and only giving money to the partners when the business could afford it, though what our business can afford versus what yours can afford will likely be very different.

Operational structure: Many feel that this portion is not always necessary; however, we disagree. Every group of partners we spoke with had something like this clearly laid out, and it made a massive difference in their ability to grow and scale.

Responsibility: Are there any specific tasks that a particular partner must personally complete on a regular basis?

Accountability: What areas of the business are they responsible for keeping track of and ensuring the success of?

Authority: What area of the business is each partner allowed to make decisions on?

Dispute resolution: If it were not for this, many of the most successful teams we have talked with likely would not have made it. There are countless ways to set this up, but everyone we spoke with had a moment in their business where a well-defined dispute mediation process became pivotal in keeping the wheels on the bus.

Part 3: The Rest of Your Lives

This all stacks up, chronologically and sequentially. Putting the proper thought and energy into Parts 1 and 2 will undoubtedly make your relationship as partners much more smooth and stable; however, there is no magic pill here. Like any long-term relationship, a great partnership takes effort and energy to ensure it endures.

From our studies, what we can determine is that keeping a partnership strong over the years has a lot to do with a few wonderfully simple ideas — our mantras of partnership.

Mind the friendship: You will be in a high-stress environment at times. Over the years, you are likely to end up in some heated moments. You were friends first; keep the friendship present and front of mind as much as you can. Remember, you respect these people and actually like them. Jack, Sean, Julio, Drew, Kevin — every single person we spoke with — made it abundantly clear how critical this has been to driving their success.

Check your ego: As an owner and entrepreneur, you likely have a very healthy ego; we certainly do. As we recommend you find people who are capable of putting their own ego aside, be careful to do the same yourself when the situation warrants it. Do not let your ego push you to arrogance or hubris and destroy your partnership.

Stay out of each other's way: This is the quiet key. You chose someone who is better at certain aspects of running your business than you are. Give your partner room to do what they do best.

Consider not drinking: This one is controversial for many owners. Dave and I have had more conversations than not about the impact of drinking in the business. Neither of us has ever seen an instance where an owner drinking while working in or on the business has had a long-term positive impact. This is an industry where drinking is par for the course for more people working in it than not.

We propose the following idea: Drinking subdues effective communication.

While the benefit is anecdotal, Jack McGarry told us his story. His experience lends robust support to the idea that, at the very least, owners should not drink while working on or in the business. Each for their own reasons, Jack and Sean decided to stop drinking. While the specifics are theirs to share, broadly speaking, for Jack, it was a decision to regain control he felt he had lost, while for Sean, it was more about not seeing any benefit to drinking. What is extremely clear is that it was not until they acted on this very conscious decision that they started finding true success in their business. Without this decision, the Dead Rabbit would likely not have achieved the worldwide acclaim that these two extraordinary men worked to attain.

They certainly felt like they were doing the right thing at the right place at the right time. Every conversation was more open and smoother. The disagreements went from heated arguments to respectful and spirited debates. The business went from surviving to thriving. Jack credits this decision to not drink as having a major part to play in the wild success of his business.

Final Thoughts

Partnerships, like any intimate relationship are complicated from beginning to end, but everything we have seen and everyone we have talked to has shown us that, when they are approached and executed well and with great thought, they take on a life that has an immeasurable but massively positive effect on the business.

At the end of many of my nights on the floor as a bar manager, I walked away feeling like I had just won (or lost) a battle. Years after I ran those shifts, I became the owner of my own business and, with that new perspective, I now know that the weight of a day, week, month, and year is indescribably heavier when the success or failure of the business rests squarely on your shoulders. Sharing that burden with the right person locked in on your side can have more of an impact on the outcome than most any other decisions you will make during your career as an owner.

Applying the Delta Construct — the mindset of a special ops team — won't prevent you from making a bad decision with your partner; however, it will force you through the right questions, which, if you ponder them thoroughly, will give you a major advantage. If you treat your partnership process, from selection through to execution, with the same severity as each member of a special ops team is selected, you will be set up for success, and the execution of your vision will become infinitely smoother.

- Partnership review:
    - Make sure you trust your partner explicitly.
    - You need to be aligned on ethics and personal values with your partners.
    - Select a partner who has strengths in skills and abilities that are vastly different than yours.
    - Set clear expectations on who will do what in the business and when.
    - Do not enter a partnership without a strong, legally binding operating agreement. Pay extra special attention to how and when profits are disbursed.
    - Each partner needs their own separate lawyer to look the agreement over.
    - Let your partner do what they do best … stay out of their way when they are driving in their lane.
    - Do not be afraid to disagree and argue; some of the best decisions can come out of a spirited debate.

**On our website you will find a
"How healthy is your partnership" quiz.**

Partnerships

HELIX Sequencing

> We found varying levels of correlation between the building blocks in each chapter and the DNA points at the end of the book. The strength of the correlation is represented by 1 to 5 circles around our 5-point Hospitality DNA molecule: 1 being a lower correlation and 5 being a higher one.

Humble Nature

We've said it before, but it's worth saying again: Check your ego at the door if you want to build a successful partnership. Teamwork, trust, and true collaboration are the keys to taking a partnership from simply existing to becoming wildly profitable and satisfying. A truly lucrative partnership needs all those involved to have a humble nature. The ability to share control with others, trusting them to do what we ultimately know they do better than us, is at the core of the best partnerships out there.

Explorer's Pursuit

Ultimately, partnerships are a risk. The Explorer's Pursuit is a trait that enables you to take some risks in your career and see where they take you. It also fills you with a thirst for learning and experiences. Follow this calling and expand your network of colleagues, travel to new places, and explore the kinds of ventures that you're interested in having. By immersing yourself in others' partnership stories and seeing what worked in different circumstances, you'll gain an invaluable perspective that will drive your choices and risk-taking, moving forward. In the journeys of many of our interviewees, relationships with future partners were often started while on their travels. Remember: no risk, no reward, and when you get a partnership right, the rewards are vast.

Lifetime of Experience

Combine Explorer's Pursuit with Lifetime of Experience and you get the perfect recipe for finding the people you will need to supercharge your business. As you spend the years gathering truths about yourself and further defining your vision for your restaurant, add in the process of figuring out the exact traits you think you need in a partner to make that vision a reality. Ask questions contrasting what you already know versus what you do not and might never understand to find gaps, which that new friend you made might fill perfectly. These impulses will guide you toward more practical lines of thought and decisions on the right person to bring into your business.

Indomitable Spirit

To make it in this industry, you must have serious tenacity. When you work with a set of partners who have vastly differing priorities at stake when it comes to running a venture, project, or business, you can expect a lot of bumps in the road. When you get the right set of partners in your business, they only amplify your Indomitable Spirit, making everything easier to handle. Of course, getting them right will also propel them ahead in the same way they propel you.

Xtraordinary Culture

Finding partners isn't generally part of a culture; however, if you pick the wrong partners, your culture, and so your business, will be constantly and potentially permanently stunted. Misalignment between partners is one of the only insurmountable issues to culture we have come across. Having a supportive, empowering, and balanced partnership with people you like and trust is essential to attaining sustained success. Consider what cultural cornerstones you both might be able to build into your operating agreement. Clear and equitable provisions for dispute resolution, crisis management, sustainable growth, responsibilities, communications, and exactly who gets what sets up a culture, at the very beginning, of mutual interest and respect among the partners. When everyone knows what lane they're in, what to expect, and what they're responsible for, it's much easier to work as a cohesive team that trusts each leader to handle their role capably.

Chapter 16

HELIX Discovery

> If we knew what it was we were doing, it would not be called research, would it?
> —Albert Einstein

So, what are the conclusions? How could we pull all this data and information together in a way that is memorable and easy to understand? We shared with you throughout the book the idea of the Hospitality HELIX through sequencing the chapter conclusions to illustrate, in the most memorable way, how to connect our chapters (Building Blocks) to our conclusions (HELIX), and how our interviewees apply this to their businesses. As we dissected our interviewees' career arcs and Building Blocks, we began to discover the themes that we believe make up the core DNA components of award-winning Hospitality talent. Ultimately, we broke it down in the form of our HELIX.

For us, the big idea of doing a research book was going where the data and information took us. Ultimately, we have access to thousands of Bar and Restaurant owners. In this journey, we really wanted to hone

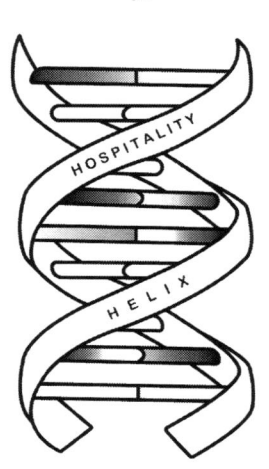

The result of our interviews and studies — the Hospitality HELIX!

in on what are the commonalities, if any, among these global award winners. There were times when things we absolutely thought would be true simply were not and we had to toss aside assumptions, and there were times where trends were staring us in the face, and we just didn't see them because it wasn't what we expected. It is true the most obvious answers are sometimes right in front of you. A little reminder about our process: we have over a hundred hours of recorded interviews. Dave and I like to be able to watch portions of different interviews and comment simultaneously at times to make sure we have alignment and agreement on what multiple people are saying. The second thing you'd find is poster board paper all over the walls to identify key notes from the individuals we spoke with, with key themes color coded. We do like our Sharpies; they help us keep the themes straight! So, the process of this book happened in a few stages:

> **Stage 1:** Selection — Who are the right people, who we have access to, who are willing to openly share their insights and knowledge with the world?
>
> **Stage 2:** Interview — What is the specific talent that propels their success, and can we explore and share that with the world so that others may benefit from their insights?
>
> **Stage 3:** Conclusions — What, if anything, do they all have in common? Are there common threads these award winners share that facilitate their success, and if so, what are they?

In this next section, we will break down in greater detail what Hospitality DNA really means and how it's created through the HELIX. And fear not, we'll do that through even more amazing stories and guidance, which we think you'll really appreciate. Let's talk for a minute about what's not on the list.

It isn't uncommon for people to hear and believe you must be formally educated in order to reach a certain level of success. While that may usually be true if you aspire to be a *Fortune*-level CEO, bar and restaurant industry achievement shows little correlation between any specific education and award-winning success. There are certainly those among the many award winners who had a hospitality-based education, but many learned on the job over a number of years. There were also those who had some sort of college degree but often in a completely different field of study.

An interesting side note: you could find evidence of certain cross-sections of interest; for example, Ivy Mix and Dave Kaplan studied art, and that influence is clearly felt in their venues. Neal Bodenheimer's degree in history informs his passion for "history in a glass," which was very similar to how Gary Crunkleton, Humberto Marques, and Salvatore Calabrese approach business — by emphasizing history and spirits. You also have those with very specific professional training, like Julio Cabrera as a *cantinero*, and those who graduated from culinary institutes. Simply put, the trend data in our evaluations didn't point to a specific education as a factor in award-winning success, but it certainly doesn't hurt either. So, for us it's a neutral proposition in terms of the HELIX. Perhaps best said, education is a wonderful thing, but learning and personal development is not exclusive to specific institutions as it relates to our award winners.

We also found no correlation to socioeconomic background. We interviewed people who grew up under many forms of governments and social structures; we see no specific correlation.

There is no data that suggests that gender is a leading indicator for a successful Bar and Restaurant career. Nor was it discussed by any of our interviewees as a significant factor in their success one way or another. This is not to say that gender issues don't exist or do not have their unique challenges. We know they do — as evidenced by Minakshi Singh's story, which is nothing short of awesome (upcoming in the chapter on Indomitable Spirit). It just wasn't discussed or emphasized by our award winners.

We also found people who grew up in extreme poverty and those who grew up with financial comforts. Again, we found no correlation. In fact, if there's an industry where you can work your way to the top, this is it! It's a no-BS business. If you can make things happen, you're in demand!

What is extremely evident is, the independent bar and restaurant industry is one of the great bastions of individual spirit and expression; the challenge becomes harnessing that individualism into something that can generate meaningful income. So that leads up to the Hospitality HELIX. In our quest to define Hospitality DNA, this is what we distilled from the research: trends that stood beyond the rest. If you have or develop these five HELIX traits, you will be in concert with some of the best operators in the world.

The HELIX Sequence

Humble Nature

> Humility, that low, sweet root, from which all heavenly virtues shoot.
> —Thomas Moore

The humility these globally known, award-winning individuals displayed was simply extraordinary. So many times, we heard about how lucky they were or they would credit their mentors, teams, and partners, and of course you would expect that, but once in a while I think we expected to hear some hubris and perhaps a little braggadocio. After all, they have certainly earned it. But we noticed time and time again astonishing humility. Perhaps it should come as little surprise that one of the greatest business books of our generation, *Good to Great*, by Jim Collins, denotes their highest achievers in terms of Fortune 500 leadership as "Level 5 leaders" (on a 1 to 5 scale), as he describes it, with Level 5 being the absolute nirvana of leadership. Here's how Collins and his team describe what they call Level 5 (1 to 5) leadership in his book *Good to Great*:

"A Level 5 Executive builds enduring greatness through a paradoxical blend of personal humility and professional will."

That is frighteningly similar to what we discovered with our process. I think it's safe to assume that there are themes of elite leadership that resonate the same, whether you are in the corporate world or a small independent business owner. People respond to certain leadership cues in a very similar way.

In fact, when we think of someone with a big ego, it's easy to visualize someone who is overtly confident, boastful, and would fit a classic know-it-all stereotype. That could certainly be the case. However, as it relates to hubris and ego, we find that people who simply won't listen — who, in their mind, have transcended the idea of learning from others — is a very common example of hubris in our industry. Essentially, they are set in their ways, and they know best. This can be tough, as success is hard earned in this industry and our history informs our present, yet it can also be extremely limiting.

If you're not already, learn to become an excellent listener — even when you're predisposed to disagree — and stay open to the idea that despite your knowledge, you may be wrong or there may be an even better way.

During our interviews, you would think success was everyone else's fault and we were speaking to the wrong individuals. But there's a critically important DNA trait here, and we believe it's vitally important to understand. It starts with motivation. To quote famous author Simon Sinek, "It starts with Why." What do we mean? Well, if you're in the industry to deliver Hospitality to others, at its core that means prioritizing the experiences of others. It's extremely hard to deliver excellent experiences to others when you're all wrapped up in yourself. Harken back to our discipline chapter. Everything fell apart — not due to poor planning and not due to a lack of knowledge, but due to compromised motivation. The *why* was a mess (and we left out a lot of material deemed inappropriate in that chapter; oh, the stories we wanted to tell!). Hubris and ego are huge limiting factors in one's success. A healthy ego is important, and our interviewees have confidence — they believe strongly in themselves and their teams — but they don't believe all the credit belongs to them, which is a huge point of distinction.

Specific to our industry, this could be a bit of a beacon. Too many TV shows that spotlight our industry do not emphasize a humble nature; indeed, quite the opposite. It's one thing to tell a story about a disastrous scenario turned around in a couple of days into a world-class operation — that's certainly entertaining. Perhaps the reason we don't see shows about the best of the best is because it's boring. No drama … no ratings, which is a shame really as it doesn't make for a great example to the vast majority of people and operators in our industry on how to achieve award-winning success. It's hard to find real Hospitality DNA in some bizarre two-day turnaround not grounded in any sort of reality. If this book serves no other purpose, we hope it achieves a certain end, a road map — a road map which, if followed, will lead you down the path of much-deserved success. It's a long road filled with adventure, disappointment, learning, and a wealth of excitement. Along that road, you now have a set of reliable, proven Building Blocks upon which to build:

- Practice a **H**umble Nature
- Cultivate an **E**xplorer's Pursuit
- Acquire a **L**ifetime of Experience
- Exude an **I**ndomitable Spirit
- Create an **X**traordinary Culture

… this is your Hospitality HELIX, the DNA that powers the best of the best.

There are no guarantees, of course. There's no accounting for all eventualities that may come our way. We know through the certainty of others what this collection of high achievers was able to achieve and their thoughts on how to do it. As William Shakespeare wrote in his play *The Tempest*, "What's past is prologue." May these collections of wisdom and experiences serve you well on your unique path to success.

Speaking of writers, Jackson Cannon is the son of a retired political writer and presidential historian who as a child was based in DC by way of California. His roots in both history and writing run deep. He shared, "Hemingway loomed large in our household growing up."

Jackson will tell you he learned how to make his first cocktail at eight years old — for his father, of course. The idea of social drinking was a significant component of his family interaction. "The idea of heavy drinking without ever being out of control was how I was introduced to culture in the social context of storytelling, the community, and the communion."

It was during his father's reading of Ernest Hemingway's *The Sun Also Rises* that Jackson recalls first learning of the Jack Rose cocktail. When Jackson pressed his father on the special ingredients of this unique cocktail, he shrugged it off as some sort of apple brandy concoction.

It is no surprise to us that years later Jackson would become a founding member of the Jack Rose Society, whose mission is to preserve the art of the American cocktail. Before we explore that further, we have some ground to cover as, unlike many, his first passion took his education and career in a slightly different direction.

He never strayed too far from his passion for spirits and cocktails. Initially, Jackson pursued a career in music, where he studied jazz at Berklee and played all sorts of music (other than classical). Like many, upon leaving school, he took his music on the road, where the entire day is sacrificed in the name of a 45-minute set. Jackson could play rock, blues, jazz, or basically anything you like. Either through music or cocktails, he's performed in every single state in the U.S. and throughout Europe.

It's fun to hear him tell stories of his performance in front of hundreds of people in a German amphitheater and then, one week later, he's playing at a New Hampshire barbecue — such is the life of a traveling musician.

In his late thirties, Jackson felt a pull back to his cocktail roots. Truthfully, he became more interested in listening to Dale DeGroff discuss the martini than he was in the latest music trends. Jackson realized that he was ready to put aside a well-established music career — this was mind boggling for his music colleagues. But the allure was always there, pulling at him, as he was slowly drawn into the cocktail world again. He wanted to work behind a bar. So he went on a quest ...

Jackson became acutely aware that he loved connecting with people. And yes, that would happen occasionally onstage as a musician. "To be candid, it happened more on the road, traveling to gigs with the band, than it did onstage with the audience." Passion set his eyes on connection. Interest set his eyes on spirits. And he was set on connecting with people. This all made running a bar the obvious choice!

"I thought for years I was spending time in bars to play music but in reality, I was playing music so I could be in bars," says Jackson.

> I thought for years I was spending time in bars to play music but in reality, I was playing music so I could be in bars.

In the pursuit of his personal renaissance, Jackson traveled to places like Turin to study vermouth, London to develop his understanding of gin, and France to learn more about Benedictine monks.

Jackson recalls the difference between when he first told stories of the Benedictines prior to his visit and the stories he told after his visit. His new stories had incredible impact — they were more authoritative and came from personal experience. That passion was contagious. Jackson's natural inclination is to gather unique experiences and expertise and reminisce about those experiences with complete strangers in an effort to create new memories with and for his guests. Spot on!

So, armed with his past musical passion and recent learnings, Jackson was ready to start his first bar. It didn't take long for the rude industry introduction to begin. Jackson recalls a time where he was only six months into his first bar management job at Eastern Standard when his partner asked for a meeting. Jackson had, in his opinion, a very solid and valuable business partner in Garrett Harker. They had the kind of relationship most would aspire to. Mutual respect and honesty were the hallmarks of their accord.

Jackson was struggling to find his footing behind the bar. It's one thing to have great knowledge of history and cocktails and a whole other thing to handle a packed bar on a Friday night when the lights go down and the music comes up. Garrett, realizing that his friend and partner was in trouble, opted for the direct and honest approach to their meeting.

> Hey, just keep doing what you're doing, and you'll fire yourself in a couple of weeks.

"Hey, just keep doing what you're doing, and you'll fire yourself in a couple of weeks."

He went on to say, "I'm not telling you this is a meeting where I do all the talking and you just listen, but it is." Jackson calls it the last great rescue conversation. Fortunately, he found his way through with Garrett's guidance. He learned how and when to apply conversation and knowledge to the guest experience. He naturally became more efficient in his cocktail creation, all of which allowed him to become the mixologist he aspired to be. Eventually he partnered with Garrett in a new venture, The Hawthorne. As with most, his first year was very much a boot camp where he had to tread water to survive — and survive he did, winning multiple awards and gaining global notoriety for expertise and execution in mixology.

The reason we loved Jackson's story is because very few people can be wildly successful in multiple disciplines. Once someone experiences success at a high level, it can be difficult to experience the rigors of trial and error, and to have to go through the curve all over again. Jackson took this all in stride and is a humble example of how to follow your passion.

It may be the biggest challenge of humility there is. Nobody cared that Jackson played for huge arenas if he screwed up their order or struggled to manage a 26-seat bar. He described this experience so gracefully, in that he leaned on people, took advice, and listened a lot. It was all that feedback and learning that got him through the toughest times. This type of learning doesn't happen for people full of hubris.

"I get so much satisfaction out of taking care of people. I crave it, and I approached my learning that way!"

He'll go on to share something else we hear repeatedly, that being his passion.

Jackson Cannon

> "I get so much satisfaction out of taking care of people. I crave it, and I approached my learning that way!"

This is fueled by his connection with others — most notably at the bar. For Jackson, those experiences were play-based — they were fun and engaging. The bar provided an opportunity and escape for deeper, more meaningful connections, which became his elixir.

"Creating a perfect old-fashioned never takes precedence over getting something that will make them happy," says Jackson.

Humble Nature DNA sequence

- Success will usually bring with it an element of enhanced ego, and there's nothing wrong with a healthy ego. Problems arise when a healthy ego turns to hubris and not recognizing when that occurs.
- Being humble can be as simple as being a good listener and a willing learner. It's very hard to grow when you already know everything.
- Have people in your orbit who can be completely honest with you, and do not punish them for it. Welcome candid feedback.
- Own your mistakes and learn from them.
- Be confident enough to ask for help; be humble enough to accept it.

The HELIX Sequence

Explorer's Pursuit

> It seems that the more places I see and experience, the bigger I realize the world to be. The more I become aware of, the more I realize how relatively little I know of it, how many places I have still to go, how much more there is to learn. Maybe that's enlightenment enough — to know that there is no final resting place of the mind, no moment of smug clarity. Perhaps wisdom, at least for me, means realizing how small I am, and unwise, and how far I have yet to go.
> —Anthony Bourdain

This is the one we didn't see coming. If there was an epiphany for us, this was it. Another thing we learned in this process was, part of doing research is the importance of remaining unbiased as to your own assumptions and letting the subject(s) be your guide. As I was sitting in the aforementioned office looking at all the poster board paper on the wall, I saw the same bright orange (my color code for travel) on every single page. It was right there in front of our eyes, yet I hadn't noticed. When I discussed this with my friend and mentor Derek Jones, he recommended a book. He said it changed his life and compelled him to attend a week-long leadership seminar at the Harvard Business School hosted by its author. The book is *The Power of Noticing*, by Max H. Bazerman. The book's focus is on exactly that: seeing the obvious and asking the obvious questions that no one else is asking. Truly, of the number of simple things that can be overlooked to disastrous ends, one example he uses that sticks out for me is the *Challenger* space shuttle disaster and the O-ring issue. This could have been prevented had the right person simply looked at the data differently. In fact, one person did see the disaster coming, but they failed to convince those with the power to stop the launch to do so, at the cost of tragic demise. I can't go into it further here. Obviously, suffice it to say it's a book worth reading! So here we found ourselves in a similar situation (not nearly as dire), of completely missing a congruent data point that nearly all of our interviewees shared: the Explorer's Pursuit! What does it mean? Dave and I had more than a few exhaustive conversations about what this meant, if anything, to the relative success of our award winners. Could it just be a massive coincidence? We obviously decided it was not; in fact, it was ultimately deemed a core component of Hospitality DNA!

Imagine working for 35 rupees (50 cents U.S.) per day as a mechanic in New Delhi. As a teenager, you are home, free of your formal education. Like many at that age, you're starting to consider what the world has in store and there is no clear path forward. Jump forward 12 years: you're running a Michelin three-star restaurant-bar in Hong Kong as a Diageo World Class champion, a Bacardi Legacy winner, and a Hernö Hero champion. How does that happen?

> "Travel has taught me massively ... I use those experiences to share with others and it allows me to relate to others."

It's hard to visualize filling in the blanks in getting from point A to point Z, but that's the story of Devender Sehgal. In all our interviews, there was no one else who more exemplified the idea of an Explorer's Pursuit — that discovery matters! This also encompasses being relentless in pursuit of your dreams. After all, we learn and grow through experience. "Travel has taught me massively ... I use those experiences to share with others and it allows me to relate to others," says Devender.

We've crafted a simple diagram that outlines the Explorer's Pursuit — this is common to most of our interviewees. We have also learned that this is an integral component to Hospitality DNA.

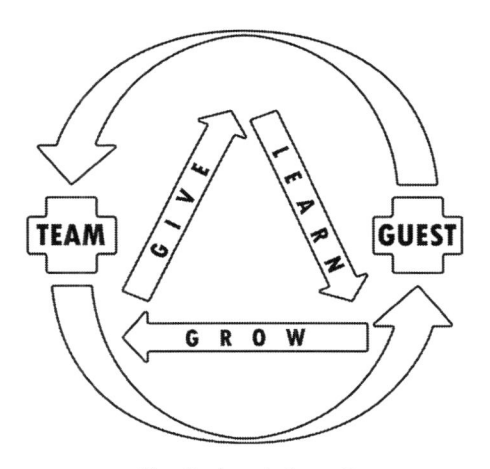

The Explorer's Pursuit

The idea here is beautiful in its simplicity. On the outside, we have a simple exchange of experiences between the guest and the team. This interaction enriches the guest experience while the guest is engaging with the staff on a very personal level. When we master this simple symbiotic process, both

> The most important thing I could focus on was to be able to relate and connect with people, because when you come from a different culture, the sooner you can connect personally, the sooner people will start to trust you, and then you can build toward future experiences.

parties benefit equally from the relationship. This in turn generates lasting bonds and loyalties for the business. The mechanics within the framework are those of *learn, give, grow*.

When these concepts are implemented in our business, they become integral to creating immersive experiences. They allow us to develop deep personal relationships with guests, leading to long-term success.

"The most important thing I could focus on was to be able to relate and connect with people, because when you come from a different culture, the sooner you can connect personally, the sooner people will start to trust you, and then you can build toward future experiences," says Devender.

Devender never adapted to what most would consider traditional learning. He learns by doing — his vehicle equates to experiences. It eventually became routine for Devender to travel at least once per month outside his own country to gain knowledge and experience he could then share with his team and valued guests.

Let's circle back to the start, when Devender had completed his formal education and was first working toward becoming a mechanic as a teen. At the time, he asked himself a simple question: Should I be working toward becoming a mechanic or the person who can afford one? There's, of

Devender Sehgal

course, no shame in being a mechanic. In fact, you can make a lot of money, depending on the situation. As it happens, in New Delhi the ceiling was so low that the circumstance demanded Devender contemplate his options.

Here in the U.S., my father made a decent living working in auto repair his entire life and provided just fine for our family. But in India, Devender's pay was literally 50 cents (U.S.) per day, which is a better rap name than a career path.

Devender landed a new job working with an event company and fast became fascinated by flair bartending and naturally began working some bar gigs. Most of these events included massive Indian weddings with as many as 5,000 people in attendance. To hear Devender explain it, weddings in India are a monumental celebration — an extremely lively and important part of their culture.

From there, his thirst to learn more only intensified, and he applied to work at Institute of Bar Operations and Management (IBOM), where he would study flair bartending techniques and work toward managing events. Devender didn't speak much English. He knew for a fact that to grow in the industry, he would not only have to learn more professionally, but he would also need to become proficient in English.

People joined the institute from all over India, and he found himself learning the language through osmosis. After a rapid progression through the institute, Devender's techniques were so impressive that he was asked to actually run the flair program — he happily accepted. He still had a lot to do in terms of learning English, so he made a deal with the students. He would teach them flair, and they would help teach him English. It was a

> "Where do you see yourself in five years?" Devender's response: "Not here."

productive agreement that rapidly accelerated his learning and made him much more marketable.

It eventually became time for Devender to leave the institute and put his newfound skills to work. He opted to apply for a job at the Taj Mahal Palace hotel. While he was interviewing for the most important position of his young career, at one point his interviewer asked, "Where do you see yourself in five years?"

Devender's response: "Not here."

Did he get the job? You bet! Devender gives great credit to his time at the Taj Mahal Palace in helping him incredibly advance his overall understanding of guest experiences and interactions. From this experience, Devender was tapped for a large-scale bar project in Sri Lanka, and as that work was in flight, he had another competing opportunity at a bar called Ellipsis in Mumbai, which he initially had to decline. He had already committed to the Sri Lanka project and wanted to stay true to his word. As it turns out, the Ellipsis project was run by Dave Kaplan and Alex Day at Death & Co — what a small world!

When the Sri Lanka project finished, Devender made a call to see if there was still an opportunity to work at Ellipsis, and fortunately, there was. At this point, Devender was extremely well schooled in flair talent and guest experience training. He would now learn mixology from the best of the best!

As Devender gained momentum and built confidence in himself, he began to enter competitions. Here are some of the competitions he entered … and won, to name a few:

- Winner: 2009 Bacardi Martini Grand Prix/Flair — India
- Winner: 2012 Diageo World Class — India
- Winner: 2015 Bacardi Legacy — Hong Kong
- Winner: 2017 Hernö Hero Champion — Sweden

Having won Diageo World Class, India, Devender was on his way to Rio de Janeiro to compete in the global finals. Again, his eyes were opened to the real potential the industry had to offer. During the event, Devender made a connection that led to an otherworldly opportunity. Although he didn't outright win the event, he did win a job offer in Hong Kong, running the bar 8½ Otto e Mezzo Bombana, a Michelin three-star location, where he would continue to hone his craft.

Devender has since parlayed that experience into an amazing opportunity running The Aubrey at the Mandarin Oriental Hotel in Hong Kong, which is yet another stunning Michelin award-winning venue. Does anyone else see a trend here? What a pursuit, indeed!

The Aubrey
Photo courtesy Mandarin Oriental Hong Kong

Harken back in the book to the different stories we were told. Consider Julio's journey from Cuba and the different countries he worked in before migrating to the U.S. Consider António and how the man from Portugal working in Denmark is traveling to Cuba to learn more about cigars and tobacco to bring that knowledge and experience back to Tivoli Gardens. Remember how Neal opened a small restaurant on the coast of Malaysia to support his SCUBA habits until 9/11 struck, when he then went to NYC and then on to New Orleans after Hurricane Katrina? How about our dear friend Angus, who lived on airplanes and in airports for over 20 years with literally no permanent address. I know of no one who has traveled more than Angus Winchester. Remember the story of Costin making ten trips from Romania to Annapolis just to spend two days in Annapolis on professional development? Mimmo Alboumeh left Lebanon to study the culinary arts in Spain and Italy, only to find himself owning three venues in Atlanta, which you'll hear about shortly!

Upon further review, travel is Hospitality in its purest form, we believe. Recall our story about the Pashtuns and how for their culture, Hospitality is a matter of life and death. What we begin to see here is, for some people, Hospitality is a way of life; it's in their DNA in the same way we discussed previously, as it relates to experience and to when most people began their journey in this profession. It's an exploration of giving and receiving experiences, and for some, pushing the boundaries of those experiences to the limit. Dave Kaplan told us his desired outcome for every guest at Death & Co was a "holy shit!" experience. You could say it's hard to deliver on those types of experiences without having an array of such experiences yourself. Dave Kaplan (we use his full name here so as to not confuse you with all the Daves around here) spoke often of "curating experiences." He sees his role very much as a curator. In order to do that, you must do some harvesting.

What's more, many of our interviewees traveled at an early age, in their formative years. This shouldn't dissuade any of us who are, say, a little more advanced, from continuing to travel, but it should be noted as a data point that the impact of travel and exploration had an effect during more impressionable years. So, what are we to make of this? We concluded, perhaps not so boldly, that exposure to diversity of cultures, foods, spirits, and ambience lends itself to creativity. Our award winners are also not risk-averse, per se; there are certain inherent risks associated with owning a bar or restaurant, given the long hours, failure rates, and stress associated with its ownership. Imagine, for example, Jack McGarry's willingness to jump on a plane in Ireland and transport his vision, along with his business partner Sean Muldoon, across the Atlantic to test his concept in the toughest bar market in the world ... that mentality epitomizes what we saw time and time again in our award-winning operators.

> The ultimate experience excites all five senses to create a sixth.

At nearly every conference or webinar, you'll hear people exclaim, "We're in the experience business," but what does that really mean? We now understand what that means with great specificity. "The ultimate experience excites all five senses to create a sixth," as Michael Tipps tells it. We've come to understand that sixth sense is feeling. The Explorer's Pursuit of award winners allows for the generation of feelings that can't be found elsewhere, feelings that are so unique and moving it generates an army of advocates.

So, here's the real tough part of the book, and you'll have to knuckle down for this one ... we encourage you to travel! Based on all the data, experience-based travel that expands your personal perspective is central to Hospitality DNA. When we take those perspectives and apply them to our business in a meaningful way, it has a significant impact; there's a multiplying effect. Not just any kind of travel, however. You're likely not going to find cultural revelations for yourself at a couples' beach resort; it's not quite that easy! But finding diverse cultures, unique bar scenes, and second-language locations are magic for the senses. Take great notes when you travel. Look up bars and restaurants on the "world's best" list, but also drop into the hidden local joints for all types of interesting experiences. If international travel is too much to undertake, get away to somewhere unique within driving distance and get out of your comfort zone to enhance your own perspectives.

Explorer's Pursuit DNA sequence

- Travel is Hospitality in its purest form. Explore early and often to garner a broad range of experiences that can be applied back to your business.
- It's challenging to give unique experiences when you lack experiences of your own to draw upon. Your exploration doesn't have to be global or exotic; we understand many have limiting factors. There are unique experiences all around us if we just look for them. The more diverse the better!
- Encourage and, if possible, support travel for key members of your team — you will soon see how Laura and Mudd fund trips for their key team members. This shows a tremendous commitment on the owners' part and in return you receive a smarter, more well-rounded team to execute your strategy … and bushels of loyalty!
- Consider all five senses when you travel. Take notes on all the interesting things your discovery provides. Smell, color, texture, sound, and taste can travel back home with you. Take special note of your overall experiences. How were you treated as a stranger, and how did that make you feel? Remember it, and own it for your place; that's the essence of hospitality.

Lifetime of Experience

> If we could sell our experiences for what
> they cost us, we'd all be millionaires.
> —Pauline Phillips

We speak at great lengths about knowledge in Chapter 1 and the ability to bolt on experience in Chapter 15 on Partnerships. We are differentiating here with the importance of pure individual career experience. A lifetime of experience was so prevalent in our interviews that we wanted to differentiate in the previous chapters between the importance of personal knowledge gained as well as the experience you can add with the inclusion of partners. As this relates specifically to what our global award winners have in common, it's an undeniable commonality of a lifetime of experience.

To show what a full lifetime of experience may look like and perhaps further emphasize the importance of mentorships, one could start with how uncannily similar many of our interviewees' careers began. For some, like Julio, it was the family business. For others, it was an available opportunity to make money at a young age. And for some, it was simply a calling. Indeed, not only do many of these operators have a lifetime of experience, but they are often teamed up with others, in terms of partnerships and mentorships — as we discussed in our previous chapters — where they start to multiply on industry experience. In some cases, partnership teams have over 100 years of combined industry experience, just to run a few venues or less. And in some cases, it is a bit of an apprenticeship under someone who has made Hospitality their master craft. This serves to, if nothing else, validate just how tough an industry this can be to achieve significant success in on your own.

We have pages of wonderful quotes from our hours upon hours of interviews. Perhaps our favorite is:

> They have the right kind of disease that is predisposed to being great in this industry.
> —Jackson Cannon

Jackson believed not only in a Hospitality DNA but also that there was an inherent need being filled by giving of oneself so completely that it has a transformative impact on others.

The living embodiment of Hospitality DNA resides in the form of Salvatore Calabrese, otherwise known as "the Maestro." As you can probably deduce, that is not the type of nickname given lightly.

Salvatore's career began at the ripe old age of 11, working on the beautiful Amalfi Coast of Italy. His dream as a youngster was to become a naval officer, but when an eye ailment prevented him from enlisting in the service, the Hospitality world benefited. A new career path was charted. The universe was awaiting Salvatore's impeccable talent!

A young Salvatore was mentored by a charming, well-traveled, Bogart-like bartender named Signor Raffaello. Signor Raffaello was popular among the lads and lasses alike. During his formative years, Signor Raffaello emphasized and instilled core values into the young Salvatore. These consisted of

- Don't forget where you started
- It's not about the people behind you but the people in front of you
- Every day is a different day
- Know how to care — each experience is unique

These became the guiding principles upon which Salvatore would ultimately transform into a world-renowned talent.

In 1982, Salvatore met his future wife. She lived in London — a faraway place — but as love often does, it propelled him to change. So, Salvatore packed up and moved to London without any concrete job opportunities. Upon his arrival, he got a job at a small bar at Dukes Hotel. He worked a temporary role because the hotel leadership had someone else in mind for the job who was currently unavailable.

Salvatore saw opportunities where others did not. He was a true believer that something special resided in this small hotel — this captured his imagination and led him to explore and appreciate the history behind this unique venue.

His mind filled with ingenious ideas, like buying old cognac and celebrating the birth year of each spirit. For example, Salvatore would buy a bottle of cognac from 1865 and discuss what had transpired in the world in 1865 — for example, it marked the end of the American Civil War and the assassination of Abraham Lincoln. They would sell shots of the product according to its age-appropriate value, which was very high, and many believed it would never sell, yet it did!

The magical culmination of connecting the history of the product, a passion for storytelling, and the quality of the spirit made these expensive bottles sell out in less than a week's time! But I'm jumping the gun here. Salvatore had to be fired first. You see, the bartender whom the hotel had been waiting for showed up a few weeks after Salvatore started. The man took over the role that was slated for him. Salvatore was released from his job and had to hit the pavement running, in search of another opportunity.

Something absurd happened along the way. The new bartender accidentally set the bar ablaze trying to pull off a gimmicky bartending trick. That didn't sit well with the ownership — the new bartender's career was short-lived! Someone needed to go find that Italian guy!

At this point, destiny was sealed with a kiss! The bar team was very delighted by what Salvatore had been building at the bar — a rich worldliness that meshed the venue with spirits and storytelling, making for a perfectly unique experience that couldn't be found anywhere else. So, they found him and of course, he accepted. But this time he had terms.

Salvatore wanted creative freedom to bring his dreams to life. When he proposed his ideas to management, they declined. Why? It was simply too expensive to invest in these rare antique spirits without any proof they would sell. In fact, why would they trust him? There was nobody doing anything of the sort at the time. In their minds, it was simply cost prohibitive.

Salvatore's next move was a life-altering gambit. With belief and boldness in hand, Salvatore took his case directly to ownership. He sold them on the idea that combining the classic ambiance of the hotel with the allure of antique spirits was a quintessential pairing that could generate renewed interest in the aging hotel bar. As you can appreciate, this did not sit well with management, whose authority he just usurped. In time, however, they would come to forgive the ambitious Salvatore and come to appreciate his vision and results.

The bar became a destination sought out by those with a taste for history, flavor, and conversation. Which is how you earn the nickname "the Maestro." As a practical matter, where they had been making £500 per table, per day, they were now pulling in over £10,000 from people wanting to experience Salvatore's version of hospitality.

> "You should never be bigger than your bar," says the Maestro.

The bar became a hangout for all sorts of celebrities like Mick Jagger, Robert De Niro, Stevie Wonder, and business magnate Jack Welch.

"You should never be bigger than your bar," says the Maestro.

In 1985, a gentleman named Stanton Delaplane walked into Salvatore's bar. Salvatore had been making a name for himself and the Dukes Hotel bar when the well-known travel writer came in and ordered a drink. "May I have a very, very dry but very, very cold martini?" he asked. As Salvatore tells it, "It took God six days to make the world, and it took me five days to craft the perfect martini."

Mr. Delaplane sipped on the first couple martinis — he'd say one was very cold but not very dry. The next few days he claimed the martini was very dry but not quite cold enough. Salvatore could tell he was not fully satisfying Mr. Delaplane's taste buds.

> "We can suggest, but we should never tell."

Salvatore describes how everyone has a different palate and we should not tell people how to drink — instead, we must aspire to only give people what they want and make them happy. "We can suggest, but we should never tell." Salvatore suggests one hand is Hospitality and the other hand is mixology — the two hands should always shake.

The Two Hands That Should Always Shake

Fridays are traditionally fish and chips day in London, according to Salvatore. When he walked through the kitchen, he noticed how the chef was dashing vinegar on the fish and chips, while he separated the two to get the seasoning just right. This gave birth to a legendary idea!

Salvatore grabbed a vinegar bottle, washed it thoroughly, and filled it with vermouth. This would allow him to get the exact amount of vermouth into Mr. Delaplane's martini. Back to Occam's razor — the simplest solutions are almost always the best. The Dukes Hotel bar is very small, sized at only about six feet. There was enough room for just a small domestic fridge, a picnic basket to hold the ice, and some glassware and liquor placed delicately on the shelves. Salvatore decided to keep martini glassware in the fridge, along with a small bottle of vermouth and gin. The next time Mr. Delaplane arrived, he would be ready!

Mr. Delaplane strode into the bar and said, as he always did ... "May I have a very, very dry but very, very cold martini?" This time Salvatore would pour the cold gin directly into the cold glass, along with the cold vermouth, which he could control to perfection.

Instead of using a mixing glass, Salvatore poured everything straight into the frozen glass and layered the vermouth on top — the liquid looked a vibrant, golden chardonnay color. Now this would allow the vermouth to play its part, emitting a lightly aromatic essence, as the aromas were not lost in the cocktail.

Salvatore had a mastery for martini mixtures, pairing a botanical combination of vermouth with gin. The mouthwatering cocktail was finished with a twist of lemon. He thought to himself, the balanced notes of the drink and all the love and care he had put into it might be to Mr. Delaplane's liking.

So, he served Mr. Delaplane his first martini of the day and Mr. Delaplane said nothing. But he did order a second, upon which he said nothing again, and after a few sips, he got up and left. Salvatore was left feeling a bit nonplussed. What more could he do to get this guy's martini just right?

When Mr. Delaplane came back, he introduced himself to Salvatore as a journalist and travel writer for the *San Francisco Chronicle*. He explained to him that after he had had his drink, he'd had the urge to go upstairs and write about it. Mr. Delaplane wrote an article on Salvatore's martini and would recommend to the world that when in London they needed to visit the Dukes Hotel bar if they wanted to try *the best martini on the planet*.

To Salvatore, this is what it means to be hospitable — filling the dream, making people feel special — and it's not about serving, it's about giving; a social place where we can deliver lifelong experiences.

Salvatore Calabrese — The Maestro
Photo by John Carey

Jack Welch once told Salvatore he was responsible for his biggest bill because during his travels, he had had so much fun in his bar. That is where he fell in love with his assistant, ended up marrying her, and later, divorced her. Not an ideal scenario, we'll grant you that, but these are the types of regulars found at the Duke Hotel bar, and the Maestro is an Italian, after all, so love is in the cards and happens around every corner.

Salvatore would end up serving the likes of President Bush, Fidel Castro, and ultimately the Queen of England, which led to his other nickname, "The Royal Bartender"! Salvatore will tell you he had to be prepared every single day because royalty could walk into his bar at any moment. Imagine this being your touchstone!

Salvatore has a lifetime of stories. I wish I could write them all out for you, but there's just so much to tell that could fill a whole other book. I do want to reserve his favorite story for you as it's an awe-inspiring one!

Salvatore had a very shy, yet highly successful English businessman as a regular client. We'll call him Mr. Smith. He was a lonely man in search of a romantic partner, and Salvatore knew it. One day Salvatore decided he would play matchmaker and introduced him to another regular who was a very outgoing "bubbly" personality, as he described it. He felt that opposites would attract, and attract they did.

Now, the relationship bloomed and quickly escalated. Mr. Smith was very nervous when it came time to propose. Salvatore said to him, "Don't worry about it. Buy the ring, give it to me, and I will do the rest." When Mr. Smith arrived the next time, he was blown away. Salvatore had elegantly decorated the corner of the bar full of beautiful, colorful flowers in a grandiose way. The proposal was romantically executed and blissfully accepted.

Years later, on the way to the hospital while Mrs. Smith was in labor, the couple stopped in to celebrate the occasion with a glass of champagne prior to her giving birth. Several years later, that baby, now all grown up, would come to be a regular at the bar where his parents met. To Salvatore, this is the splendid standard to which he aspires.

L-DNA sequence

- Knowledge and wisdom are often a product of time. Yes, you can accelerate learning, but you can't shortcut it. Experience was the first and most evident DNA trait we discovered. Interview after interview featured a lifetime of experience. Take it all in and multiply through personal development, partnerships, and mentorships.
- Seek knowledge and advice of others inside and outside the industry. It's good to find the occasional outside voice or someone who has a completely different perspective from your own.
- Surround yourself with knowledge and talents that you may not otherwise possess. Partner wisely!
- Be a mentor! We've had some of our own greatest learnings from being a coach and a teacher. As an example, we can assure you that this book would never have happened if we hadn't jumped into the opportunity to help others ourselves, in this regard.

Indomitable Spirit

> If you find a path with no obstacles, it
> probably doesn't lead anywhere.
> —Frank A. Clark

In the continued search for commonality among our interviewees, we continued to hear amazing life stories, as we're sure you've appreciated as much as we did. It's incredibly important to note that during the interview process, while our interviewees would chronicle the details of their professional and sometimes very personal journey, not a single person complained about the multitude of challenges they had faced. There were no gripes about how tough or how unfair their situation had been. They seem to understand their journey was a key component of a necessary process that is part of who they are and defines their success.

We think it's also critical to note that not all of our interviewees experienced immediate success, nor were their journeys easy or without struggle; in fact, just the opposite. In almost every case, not only did they experience significant challenge and struggle but complete and total failure as well. New venues that failed, partnerships that had to be dissolved, financial woes — you name it, we heard about it. Interestingly though, they would never dwell on it. Almost to a person, it served more as a bookmark in their story — something to be learned from, something that helped them become better forward and not on their heels.

In this chapter, we want to highlight some of the most compelling "bookmarks" for you. These captivating journeys are unique in many ways, so you'll appreciate what makes them special. These heart-warming stories serve to remind us that when adversity strikes, we must stare it down, no matter how tough, and let our Indomitable Spirit prevail!

For starters, I'm happy to share with you the story of Mimmo Alboumeh. Mimmo is originally from Lebanon and grew up when severe civil war was taking place. That in and of itself was enough to bear. Around this same time, Mimmo's father tragically passed away when Mimmo was only 13 years old.

To help take charge of the family's financial situation, Mimmo worked in the restaurant business as a young teen. He quickly fell in love with food and truly savored the wide array of flavor profiles and textures. Due to his situation, Mimmo frequently traveled to spend time with extended family in Italy and Spain. It was in these picturesque landscapes where he learned about the culinary nuances of these regions and picked up the languages as well.

Spain is the beautiful country where Mimmo was formally educated in hospitality. When you visit one of his venues, you will immediately sense the impact of his time training and learning across three cultural dimensions — Italian, Spanish, and Lebanese.

In his twenties, Mimmo decided he wanted to bet on himself and try his luck in the U.S. He thought it was of the utmost importance in life to take some chances and even embrace a certain amount of risk in the journey. But he differentiates between risk and gambling. Mimmo never saw his pursuit as a gamble; it was, however, a calculated risk — one in which he liked the odds!

> "You have to take care of people and they will take care of you."

Today, Mimmo lives in the U.S. and owns multiple venues with numerous concepts. He is a "celebrity chef" who spends time on the local market channels, as well as being one of CNN's resident experts.

Mimmo is quick to emphasize how his diversity of experiences has significantly impacted his business mindset. Mimmo has high energy and is passionate about every aspect of his business. He's clear about expectations with his team and serves as a willing mentor to those who work for him. Mimmo believes strongly in the power of people and the integral nature of their impact on the guest. "You have to take care of people and they will take care of you." He is eager to share knowledge with his team. Mimmo believes, with the proper approach to life and relentless spirit, people can achieve whatever they want in business and life.

Mimmo was quick to emphasize that the loss of his father at such a young age was devastating, especially given the totality of the Lebanese situation at that time, but it was during those events that his perseverance and tenacity bloomed. Award-winning success is clearly, in part, what you're made of — your internal DNA. It's also largely impacted by environment — the external: What are the circumstances presented in your life journey, and how do you handle them? There's a classic quote from Charles R. Swindoll: "Life is 10% what happens to you and 90% how you respond to it." That's the underlying theme of our Indomitable Spirit discovery. For Mimmo and others, it's all about how we respond. We can't always control what happens to us, but we do get to own the response. For Mimmo, it was a devastating 10% that provided the impetus for his extraordinary 90% response, which led him to where he is today.

Mimmo's story is extreme and not one you'd wish on your friend. Mimmo offers us his keys to facing down challenges:

- Appreciate the small things like kindness (giving and receiving)

- Take care of the people who take care of you
- Embrace differences and learn from different cultures
- It's not what happens to you, it's how you respond

Mimmo Alboumeh — Botica, Atlanta
Photo by Hailey Curtis

Throughout the book, we've communicated about countless enlivening journeys. These spanned across spheres of the personal, the professional, real-world experiences, and intense obstacles. It is the incredible determination people have to overcome these challenges that truly sets them apart. It is those individuals *who radiate an Indomitable Spirit* who face roadblocks without ever compromising their spirit!

We found no better example than Minakshi Singh. Minakshi exudes a unique happiness, a big smile, and a strong spirit — we felt this the second we met her. It was clear in an instant why she would be successful in this industry. She has a wonderful story that ends with her bar, Sidecar, being voted the number one bar in India and one of the top 50 in Asia by *DRiNK* magazine.

Now, you may think, Ah, no big deal. Lots of people could be voted best bar in one of the most populated countries on the planet — maybe not! What if I told you women weren't allowed to own a bar? What if I told you, it was socially frowned upon at best and illegal at worst for a woman to own and operate such an establishment? It was at that point we began to realize the gravitas of her story. So how did she get here?

Minakshi's career began like that of many of our award winners: as a teenager looking to make some extra money. She had a few choices and opted for a job working in the event space with a gentleman named Yangdup Lama.

Recently, Yangdup was featured as a "Top 100 most influential people" in *DRiNK* magazine's annual list. At that time, however, Yangdup didn't own any bars and was trying to make his mark in the event and hosting space. Little did Minakshi know, her first boss may have been her last. This is because, over 20 years later, they are now business partners and are featured in some of the most elite lists in the world.

Around the turn of the century, Minakshi was trying to make some money to help with her pending acceptance to university. She had opted to study hotel management. During her time in college, she continued to work in the bar game. She would describe working during these times as "a rush" because she embraced the late nights and the hard work. During this time, the idea of owning her own place began to take form.

Having earned her degree as a university graduate, Minakshi took her practical experience and education with her upon joining the Pernod Ricard organization. From there, she would eventually move over to Diageo where she continued to grow professionally, travel, and execute brand-based support initiatives for the organization. This is where the compelling story begins to unfold.

Upon winning an internal annual award at Diageo, she had requested a meeting with her boss. He had a career path charted out for Minakshi that would be the envy of any mid-level manager in one of the largest companies in the world. It was at this point that she opted to inform her boss, whom she liked a great deal, that she would be leaving the organization to pursue her dream of running a bar of her very own.

An Iindomitable Spirit indeed! Imagine the stakes: a job most would kill to have, a promising future, a boss she respected — yet this was not the dream.

A special component to this story is Minakshi's father. In India it would have been traditional for her to keep the job, get married, have children, and help support the family — a bird in the hand — the safe route. However, Minakshi's father had just retired and decided to open a school where he would finally pursue his life's passion of teaching. He encouraged Minakshi to pursue her dreams, just as he'd wished he had done years earlier. His life experience and guidance was enough to put her decision-making over the top; it gave her certainty.

Over the years, Minakshi had kept in touch with her first boss, Yangdup Lama, as you recall. Her first call was to reach out to Yangdup and see if he might be interested in a partnership to launch a bar of their very own. He eagerly agreed, and together they launched a concept called Cocktails and Dreams ... yes, Coughlin's Diet!

India comprises 29 different states, all with their own unique laws and regulations, as you would expect. When Minakshi would meet with local officials about opening her bar, she would often be met with rejection. She learned quickly that she always had to have Yangdup with her, so the local officials would be willing to engage in conversation.

It was so counterculture for a woman to own a bar that once she was able to get a meeting, the officials would look at Yangdup, even when they were speaking directly to Minakshi.

She remained undeterred and persevered through seemingly endless administrative toils to eventually launch Cocktails and Dreams in the tech center of New Delhi. Minakshi had always envisioned a Western-style bar that was casual and inviting to everyone. This type of bar is not necessarily typical in India. She had envisioned a place where a woman could go on her own and have a beer, which is not "normal" in Indian culture. They also wanted to create an atmosphere that had a neighborhood hangout feel — very Western.

Her concept was unique enough that even in the modern tech center of India, there were days where the venue made literally zero revenue. The dream did not become an instant reality. Times were tight, and their success was tenuous at best. But day after day, the pair staffed the bar and bussed tables in an effort to ensure they executed their vision of the personal connections they longed to form with guests.

In fact, it was also extremely unusual for the owners to be executing such roles in a bar in India. In time, as they connected with guests and created regulars, the guests were always shocked to discover they were being served not only by the owners, but by a female owner as well! Minakshi was breaking the barriers — her mind was set on living her dream.

Keep in mind that India has a very specific, very traditional service culture, and it's simply not in keeping with being the owner doing the work that would ordinarily be done by servants.

The HELIX Sequence

Success is measured by certain cultural markers that include dress, servants, and the like.

Minakshi and Yangdup's countercultural, Western-style bar eventually became a smash hit through grit and perseverance, which led to the opening of their second bar, Sidecar.

Sidecar put the duo on the global stage and was voted the number one bar in India, number fourteen in Asia, and one of the top fifty in the world! Sidecar is a super-unique venue that prides itself on being "a bartender's bar." It is a stunning two-story venue that includes a carefully curated bookstore on the first floor where guests can settle in for a cafe-like experience if they so choose, or they can go upstairs to the bar and extend the evening with a world-class experience. It's a very special place that is very much a reflection of Minakshi's vision, values, cocktails, and dreams!

Minakshi Singh
Courtesy of Terai India Dry Gin

The moral of Minakshi's story is, realizing a dream is likely going to be extraordinarily difficult, and at times the process can be unfair. It will require risk and sacrifice, and one should be well prepared for disappointment along the way. We have to face down those challenges while maintaining our hospitable nature. It's who we are; it's what we stand for.

What we learned throughout almost every interview was, dream chasing is a relentless pursuit. The Indomitable Spirit is what powers us through the ups and downs — facing down the absolute toughest and worst circumstances to make it happen for yourself and others. Think of Mimmo and his family situation or Minakshi facing down massive cultural barriers and walking away from a cushy dream job. Recall Julio's escape from Cuba and Katalin's trek across Europe to find out she had gotten the dishwasher job. At one point, Devender was homeless, without any idea where his next meal was, let alone a dream job. Or imagine losing your life partner to cancer, like Jen Hidinger-Kendrick. These stories are heart-wrenching and could easily and understandably break one's spirit. This is where it became clear to us that having an Indomitable Spirit was one of the five key components to award-winning success in our industry. It lends itself to a certain level of appreciation for the attainment they achieve. It also helps build a Hospitality heart, one that can easily empathize with the situations that employees or guests may find themselves in. Once again, we've learned that this isn't "the service industry"; rather, it's an industry of willful giving. These award winners gladly and willfully give of themselves in the name of lifting up guests and others while they are in their care, if even for a short period of time.

Indomitable Spirit-DNA sequence

- Life requires internal fortitude, as dreams and award-winning success aren't easily realized. In this industry (and others), most fail many times before basking in the glow of high achievement. There will be disappointment, letdowns, and challenges. Be mentally prepared when they occur. Failure can be a great teacher to a willing student.
- Surround yourself with two kinds of people. First are those who believe in you and your dream, as you do! Second are those who have achieved the things you aspire to. The latter can serve as friends and mentors with the ability to greatly accelerate your success.
- Keep smiling! The power of kindness and positivity are boundless. Neuroscience supports the exponential effect of positivity and kindness toward others and its reciprocal nature. It's no wonder that having an Indomitable Spirit is a core component of Hospitality DNA.

Xtraordinary Culture

> The idea of culture is total bullshit unless
> you completely and totally buy in.
> —Riz Shaikh

The most powerful thing we do as business owners is to build our culture. I was recently asked, *What is culture, anyway?* and in a skeptical tone.

My response was, culture is simply the day-to-day actions in your business, which are set by ownership expectations.

Make no mistake, owners set the culture. How people behave is a direct reflection of how we choose to run the business. Our behaviors as leaders set the tone for everything that happens and ultimately it will be those behaviors that the staff follows — not words.

It was sometime in the mid-'90s when people started defining culture more meticulously. We started hearing about things like mission statements, company vision, and core values. If you worked in an office of any size in those days, you were certain to see a poster on the wall, most likely of an eagle, challenging you to fly high, or perhaps a Grand Canyon photo daring you to "Accept the challenge." These inspirational posters adorned office space worldwide; now you can find them at your local thrift shop for $2 in the home decor section. So, what happened? Are mission statements wrong, core values pointless? Does a waterfall not start with but one drop of water, as was explained to P.K. in the movie *The Power of One*? Should we not aspire to soar like an eagle? Well of course we should, but what we learned over time is that words and talk, without an underlying commitment to support the claims, are cheap at best and actually serve to undermine the business, at worst.

> An HR department can't set company culture, and a few pictures on the wall will only serve to inspire an eye roll if they do not truly describe the actual culture of the company.

An HR department can't set company culture, and a few pictures on the wall will only serve to inspire an eye roll if they do not truly describe the actual culture of the company. Culture is defined in our everyday actions and behaviors. It's what we DO that defines our business much more than what we say. Do words matter? Of course, words can inspire us to greatness, but they can also suck our will to live dry. However, if you want to get to the heart of what makes a company or venue great, watch how they behave, and you'll begin to know their culture.

From time to time, clients will call and ask us about a critical decision they are considering. Perhaps they are interviewing a potential general manager or looking to purchase an existing venue and they want an independent opinion on whether or not to move ahead. The great thing about our industry is, you can pull up a chair at the bar or be seated at a restaurant and immediately watch culture happen. So when people ask our opinion on whether there is a fit, we'll tell them to go spend a few hours there during a slower day and then a busy night, and they'll get a great feel for the culture of that business. Essentially don't just believe the interview; you don't have to! Go see the place this person comes from; or if you're considering a purchase, go spend time getting a feel for who frequents the venue, and why. See how the staff behaves. Think about how many times an interview does not at all reflect the realities of a venue, a situation, or a person, which ultimately only leads to faster turnover or less-than-ideal purchasing decisions.

We had anticipated our interviewees would have deep insights into culture building and very purposeful culture statements that defined what they were all about: What is their "why"? However, during the interview process, when we would ask the question or seek definition on culture, most would begin to describe how they felt about the business and what they hoped to accomplish and very little by way of a standard practice. In other words, they knew how it felt and how it should look but with very little actual definition. It's more common than not that independent Bar and Restaurant owners *are* the culture of their venues. The venue and the culture therein take the form of the owner's personality itself, which can be extremely dangerous on multiple levels. What if you have a passion for owning a bar and you're a reasonably good business person but you're somewhat unlikeable? You might want to think twice before opening up a hospitality-based venue because without a formalized living, breathing, hospitality-based culture, the business will undoubtedly take on the form of the owner's personality and interests. On the other hand, what if you are the life of the party — the person everyone in the room wants to be around? You enjoy tilting a few in the venue, thank you very much. What happens when you leave for a month to go research mezcal in Oaxaca? I can tell you ... the party rages on!

Another scenario where personality-based culture can be dangerous is the absentee ownership or "investor" model, which we will also see from time to time. When this occurs void of an enforceable culture, the business will take on the personality of the GM or whoever is ultimately the day-to-day authority. These personalities can be amazing if you're lucky, or they can be disastrous if you're not.

You get the point: personalities can be mercurial or temporary, while culture stands the test of time. Award-winning operators take their version of Hospitality seriously and with definition, which we highly encourage for every business. Formalize what you stand for: live it, teach it, enforce it, reward it.

> Culture is a direct reflection of ownership.

> Culture simply defined is the day-to-day actions you find acceptable.

> Get specific—define your culture, because culture will ultimately define you.

Laura Newman and Larry Townley are a wonderful example. Many of our award-winning operators have some connection to New York City. For years, NYC has been the pressure cooker of the Bar and Restaurant industry. There's an old adage: "The hotter the fire, the stronger the steel." This rings true, as many of our interviewees had some rich roots and experience grounded in the Big Apple.

Case in point, Laura Newman worked at hot spots like Bacchanal, Mother of Pearl, and Cienfuegos. Laura also met her future husband in New York, who also worked in the bar scene. Larry Townley's nickname is "Mudd" — so we'll refer to him by this highbrow nickname, which is one of our all-time favorites!

Laura moved to Alabama to open her first bar, Queen's Park, in the booming downtown Loft District of Birmingham. Laura is a Diageo World Class champion — a "tough as it gets" accomplishment for winning the annual bartending competition awarded by Diageo. Among her many notable accolades, Laura is also a certified sommelier and holds a degree in Hospitality management from the Institute of Culinary Education.

As self-professed culture champions, we were quickly won over by Laura and Mudd when we first met them.

I recall meeting the dynamic duo at a Hospitality conference. Throughout the weekend, they asked poignant, meaningful questions related to their staff. This topic is something we always find intriguing and attractive because all too often in our industry, staff is treated as disposable or as interchangeable parts. There's a built-in expectation that staff will always churn, so why invest? It most certainly doesn't have to be this way.

When we sat down with Laura and Mudd, they revealed very forward-thinking processes relative to culture building and staff training. These progressive ideas are some of the best we've seen! We're very thankful they were willing to share the details of how they think and behave in their business. One of the easiest

Hospitality DNA

ways to see the impact of their culture-building efforts is to look at the concept of staff turnover.

> If you're looking for the best measure of your cultural efficiency, turnover is a magnificent place to start.

Laura and Mudd embodied a culture so strong that it beats the industry turnover average of 70% by a seven-time multiple!

It's not unusual for us to find businesses with 100% turnover or more. The worst we've seen was a business we helped that had over 200% annual turnover. We were flabbergasted by the amount of time spent on hiring, training, and retraining! The massive turnover was so bad that it was crippling every aspect of the business, like a domino effect. Guests suffered, profits were suppressed, and morale languished.

If you're looking for the best measure of your cultural efficiency, turnover is a magnificent place to start. Interestingly, in a larger company, turnover is one of the most important measurement indices of a management team. However, we find that in hospitality, turnover data is shockingly overlooked and rarely measured.

The turnover equation is as simple as this:

$$\frac{\text{Number of employees who left during the year (30)}}{\text{Number of employees at the beginning of the year + Number of employees at the end of the year} / 2 \\ (200 + 195) / 2} \times 100 = 15\%$$

Xtraordinary Culture Turnover

Laura Newman (middle) and the Queen's Park team — Birmingham

World class turnover is 10% or lower. If you want to set a world class goal for you and your leadership team, start here. Low turnover allows for great productivity, and almost every company that generates great productivity also generates great profits. Why? Because ownership is constantly working on forward-thinking, progressive ideas that improve the business rather than running on the treadmill of redundant staff churn. Because they aren't constantly involved in the time-consuming process of looking for and training new employees, they can focus on other aspects of their business. Hospitality operators very rarely speak in terms of measured turnover and productivity, except for the elite operators. They get it, and this is how …

Getting the culture right and the turnover low has allowed Laura and Mudd to focus on the strategic aspects of the business and hasn't had them tied up behind

> Honor your roots, and you'll grow from the ground up.

the bar or executing managerial duties. Their employee turnover, which they measure, runs in the 10% range — simply extraordinary for our industry. The culture they've built has accelerated their success to levels even they couldn't anticipate. So how do they do it? As with most highly successful cultures (as measured both financially and in terms of well-being), we find a few common threads that include training, trust, and empowerment. As you read in our chapter on Scalability, you'll find you can't scale personality. Award-winning hyper-successful people come to realize that culture in many ways is the key to everything.

According to Laura, at the core of the culture at Queen's Park is a guiding principle of "What we had never been offered as a bartender or manager when we served in those roles."

There's not a better story we found of "Don't forget where you came from." The gem of wisdom here: honor your roots, and you'll grow from the ground up.

Laura knew they didn't want the bar to be about them; they wanted the concept to stand on its own. In an innovative way, this would allow for scalability. Although, the duo isn't sure they want to scale this particular concept due to its complexity, which is even more evidence of honest progressive thinking.

The culture at Queen's Park is all about empowering and educating the staff. There's a commitment, both financial and emotional, to safeguard the team in an upward growth trajectory. The hidden win here becomes the amount of productivity gained by ownership, which quickly becomes a success multiplier — which we've spoken of many times throughout the book.

Imagine a world where you continuously make more and work less! Never say never; here's why. If for one second you don't believe it's possible, I can tell you that triumph prevailed. In 2020, this team beat their year-over-year revenue numbers, which were already at an all-time high in 2019, smack dab in the middle of a pandemic with very limited outdoor patio seating, which was part of the 2019 number.

Sounds improbable if not impossible, right? How do you build the kind of team that makes this kind of result possible? It takes vision, hard work, and commitment that most just aren't willing to do. The extra effort it takes to get you there requires long-term thinking over short-term gains.

The first thing Laura and Mudd do is *invest* in their team — it's their number one priority. Twice a year they close their venue and go on an exploratory trip together. Recently they went to NYC, where they visited 40 venues in just a few days, although they will be toning this down in the future, as it was a little ambitious by their own admission.

They also brought in guest speakers who shared their vision and guidance during the trip. In the name of sanity, this culture-building strategy has been refined to include fewer visits and more speakers, going forward. The team claims the plan to visit 40 venues in NYC over such a short span was well intentioned but was actually harmful to learning. We don't learn well when we are exhausted (take note).

Each team member also gets to pick a personal exploration where they can travel anywhere in the U.S. to an event of their choosing. Airfare and accommodations are all covered by Laura and Mudd. We were blown away by this. They sound like a dream employer!

Let's take a step back. In terms of culture, who we hire is vital. Laura and Mudd will not hire someone at Queen's Park who doesn't have management potential. This is the first time I heard this within the world of hospitality, specifically.

One of the most successful people I ever worked for — let's call him Derek Jones for fun — said to me once, "Never hire someone into a role of importance where they can't at least make one more step." Such a simple and meaningful way to think about motivation and talent evaluation! Always build a team that's capable of doing more than what they're being asked to do at the time. This allows for additional flexibility, productivity, and responsibility, which our industry rarely considers.

> "Never hire someone into a role of importance where they can't at least make one more step."

We want people who are motivated and capable of increased authority and responsibility. This means organizations need people who can move both horizontally for experience and vertically for responsibility.

A team full of true-blue and clever employees allows you to do the things that *you want* to do versus a ton of things *you have* to do — pure incentive for the ownership team. When we can count on stellar staff, we're firing on all cultural cylinders. Indeed, if we really get it right, our staff begins to outperform the potential that ownership had originally envisioned for the business: success multiplier!

During the trips, there is a fun activity that Laura calls "the rose and thorn." This is a review where each team member shares their favorite part of the day — the rose — with the thorn being that which they enjoyed the least. They are encouraged to use these *nuggets of newfound wisdom* and apply them to enhance the venue upon returning and suggest how to improve future trips.

These programs are designed to empower the staff with new and great ideas that Laura and Mudd can trust them to implement. During enriching explorations like these, we can count on having eureka moments. What we know about any idea is that the more somebody owns an idea, the more likely it is to be successful; the highest success comes when it is one that comes directly from the source. The more filtered an initiative is, the less likely it is to be successfully implemented. Basically, people will fight harder to find a way to make their own ideas work, pushing to prove themselves right, no matter the effort. When someone else comes in with a different or contradictory idea, even when that other idea is better, we tend to want to continue to push our own "good idea." By creating a systematic process where staff is empowered to have and implement their great ideas, the business benefits.

> Of course, not every idea will be a winner; however, allowing for failure in moderation while fostering a full-scale ownership mentality has a multiplicative impact on growth potential and breeds responsibility.

Of course, not every idea will be a winner; however, allowing for failure in moderation while fostering a full-scale ownership mentality has a multiplicative impact on growth potential and breeds responsibility. This is a beautiful example of successful culture building without a lot of complexity.

Our recommendation — coming out of literally hundreds, if not thousands, of conversations — is to formalize your culture. Get your culture in writing so that it can be taught and executed in your absence. Know exactly what you stand for and how you plan to go about ensuring it through your team. You can start defining your culture by getting clear on a few critical questions:

- What are we?
    - Get super clear on what you are trying to achieve; keep it simple
    - Refer back to our chapter on Clarity and Immersion

- Who are we?
    - Define what you stand for
    - Establish hiring standards
- How do we do it?
    - Define it
    - Measure it
    - Enforce it
    - Reward it

We strongly recommend implementing a turnover metric that you measure and reward monthly. Remember, low turnover is a key driving force on you, your management team, and your guest experience. Then invest in your team so that they are motivated to stay and exhibit an ownership mentality. Track things such as positive and negative reviews, and go over these with the team as coaching points. Implement guest rewards and track returns, program activations, and redemptions.

If you want to live a fundamentally different life, it starts with culture and team building. When you are surrounded by great, tenured, motivated talent, you WILL live differently, they WILL live differently, and guests WILL experience differently. This is essentially the dream. We can't emphasize enough, if you don't have a formalized culture and if you don't measure cultural outcomes, you will not reach your full potential.

You simply can't get through any conversation with these folks without having to hear about their teams, how vital they are to the business, and how important their partners are. Candidly, if there's a subtext here it would be humility. It is simply astonishing how humble these operators are — how willing to give away credit and accept little responsibility for success and tons of it for failure. All cultures are unique — some much more than others — but each of our award winners had extreme clarity and vision for exactly how to behave in the business and how that behavior translated to the guest experience.

A very important note to remember about culture is, everyone has one. The question is, is it the one you want? Is it the one that produces the very best results for you and your business? If so, make sure it's well documented and celebrated. If not, formalize a new one and make it part of the processes as we discussed in our chapters on training. In addition, remember the importance of culture in your scaling efforts. *We can't scale personality* is a key takeaway from our Building Block chapters. In order to grow your great ideas, they have to be planted in fertile ground. You can certainly have a beautiful flower in a pot and nurture it, but its capacity for growth is extremely limited. It is oft said, culture conquers all, and we agree. Your culture is just a fancy way of saying this is how we do things around here, but the details within that statement are everything for you and your business. Think of the clarity Lil had in imagining Coyote Ugly and the intensely specific way she expected her Coyotes to conduct themselves, even in raucously turbulent environments. It would be a huge mistake to think that it was all just controlled chaos at any time; not at all. There was a very specific formula to what made it all work. Consider Michael Tipps and Shoo Shoo, Baby, where every consideration is made down to the size, shape, attire, and dialogue you receive from the bouncer before you ever even enter the venue. What is an upscale dive bar anyway? You'll know exactly what that means after leaving Michael's place! Do you remember the tens of thousands of dollars Jack McGarry invested in training platforms for his team so that they could execute upon an authentic 21st-century Irish pub experience and win Best Bar in the World? You may not know exactly what a 21st-century Irish pub is before you walk in the door, but when you leave the Dead Rabbit, you'll understand exactly what that means.

Hospitality DNA

The Aperture Effect

In doing the interviews with our amazing award winners and writing our conclusions, we came across an interesting juxtaposition, which we're calling the *aperture effect*. An aperture is essentially the amount of light a camera lets in through its lens, which then determines the quality of the photo. If we let in too much, it can overexpose the photo, and too little, and we're left in the dark.

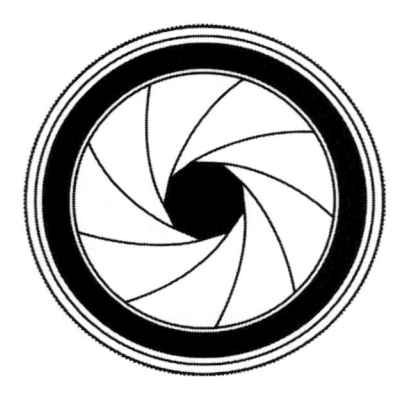

We noticed, in our chapter on partnerships, that we saw our most successful operators had a very tight focus; they let very little light in, which is to say, the spectrum is tight. There is tight agreement on critical matters such as ethics, vision, common goals, and agreeability that create tremendous business bonds. We do want to diversify on talent but in a very specific way; the details are very tight and, in many ways, nonnegotiable in terms of strategy and ethos.

In contrast, when it comes to experience, we want a very wide aperture; we want to take in as many experiences as possible. We want to experience a broad range of personal and professional experiences that allow us to learn and grow. That's the spectrum at its widest view, and not only do we encourage this for ourselves but for our partners as well. These are the two extremes in the aperture effect, and the picture it creates is a special place called culture.

You'll notice culture and experience make up two of the five main components of the Hospitality HELIX. The aperture effect gives us some construct around the connection between these two critical strands of Hospitality DNA. The culture that is created is a combination of the vision and ethos of leadership combined with the experiences gathered over a lifetime. The intersection of the two sets the footing for our culture. That culture creation is what our employees come to experience every day on the job and what our guests come to expect on each visit.

Over time, we encourage the constant expansion of the outer aperture. We want to persist with our Explorer's Pursuit and widen the aperture by exploring and discovering new cultures, ideas, and concepts, all of which can be applied and adapted to our business.

As we continue to learn and grow, over time the inputs or experience become wider and wider, and ideally our focus will become tighter and tighter as we gain knowledge and confidence in how we find success in the business.

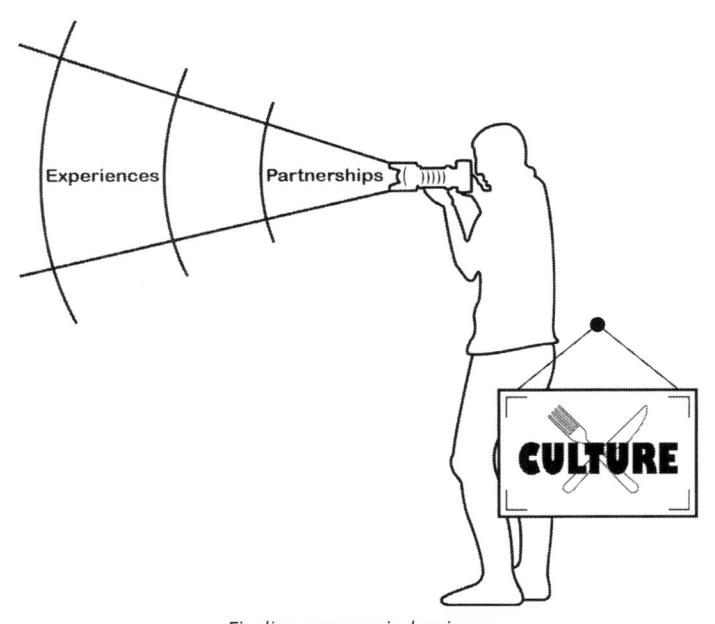

Finding success in business

Keep in mind, it would be easy to confuse having a tight focus among partners with a lack of diverse experience. Don't make that mistake. The tight focus among partners is a matter of values and vision. We devoted an entire chapter to partnerships for a reason; it came up in every interview and, to a person, the value of a healthy partnership was paramount. The tighter the values and ethos, the more likely the partnership was to thrive, and the more those things diverged, the less likely it was to be healthy relationships.

At the same time, we discussed at length the value of travel and an Explorer's Pursuit. It's simply not viable for some to travel to exotic locales and take vast time away from the business. Bear in mind, diversity lives all around us. We can find incredibly diverse cultures, venues, and experiences right in our own backyard; we just have to pursue them. So, open the aperture. Get your perfect picture!

Xtraordinary Culture DNA sequence

- Great culture generates great productivity, great productivity generates great efficiency, and great efficiency creates great profitability.
- Our interviewees were reluctant to take any credit for their success directly. "I am lucky to have a great team" is thrown around a lot. This type of attitude will endear people to leadership. It tears down barriers to achievement and fosters an attitude of ownership and sharing. Allow for better ideas than your own, learn to hire well, and trust your hiring decisions in the business. Remember the success multipliers!

- Culture is built off a platform of learning. Use your experience to set your ideal culture for your business as it will be the most important thing you do as a leader.
- You must be the champion of your own cause, and your cause is your culture. In that vein, we simply cannot look to others to build a culture for us as they will build upon *their* lifetime of experience and foundations, not yours. Culture doesn't just happen and can't be hung on a wall; it's a reflection of what we stand for as leaders.
- Define your culture. Measure and reward cultural indices. A significant mistake many people make in terms of culture building is that they have no metric to support it. A great irony in our industry is how often people tell us how important their teams are but have no way to measure the impact they are having on them. Remember, what gets measured gets done, and people tend to manage to what they are compensated for. It's always a good idea to have culture components built into compensation structures.

Conclusion

We'll be brief. I'm confident we've exhausted our guidance in the chapters. We're profoundly grateful and honored to be able to share these extraordinary stories of hope and success. It's been an absolute thrill to get to know our interviewees, and the discovery of the HELIX is something we never could have anticipated. We learned so much ourselves and discovered so many new ways to teach that the work has inspired more work … funny thing, that is.

This industry is unique, special, and intense, and in the volatile mix come these special people committed to delivering on a promise, a promise of giving to others. When we get it right, magic happens; success happens.

If you'd like to contact us directly, please visit us at www.DaveAndDave.co and check out our Hospitality DNA coaching programs for managers and ownership. We're here to help. You can also contact us about speaking engagements and educational opportunities.

Feel free to engage us on our socials as well! And if you happen to see us at a trade show or convention, please come say hello!

Acknowledgments

A huge thanks to our families, first and foremost, as always. Of course, to all the participants for being so gracious and willing with their time and experiences — without you this doesn't happen! You set the standard for what our industry aspires to exemplify.

A very special thank you to Angus Winchester for pointing us in the right direction when needed and writing the foreword, which set the tone for the entire book.

Special thanks to Rob Kosberg, Bob Harpole, Matthew Schnarr, May Cheng, Steve Fata, Kathleen Shewman, Lizze Slocum, Meghan McDonald, Liz Huston, and Cole Kosberg at Best Seller Publishing for all your help and support; otherwise this would have been messy.

Our sincerest gratitude to MD. Imranul Haque, our graphic designer and illustrator based in Bangladesh.

Last but not least, thank you to all of our colleagues and clients at Barmetrix. You are the inspiration!

Online Resources

On our website, we have two complimentary quizzes if you want to continue your Hospitality DNA Journey.

DaveandDave.co

Hospitality Quiz

Partnership Quiz

Buy the Bar Shift

DaveandDave.co

Made in the USA
Columbia, SC
01 May 2023

82009ff9-369a-49e9-92a6-5d504a82272cR01